David Boyle

The Township of Scarboro

1796-1896

David Boyle

The Township of Scarboro
1796-1896

ISBN/EAN: 9783337059521

Printed in Europe, USA, Canada, Australia, Japan

Cover: Foto ©ninafisch / pixelio.de

More available books at **www.hansebooks.com**

THE TOWNSHIP

OF

SCARBORO

1796—1896

EDITED BY

DAVID BOYLE

PRINTED FOR THE EXECUTIVE COMMITTEE

BY

WILLIAM BRIGGS,

TORONTO.

1896.

To the

Sons and Daughters of Scarboro

AT HOME AND ABROAD,

THIS BOOK

IS RESPECTFULLY DEDICATED

BY

THE EXECUTIVE COMMITTEE,

WITH THE

VERY FULLEST AND HEARTIEST CONFIDENCE, THAT ALL

WHO BELONG TO

THE OLD TOWNSHIP

WILL ACCEPT WITH PARDONABLE PRIDE

THE RECORDS OF A RURAL COMMUNITY,

THAT HAS EVER BEEN ACTUATED

BY A SENSE OF DUTY,

EFFORTS MADE TOWARDS THE REALIZATION OF WHICH

HAVE ALWAYS BEEN CROWNED WITH

SUCCESS.

1796–1896.

Scarboro Centennial.

"ONE hundred years!" How easily 'tis said—
How slight an effort of the gift of speech!
Not many letters to comprise it all.
A little child can lisp them o'er with ease,
But who can grasp the fulness of the time?
Or who can measure all that it contains?
Its symphonies and mournful cadences,
Its echoes of the past that thrill the ear,
That stir the heart to richer, fuller life,
And cause the pulse to beat with quicker throb
As we do muse on days that long are past?—
Days that were bright with honest, sunny smiles,
Or clouded o'er with sadness, or with pain,—
Days full of memories of varied scenes
Illumined by the acts of friendship true
Of those whose lives were joined to ours in love—
But who have left us for a little while,
Until the call to us shall also come
To enter on a higher, nobler life
That knows no end, that is not measured by
A term of years, but where ten thousand times
Ten thousand centuries are but a drop.
In the vast ocean of eternity!

—R. DAVIDSON, *Ingleside.*

PREFACE.

ONE hundred years ago to-day, Robert Burns had but a few weeks to live; Thomas Carlyle had spent only six months of discontent in this world; Napoleon Bonaparte had just assumed command of the army of Italy, and was no doubt even then forming plans for the conquest of Europe; the United States was in its infancy, with General Washington as President; General Prescott was Governor of Canada; Simcoe was at the head of affairs in Upper Canada, Newark being still the capital; and George the Third reigned, King of Great Britain and Ireland.

The year 1795 had proved one of great agricultural depression in the British Islands. Peace prospects were slender; business was unsteady, when not actually stagnant; labor, consequently, was not in much demand, and famine stared thousands in the face. In such circumstances it was but natural that many persons, especially the more adventurous and enterprising, should look abroad for that measure of comfort and success, the prospects of attaining which seemed to be so uncertain and so distant at home. Of this class, as is hereinafter recorded, were the very first settlers in Scarboro.

It is in commemoration of this settlement, and at such a time, that the people of Scarboro have had the present modest volume prepared in connection with their celebration, the object being to bring together in a handy form the various records of local events and bits of personal reminiscence, many of which, in course of time, would otherwise be lost or forgotten.

The time is past when history was supposed to be merely a record of political events, of campaigns in the field of war, and of great discoveries. Important as these are, they do not by any means constitute the sum total of history; and hence we find considerable attention now being given to sociological features in the growth of nations; and as nations are but aggregations of communities, it would seem that intelligent citizenship implies a knowledge of facts pertaining to the development of institutions and industries in young settlements of modern, as well as of ancient date.

In most townships, the people as a whole, or groups of them, have much in common regarding origin and circumstances; and as time advances, general interests become mingled through marriage, business, and social relations. Such municipalities, therefore, almost naturally suggest themselves as fields for the convenient grouping of local records.

The plan followed in this book is to present the subject under separate heads rather than as a continuous narrative, and no attempt has been made to produce anything but a bare statement of facts, beyond supplying introductions to the chapters, and such connective passages to the information collected as seemed necessary to put the material in tolerably readable form.

When the writer undertook, quite unexpectedly, to perform this work, he feared his ability to complete it in the time at his disposal, and for this reason felt himself fortunate in gaining the ready assistance of two well-known literary ladies, both of whom are deeply interested in everything that relates to Canada and Canadian history, local as well as general.

Mrs. S. A. Curzon,* President of the Woman's Canadian Historical Society, has prepared the chapters on "Domestic Life," "Churches and Ministers," "Societies," and the chapter relating to the Centennial proceedings. Miss M. A. FitzGibbon,† Secretary of same organization, has written the chapter devoted to militia matters, and that containing brief references to pioneers and their families. The work of each lady will speak for itself.

Collected as the information was, somewhat hurriedly, by the committees appointed for this purpose, it is quite certain that numerous omissions, and perhaps some errors, will be noticeable. In the face of many difficulties, however, and the expenditure of much time, the committees performed their work well, and it is only fair to state that special thanks are due to the Chairman of the Executive Committee, Rev. D. B. Macdonald, without whose untiring efforts, and excellent organizing ability, it would have been impossible at this juncture to bring together the material required for the memorial volume, now fully twice its originally intended size. To him also the editor is indebted for much of the information contained in several of the chapters, and for valuable assistance rendered in various other ways. Messrs. J. C. Clark, David Martin,

* Mrs. Curzon is the author of "Laura Secord, a Drama, and other Poems," and many short addresses and papers on historical subjects.

† Miss FitzGibbon is the author of "A Veteran of 1812," "Home Work," "A Trip to Manitoba," and several magazine articles.

Dr. O. Sisley, A. W. Forfar, J. C. Cornell, R. Malcolm, and A. J. Reynolds, all supplied admirable epitomes, either of general subjects, or concerning the several districts they represented.

To Mr. Clark also is due the credit of having photographed most of the views that are reproduced in the book.

It should be mentioned that the poems given at length are by natives, or former residents of the township.

It is much to be desired that every other township in the Province should take steps to crystallize in type the knowledge that now exists chiefly in the memories of the oldest people, and to bring together the numerous scattered references to municipalities, as these may exist in writing or in print.

That this embodiment of what relates to Scarboro will in some degree meet with the approval of those for whom it is more particularly intended is the sincere hope of the editor,

DAVID BOYLE.

TORONTO, June 10th, 1896.

CONTENTS.

CONTENTS.

ILLUSTRATIONS.

CORRECTIONS.

Read *made* instead of "ceded," third line from foot of page 28.

Read *folk* instead of "folks," third line from foot of page 98.

SECTION OF SCARBORO HEIGHTS.

TOWNSHIP OF SCARBORO.

CHAPTER I.

TOPOGRAPHY AND GEOLOGY.

"In Nature's infinite book of secrecy
A little I can read."—*Shakespeare.*

APPROACHING Scarboro from Lake Ontario, one cannot but be struck with the boldness of the shore line, as compared with the rest of the coast, both east and west of this township. The cliffs, or Heights, as they are called, consist of boulder-clay and sand, somewhat irregularly stratified, forming what is known geologically as "drift," that is, the result of interglacial deposition during indefinite periods, in some equally indefinite past, when ice-fields spread themselves over the northern part of the continent, sending immense branches as far south as the state of Kentucky. On no other portion of the north shore of Ontario can the phenomena of such deposits be better studied than along the face of this cliff from Port Union westwards to Victoria Park.

In a paper* read before the Toronto Mechanics'

* The paper appears in the *Monthly Review*, of June, 1841, published in Toronto at that time, but subsequently removed to Kingston, which had been chosen as the capital. This number of the magazine was brought to light by Mr. J. C. Clark, of Agincourt, and by him kindly lent for perusal.

Institute in 1841, by Mr. John Roy, Civil Engineer, on "Toronto Harbour," the writer referring to a time when he claims "that the whole of the waters from the west, including the Mississippi waters, were discharged by the Niagara River, and through Lake Ontario, up to the period Lake Ontario subsided to its present level," and when, "therefore the quantity of water which flowed through the chasm must have been more than double what it is at present," expresses his belief that the current acting on the bottom of the lake was sufficiently powerful "to throw up the materials excavated on the north shore," and that as the level of the lake gradually fell, a series of ridges was thus formed, until the time came when the water being only some 200 feet above its present level, gave the Niagara current "a vastly greater power to act upon the bottom of the lake than any of the three former subsidations; for the current had not only a greater downward bend, but also the waters of the lake were greatly reduced in depth; consequently, we find vastly greater deposits of the excavated materials upon the northern shore of this elevation. Those heights in Scarboro which project forward [*sic*] to the lake, the hill upon which Captain Baldwin's house stands, and the ridge upon which Dundas road runs along the head of the lake, all belong to this era."

Mr. Roy's theory is as bold as it is absurd, but the quotation serves to show that more than half a century ago attempts were made to account for the existence of Scarboro Cliffs and other escarpments on the north shore.

In 1854, Prof. Henry Youle Hind and Mr. Sandford Fleming made a study of the Heights with relation to their influence in the formation of Toronto Island, or

Hiawatha Island, as it has sometimes been called; and five years later, the distinguished Scottish geologist, A. C. Ramsay, referred to them in the Journal of the Geological Society, but it was not until 1876 that something approaching an exhaustive scientific examination of Scarboro Heights was carried on by Mr. G. J. Hinde, an English geologist spending a few years in this country.

Mr. Hinde believed firmly that the beds of the great lakes had been scooped out, through the tremendous grinding force exerted on the rocks by moving ice-fields from 3,000 to 5,000 feet in thickness; but it is unnecessary that we should adopt this view in our consideration of the facts he reached regarding the nature of the cliffs, which are, after all, only a section of what constitutes the township at large. He writes:* "The present basins of the lakes, however, by no means represent all the hollows made in the old rocks by the glacial ice; many of these have been filled up by till and stratified deposits, and until borings are made must remain unknown.† Thus, Dr.

* Page 12, "The Glacial and Interglacial Strata of Scarboro Heights, and other localities near Toronto, Ontario," by Mr. George Jennings Hinde. Toronto, 1877.

† Mr. Hinde was unaware that at least one boring of fully a thousand feet had been made near the village of Highland Creek in 1866, when an attempt was made to "strike oil." Unfortunately the log of this boring has been lost. Mr. Wm. Helliwell, in whose possession it was, vouches for the accuracy of the following statement, from memory:

Sand and gravel (surface)	5	feet.
Blue clay	50	"
Limestone	750	"
Soapstone	100	" (?)
Rock salt and cavities	97	"
	1,002	"

Sterry Hunt has shown that the palæozoic rocks on the shores of Lake Erie are covered with glacial and stratified clays to a thickness of 100 to 200 feet beneath the lake level; whereas the lake itself in most places is not more than 70 feet in depth. There is, however, to be considered, the fact that the present depth of the lakes is probably very much less than their originally excavated depth by the glacier, for stratified deposits of clay and silt brought down by the rivers, etc., have been gradually accumulating in their basins [beds] since the time when the glaciers which filled them were dissolved.

"At the Scarboro Heights there is one of these filled-up glacial hollows. The palæozoic rocks were eroded by the first glacier deeper than the present lake level: without a boring it is impossible to say how deep the hollow may have been. With the exception of a short distance at both ends of the section and a space in the central portion, the basal beds of the Scarboro Cliff are composed of beds of stratified clay. . . . Before describing the fossils contained in the clay beds, I wish to mention the beds of sand and sandy loam which rest conformably on the upper surfaces of the clayey strata. These sand beds are of a yellowish tint; the strata are horizontal, and appear, like the clays, equally free from pebbles or boulders. Their maximum thickness shown in the cliff is forty feet, but they have evidently been eroded, and in some places completely removed, and their original thickness may have been much greater. . . .

From this it would appear that Mr. Hinde's theoretical hollow must have extended a long way into the lake, and that the deposit would thin out nearly to the surface, a little farther inland than this point, for the boring was made less than two miles from the lake shore. Several borings at intervals of some miles would be necessary to afford the required data.

"There is thus exposed at the Scarboro Cliff, beds of clay and sand of interglacial age, 140 feet in thickness, leaving out of account the extent to which they may reach below the lake level, and the amount which may have been eroded from the upper surface."

The fossil remains found consisted mainly of low forms of vegetable and animal life, including soft woods, wings of a beetle, two or three crustaceans, and two kinds of shells. "Both the plant and animal remains so far discovered in these strata conclusively show that they are of land and fresh water origin; not a trace of any marine organism has been found in them."

Without entering further into details, it may safely be assumed from the evidence in our possession, first, that the cliffs on the lake shore merely show in part the section of a deposit that once extended far away into the lake, a portion of which deposit now forms, perhaps, the greater part of the township at the south; second, that the beds of clay and sand were laid down in fresh water; and third, that the tenacious quality of the deposit has enabled it, as a mass, to withstand the erosive forces which have carried away the material on the limits of the hollow in which the clays were originally laid down—hence the elevation along the lake shore.

The following table has been prepared by Mr. Hinde to show the succession of strata forming the Heights:

7 stratified sand and gravel, post-glacial -	50 feet
6 till or boulder clay - - - - - -	30 "
5 laminated clay and sand, interglacial - -	90 "
4 till or boulder clay - - - - - -	70 "
3 interglacial fossiliferous sand - - - -	40 "
2 " " clay - - - - -	100 "
1 till or boulder clay, below lake level - -	..
	380 "

It will be observed that the total here given exceeds by nearly one hundred feet the greatest altitude (290 feet) reached by the cliffs, but this is because the measurements of the several beds have been taken at their thickest parts, and these do not occur immediately above or below each other (see diagram, p. 9).

Close to the lake shore the surface is much broken with ravines from fifty to a hundred and fifty feet in depth, especially near the south-west angle; and along the banks of the Rouge on the eastern side, the surface is somewhat rugged, but, in general, the township may be described as undulating or "rolling." The southern portion is sandy, although with the excellent system of farming, for which the township as a whole has been so long celebrated, good crops are produced close to the lake shore. To the north of this light belt the soil becomes heavier, and in some places appears as a rich clay. These alternations are just what might be expected from the character of the deposit that forms the whole or the greater part of the township.

Scarboro is well watered. Highland Creek, which rises near the north-west corner (in Markham), drains, with its numerous branches, fully half of the township, traversing a diagonal course and entering the lake at Port Union near the south-east corner. The Rouge, rising in Markham, also takes a course (with its several feeders) from north-west to south-east after entering Scarboro, and reaches the lake through Pickering. On the west side of the township a branch of the Don flows generally southwards until it enters York, where it takes a westerly course to join the main stream.

Springs of pure water are very numerous, and no

difficulty is experienced in procuring an abundant supply at depths of from twelve to seventy feet. On lot 14, con. 4, there are two springs which, from an early date, have had curative properties attributed to them. Gourlay, in 1822, referred to them as "medicinal springs," and adds that they "begin to be resorted to by persons affected with rheumatism and other chronical complaints. An eminent physician of York is said to have received much benefit from the use of the water."*

In the neighborhood of Ellesmere is a large number of springs. On lot 27, con. 2, one close to the creek, strongly impregnated with iron, discolors the vegetation. A short distance down there is a large gushing spring in the bottom of the creek, and on lot 28 is another, the water of which colors everything red. A few rods farther down there is one which some years ago was supposed to contain sulphur; the water is very clear but has an unpleasant smell. The creek has encroached so much on this spring lately that the latter is almost lost to view. For about one-eighth of a mile beyond this, numerous springs issue from the banks of the stream, and in many places the bottom is of a marly nature and so soft that a pole may be pushed down six or eight feet. About forty years ago, Mr. Andrew Young dug a well on lot 29, con. 1. Twenty feet down the workers struck a soft place, and the water rapidly rose several feet to the surface. Another well bored twenty feet farther north and a little deeper, also filled at once and ran over as did the first, and both have continued to flow. These two wells are at the head of the west branch of the Highland Creek.

* "Statistical Account of Upper Canada," Vol. I., p. 145.

On lot 29, con. 2, there is a flowing well, the water of which if confined would rise about five feet above the ground. The bore of this one is only about an inch and a half, but it is estimated that at least twenty thousand gallons of water flow from it daily. Nearly one hundred yards to the south-east, on lot 28, is another well with an inch and three-quarter pipe, from which flow about twenty-five thousand gallons a day. It is on ground nearly five feet lower than the former, and is eleven feet deeper.

Numerous springs along the creek on lots 25 and 26 have dried since the bush was cleared.

THE OIL COMPANY.

In the year 1866, when the oil fever in Canada was at its height, the Scarboro Oil Company was incorporated with a capital stock of $4,000, which was divided into 160 shares of $25 each, to sink a well at Highland Creek village. The Board of Management consisted of:

President, - - - - - -	Wm. Helliwell.
Vice-President, - - - - -	Wm. Rolph, Sen.
Treasurer, - - - - - -	Thos. Elliott.
Secretary, - - - - - - -	Donald G. Stephenson.

Directors.

Messrs. Wm. Helliwell, Wm. Rolph, Sen., D. G. Stephenson, Wm. Tredway, Wm. Westney, Geo. Chester, Jerry Annis, Jas. Humphrey and Andrew Annis.

The company leased a site for operations from Messrs. Gooderham & Worts and Mr. Wm. Helliwell and wife, on lot 8 in the 1st concession of Scarboro, for a term of forty years at a yearly rental of twenty cents, beside a royalty of a 160th part of the proceeds. The directors made a contract with Mr. Hood, of

Toronto, to bore to the depth of 1,000 feet. This was effected without finding oil, although brine of the strongest character was brought up in the sand pump, but it was too much impregnated with carbonate of lime and of magnesia to be suitable for making salt. When the contractor was down about 600 feet, one Harry Key, a waggon maker, occasionally poured a gallon of oil into the well at night, thus causing considerable excitement in the neighborhood. It failed to occur to Key and others that wells did not yield refined oil.

A difference of opinion having arisen between the contractor and the directors as to the depth reached by the drill, careful measurements made by Messrs. Wm. Tredway and Geo. Chester showed that it had penetrated 1,002 feet. It is to be regretted that notes of the boring made at the time have been lost, and that there is no statement of the analysis of the brine. Mr. Helliwell has supplied from memory the figures touching the strata passed through, and these are given herein on page 11, foot-note.

Notwithstanding the failure of the company to realize their reasonable enough expectations, the pluck and public spirit of the stockholders are to be commended. Unlike those who hope to find coal in Ontario, the Scarboro Oil Company had not only the theories of science, but the facts of experience in their favor, and failure to strike oil at a thousand feet does not prove that petroleum may not exist at even a less depth not very far away. That the boring was made through soapstone, would seem to indicate that possible oil-bearing rock had been passed.

In the annual report of the Geological Survey of

Canada, for 1890-91, Mr. Brummell writes of a "Well at Highland Creek": "I have been unable to obtain any authentic account of operations at this point, and give the following as the result of inquiries made at different times and of various persons. The information shows that a well was sunk near this village, during either 1866 or 1867, to a depth of 682 feet, penetrating the Trenton limestone to a depth of 434 feet, in which formation it is reported that large quantities of gas were struck.

"The record of the well is reported as follows:

Surface (blue clay) - -	48 feet.	
Shale, black, - -	200 "	Hudson R. and Utica.
Limestone, - - -	434 "	Trenton.

"The fact that this well was at once abandoned shows that there was, as is usual in this district, but a small flow of gas."

This statement only renders matters more confusing. Not only was gas not sought for when the Highland Creek well was bored, but the records of strata penetrated are totally dissimilar and Mr. Brummell's figures are little more than two-thirds of those supplied by Mr. Helliwell (p. 11), whose statement that the soapstone penetrated measured one hundred feet in thickness, is astounding. No carefulness can be too minute in recording particulars relating to deep borings, copies of which should be forwarded to the Department of the Bureau of Mines, Toronto, and to the Geological Survey, Ottawa.

A complete list of the shareholders of the Scarboro Oil Company will be found in the Appendix. Their enterprise was a praiseworthy one, and their names should not be forgotten.

CHAPTER II.

BEFORE THE WHITE MAN.

"Tribe was giving place to tribe, language to language; for the Indian, hopelessly unchanging in respect to individual and social development, was, as regards tribal relations and local haunts, unstable as the wind."

—*Parkman.*

WHEN Canada was taken possession of by the French near the middle of the sixteenth century, it is probable that nearly all the peninsula formed by the great lakes, and a wide strip extending easterly along the shores of Lake Ontario and the River St. Lawrence, were occupied by members of the powerful Huron-Iroquois Indians; the rest of the territory (forming Upper Canada at a more recent date) having been in the hands of the Algonkins, who were less disposed to occupy fixed places of abode, for it is well known that the former people settled themselves in what by courtesy we call villages, consisting of rudely constructed houses built, or put together with poles and sheets of bark in a sufficiently permanent manner to last for a few years. Many of these dwellings, being intended to accommodate several families, were, according to our ideas, of disproportionate length when compared with their breadth, measuring from fifty to three hundred feet in one direction, and not more than fifteen or twenty in the other.

All now remaining to indicate the sites of these "long houses" are rows of ashes mingled with charcoal and fragments of bone, shell and coarse pottery. When the floors of such huts became inconveniently filthy, rather, perhaps, because of the quantity than the quality of the deposit, the village was removed to some other eligible situation, the old name being retained. These removals have led to considerable confusion arising from the accounts of travellers, who mention this or that village of a given name, in places several miles apart, because the references have been made at, and to, different periods.

It will be seen that this mode of living implies some other differences in customs when we compare the Huron with the roving Algonkin. The comparatively settled life of the Hurons afforded an opportunity to perform a few agricultural operations of a simple kind. Perhaps it was the desire to grow corn, pumpkins and beans that led to the fixity of habitation. However this may have been, the women of the village led a much easier and, on the whole, a more comfortable life than their unsettled Algonkin sisters, and they were thus enabled to devote considerable time to the production of pottery, the making and adorning of garments, and the forming of numerous tools required to carry on these operations, assisted, no doubt, in the last-mentioned, by the men of the tribe. Ceremonial observances must also have been modified if they did not sometimes actually originate as a result of this village habit, and in none of these was this more marked than in the modes of burial.

The Hurons first interred bodies singly, or exposed them on a scaffold, or in a tree, until the flesh dropped from the bones. At intervals of ten or twelve years was held the Great Feast of the Dead, one of the most important and most impressive ceremonies performed by this people, and one, too, peculiar to themselves. A large pit having been dug, usually on an eminence, the collected bones of all who had died since the holding of the last "feast" were thrown into the excavation, while the shamans, or medicine-men performed their incantations, and the assembled people howled and gesticulated to terrify the bad okis, and probably burned tobacco to win the favor of the good ones. It is the occurrence of such communal graves, bone-pits or ossuaries, that leads to the popular conclusion accounting for the presence of so many skeletons as the result of battles fought close by.

The inveterate foes of the Hurons were the Iroquois, a people of their own kith and kin. We have no means of knowing for how long a bitter warfare was carried on between the two branches of this great family, but while it lasted it was most remorseless, until in 1649 the Hurons, or Wyandots, as they were also named, were almost exterminated, the few survivors being driven out of the country. It is chiefly of these people that we find remains in the form of stone, shell and bone relics in this part of Ontario.

The Iroquois having accomplished their purpose in the destruction of the Hurons, and their attention being otherwise engaged until they ultimately became involved in the colonial troubles between the British and the French, found no time to repel the hordes of Ojibwas* who, spreading themselves southwards, soon

*Also spelled Ojebways, Ojibbewas, Chippewas, and various other ways.

occupied all the abandoned territory of the Hurons and Neutrals, to the very margins of Erie and Ontario.

It was with this branch of the enormously widespread Algonkin family that the British settlers came into contact, and with its members that our early legislators had to deal in acquiring peaceful possession of the soil for agricultural purposes. Our governmental transactions with the aborigines have always been characterized by fairness, if not generosity, but it is doubtful whether those who procured cessions and surrenders from the Mississaugas (by which name our Ojibwas were known) would have treated them so liberally had it been apparent that these Indians themselves were, comparatively, new-comers, whose occupancy did not extend further back than from fifty to a hundred years.

That few relics of the kind mentioned belong to this people will appear evident when it is borne in mind that, during the whole time the Mississaugas have had a foothold here, communication with the whites enabled them to procure necessary articles of a superior kind to those of their own production.

The area now embraced by Scarboro township was undoubtedly a desirable one for the Indian. The lake-shore cliffs formed an admirable defence against attack from the south, so that enemies from that quarter must needs have approached the villages by a circuitous route; there could not be better soil for their extremely simple method of cultivation; extensive forests of magnificent pine, with here and there clumps and ranges of hard-wood trees in great variety, afforded ideal places of domicile; small fruits were plentiful, and numerous streams supplied fish of different kinds in abundance, while game, we may presume, was not difficult to procure.

General evidences of Indian occupancy have been observed in many parts of this township, but most of the traces serving to point out village sites, potteries, or corn patches, have long since been cultivated beyond recognition. Among the localities showing proof of aboriginal residence are lot 25, lot 30 (north half), and lot 32 (south half), on the 2nd concession, where relics have been picked up; while on lot 25, concession 1, a number of graves have been found.

Large ash beds, half an acre in extent, may yet be seen on the farm of Mr. Martin Willis, lot 13, concession 2.

Indian relics have been found on lot 25, the north half of lot 30, and the south half of lot 32, all on the 3rd concession.

Relics of various kinds have been found on lot 31, concession 4, where there seems to have been a camping ground. A specimen bearing a highly polished surface was found here. No ossuaries, or single graves, have been discovered in this neighborhood.

On lot 25, concession 4, and lot 23, concession 3, old camping grounds have been recognized. Another camping ground was seen on lot 22, concession 5.

A Mississauga camp, consisting of bark lodges affording shelter to forty persons, is reported to have existed on lot 29, concession 3, as recently as 1835. In connection with this encampment, perhaps the last of its kind in these parts, Mr. J. L. Paterson relates that his father saw one of the Indians seize a red-hot brand from the fire, and apply it to stanch the bleeding of one of his wrists, from which the hand had just been cut off in an encounter with another member of the band.

At the place known as Bead Hill, specimens connected with the Mississaugas have been unearthed, consisting of "Queen Anne" gun-barrels with copper sights, hunting knives, copper kettles, and other articles of European manufacture. Along the hill formerly known as the Hog's Back, an Indian trail runs toward the west.

The Rouge yields many evidences that its banks were, of old time, frequented by the red man, Algonkin as well as Huron and Iroquois. Perhaps the earliest printed reference to this fact is to be found in a small volume by William Brown, printed in Leeds, England, in 1849. Some of the men employed in his saw-mill discovered a quantity of human bones on the bank of the stream, and from time to time stone and bone relics have been found at intervals along both banks of the river.

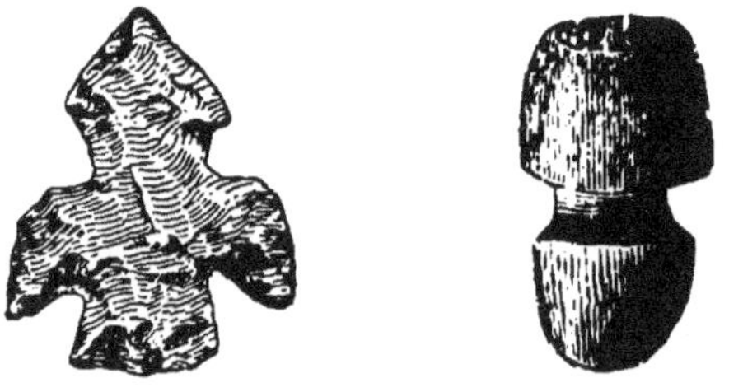

CHAPTER III.

FOUNDATION AND SETTLEMENT.

"We cannot overstate our debts to the past, but the moment has the supreme claim. The past is for us, but the sole terms on which it can become ours, are its subordination to the present."—*Emerson.*

BEFORE 1790 this part of the Province was known to trappers and Indian traders only, and but for the selection of Toronto by Governor Simcoe as his new capital, it might have remained unoccupied by the whites for another quarter of a century or even more.

Having determined upon calling the seat of government York, in honor of the Duke of that title, it was natural enough that, influenced as he was, he should adopt other names connected with the English original, and we accordingly have Whitby, Darlington, Pickering, Markham and Scarboro. In like manner the French St. John became the Humber, the stream to the east he called the Don, and the Rouge he dubbed the Nen.*

*In Chewitt's map of 1813, but probably as a misprint, this river is marked the *New.* The graceful writer who treats of this neighborhood in the second volume of "Picturesque Canada," speaks of "the well-wooded Heights of Scarboro, which early French explorers called Les Grandes Écores. This the Loyalists Englished into 'The High Lands,' so that the stream flowing through the Heights is still called 'Highland Creek.' A little to the west of the Seneca village [Ganeraské, now Port Hope] was a stream that

When the townships along the lake front were laid out by Surveyor Augustus Jones, in 1791, it is said that Pickering, Scarboro and York were respectively named Edinburgh, Glasgow and Dublin. The people of this township may congratulate themselves in having now a more appropriate name in Scarboro,*

gave kindly shelter to distressed canoes; and so by Indians of the next century and of a different race, it was named Katabokokonk, or the 'River of Easy Entrance.' In making its way to the lake, it pierced a hill of red tenacious clay, which sufficiently colored its waters to justify the old French name, *Rivière Rouge*. In his attempt to reproduce in Upper Canada the east coast of England, Simcoe re-christened this stream the Nen, just as he had converted St. John into the Humber, and La Grande Rivière into the Ouse. But like the Grand River, the Rouge fortunately survived the palimpsest maps of Governor Simcoe. It is still the Rouge, and the name is interesting as the sole trace now remaining on this north-west shore, of the old Sulpician Mission and of Louis the Fourteenth's domain."

* *Scarborough*, Isaac Taylor tells us in his "Words and Places," is a word of Norse origin, *Scar* meaning a face or cliff, from *skera*, to shear or cut asunder. In a foot-note he refers to the cognate words in Gaelic and Erse, *sgeir*, a cliff, and in Anglo-Saxon, *sciran*, to divide. "Hence," he says, "the *shire*, a division of the kingdom, the *shore*, which divides land from sea, the *skewer*, the plough*share* and the *shears*, instruments for dividing, and a *share*, a divided part. A *shower* consists of divided drops of water. To *score* is to make notches on a stick, and the numeral, a *score*, denotes the number of notches such a stick would contain. A *scar* is the mark where the flesh has been divided. A *shard* is a bit of broken pottery. *Shear*, *sharp*, and *skarp* denote that something has been cut off. *Sewer*, *scare* and *scour* are from the same root."

Borough is connected with *beorgan*, an Anglo-Saxon word meaning to cover, to hide or to protect, and probably also with the German *burg*, a town. Other forms of *borough* are *burgh* and *brugh*, all originally pronounced with a final guttural, which, passing into hard "g" in English, has at last become silent, unless we regard the short final "o" in Scarboro as all that is left of it.

At a meeting of the General Committee to collect information for the history of Scarboro, held in St. Andrew's Church Sunday School, Bendale, in January, 1896, it was decided that in the preparation of this book, the name of the township should be spelled *Scarboro*.

although it is to be deplored that the custom of importing old world place-names to America has been so persistently followed, and too often with an entire disregard to the "eternal fitness of things."

Jones surveyed only a portion of Scarboro bordering on the lake, and for some reason unknown, made the concessions to run east and west instead of north and south, as is usually the case. He seems to have been determined also that the township should not lack highways, for the side lines are placed at intervals of half a mile, and along each of these a road is opened.

On account of the line followed by the lake shore, extending in a south-westerly direction, the township is considerably longer on the west than on the east, and concessions A, B and C do not extend all the way across the township. Concession A is only a small triangular portion. North of concession D, the others are numbered from one to five and as they are the result of a different survey, the side roads are not in line with those to the south.

Shortly after the preliminary survey was completed, some grants of land were made in recognition of military services during the American war, and to United Empire Loyalists, but the township does not appear to have suffered much from the locking-up of extensive tracts held by non-residents, unless near the front, along the leading roads. Between 1820 and 1830 The Canada Company secured a few hundred acres, a grant of 384 acres was made by the Legislature for the support of grammar schools,* and King's College

* From the "Final Report of the Commissioners of Inquiry into the affairs of King's University and Upper Canada College," by Dr. Joseph Workman, in 1852, we learn that so recently as 1850, of this land there remained 120 acres unsold.

came in for considerably over 2,000 acres. (See Appendix A.)

In March, 1796, David Thomson and his wife found their way hither, apparently having followed the Indian trail which was subsequently opened as a highway and known as the Danforth Road.

Particular reference to the Thomsons and other pioneer families will be found in the following chapter.

It is worthy of note that Scarboro does not appear in any of the cessions made by the Indians. What is called "The Toronto Purchase," made in 1787*, did not even extend eastwards as far as the town line between York and Scarboro townships.

Correspondence with Dr. Douglas Brymner, the accomplished Dominion Archivist, and Mr. Duncan C. Scott, Secretary of Indian Affairs, has elicited that neither in the Department of Archives nor in the Indian Department is this territory mentioned. Dr. Brymner, after making a thorough search without being able to meet with anything bearing on the point, referred the writer to Mr. Scott, who replied to the effect that this matter had frequently been under the consideration of the Indian Department, and that while there is what may be called a tradition in the office confirming the belief that a cession has been made, there are no documents so testifying.

It is probable that some verbal or otherwise informal transfer of this, and a wide strip extending eastwards along Ontario and the St. Lawrence, was ~~ceded~~ made to the British by the Iroquois, who claimed it as a hunting ground even after the Treaty of Paris in 1763.

* "Surrendered by the Mississaugas on the 1st Aug., 1805, for 10s. & divers good & valuable considerations given on the 23rd Sept., 1787."

OLD SETTLERS.

1. Mrs. W. Paterson. 2. Mrs. A. D. Thomson. 3. Th. Brown. 4. C. Lamaroux. 5. John Martin. 6. J. A. Thomson. 7. Chris. Thomson. 8. R. Hamilton. 9. Mrs. J. Elliot. 10. S. Thomson. 11. A. Johnston. 12. Mrs. A. Bell. 13 Mrs. Sisley. 14. C. C. Bowen. 15. F. Thompson. 16. A. Forfar. 17. F. Armstrong. 18. A. Paterson. 19. S. Kennedy. 20. H. Hogarth. 21. C. Pilkey. 22. Mrs. E. Secor. 23. John Tingle.

CHAPTER IV.

THE PIONEERS.

> "With aching hands and bleeding feet
> We dig and heap, lay stone on stone;
> We bear the burden and the heat
> Of the long day, and wish 'twere done.
> Not till the hours of light return
> All we have built do we discern."
>
> —*Matthew Arnold.*

HISTORY that is to some extent within our reach, incidents that are within the memory of the very aged, tales told us by those only lately gone from among us, have a special interest, a personal significance. As we trace the sequence of events, look down the vista of the vanished years, and revive the memories of men and women who have lived and died doing their duty in preparing the way for us, we make their lives our own. We learn how by perseverance, loyalty and love they laid a firm foundation for the building up of a vigorous national life.

The more we study the past the better we shall appreciate the present, and realize the importance of our influence upon the well-being of the future.

Through hardships patiently endured, and difficulties boldly met and overcome, our fathers laid the foundations of our present prosperity, and a just pride in the integrity of the Empire which their loyalty preserved, should incite us to weld its several parts more closely to each other, and thus in our turn leave that which makes for a great peace-binding, war-controlling, national heritage to those who follow us.

A hundred years ago our fathers felled the first tree and made the first clearing wherein to plant a home on the forest-crowned heights, and in the picturesque valleys of our township.

To-day, in the crowning year of the century, we have well-tilled farms, handsome residences, educational advantages, religious liberty, every necessary and comfort of civilized life. The advance of science has provided an ample field for the exercise of talents given us, and made opportunities of which we may avail ourselves to earn an honest living, and by individual exertion and ability rise to wealth and position.

Although there are other names in the township preceding his in the records of land grants, David Thomson was the first actual settler within its boundaries.

A stone-mason by trade, and possessed of the solid, practical education common to all Scotchmen, David Thomson came to Canada in 1795.

Born in the parish of Westerkirk, Dumfriesshire, in 1760, he, and his wife Mary Glendinning, brought four children (James, Andrew, Bella and Richard) with them to the New World, Richard being only eighteen months old. A Freemason, a Presbyterian, and a Conservative in politics, David Thomson came, as did all of his countrymen, imbued with that patriotism and love of free institutions which have ever been characteristic of the Anglo-Saxon race.

Coming by way of Quebec, he, as many other settlers at that date appear to have done, went on to Niagara, which place had until then been the seat of

Government. He arrived just at the time this was being removed to York, and was at once employed as head mason in the erection of the new government buildings.

Some of the records speak of his working at the fort, others on the parliament buildings. It is probable he was employed on both.

The residential part of York was that portion of the city of Toronto lying nearest the Don River. The marshy shores of the bay, hemmed in as it then was, by the peninsula of sand which is now our Island, and by the low, often submerged lands, fostered malaria and generated a low fever and ague from which many suffered greatly. Mrs. Thomson's health was so affected thus, that they had been only a few months in York when her husband saw that he must look for a healthier locality in which to settle. The township of Scarboro had recently been surveyed and thrown open to settlers, and David Thomson turned his prospecting steps in this direction. Following the road which was then little more than an Indian trail through the woods, he crossed the intervening sand-plains until he struck the better soil in the valley of Highland Creek. Here he found the necessary conditions for success in a new settlement—rich soil, land well drained, and unlimited water power. There was also the advantage of an abundance of valuable pine.

Selecting a spot about two and a half miles from the lake shore, as the crow flies, and adjacent to a clear, running spring, the first white settler in the township struck the first blow towards establishing his home there. The spring had evidently been used and kept open by the Indians who in days gone by had made this spot their resting-place.

David Thomson was not alone. He had evidently brought others with him, possibly James Elliot, who is mentioned as the owner of the ox-team and sled by which the family and their household goods were conveyed to their new home shortly afterwards. During the first day the men not only chopped the trees, but with them constructed the walls of the small log-house. The logs were left in their natural state, rough and unhewn, and after cutting out the apertures for the door and windows the men made a fire inside, ate their supper, and set a watch to keep off the wolves while the others slept after the hardest day's toil they had ever performed.

What a picture for the painter! The rough walls, the drowsy watchman, the blazing fire casting its bright light on the recumbent, yet half-alert figures of the tired men inside, and, outside on the dense forest, ever and anon revealing the sneaking forms of the hungry wolves, that would fain have questioned the right of the pioneers to invade their domain.

The terrors of that night were never forgotten, and it was not until one of the great oxen, by whose aid they had hauled the logs, lay down across the half-barricaded doorway and thus interposed a barrier between them and the wolves, that the men slept soundly at last.

A few days, however, enabled them to make all ready to go back to York and bring Mrs. Thomson and the children. The path was carefully selected, the men breaking the twigs of the trees along the route through the woods, and "blazing" the way to guide their return.

They were accompanied by John Thomson (afterwards known as "Thomson of the Bay," probably to distinguish him from another of the same name), and James Elliot.

The comparison between the life in Scotland and the strangeness of the experiences in the woods of Canada, must have made a profound impression on Mrs. Thomson's mind. The "Mother of Scarboro," as she is invariably called, was no doubt possessed of indomitable courage, as well as a strong and abiding trust in the protecting arm of the Almighty. She must have had a firm nerve and boundless love for husband and children to carry her through the first seven months of her life in Scarboro. She was often alone from week's end to week's end with her children in the forest log-house, while her husband worked for the means of living at his trade in the town, returning with the week's provision on his back on each recurring Saturday night.

What must have been the joy of the greeting with which the weary bread-winner was met! How longingly the wife must have watched for the figure coming into the little clearing beyond which she and her little ones dare not venture! How precious must the Sabbath days have been, and with what anxious thoughts did the brave woman bid her husband good-bye on the Monday morning!

She used to say, "Often in those early days the cottage was surrounded by wolves, some on the roof, others gnawing and scratching at the door."

One day Mrs. Thomson heard a commotion among the domestic animals in the enclosure; she ran out, and seeing a bear about to carry off a pig, she struck him with an axe and made him drop his prize. The bear made off to the woods, and one of the men followed, but failed to kill him.

During these first seven months of their life in the township, Mrs. Thomson had not seen another of her own sex, until one day an Indian woman came into the cottage. The face was strange, the language spoken unintelligible, but Mrs. Thomson welcomed her gladly. Albeit, of an alien race and color, they were women, and they understood one another by the freemasonry of sympathy divinely implanted in the breast of woman.

Two years after their arrival in the New World a daughter (Janet) was born to the Thomsons, the first white child born in the township.

It would be difficult to give a detailed account of all the privations and daily difficulties of this pioneer life in the woods—the mother alone with her children while the husband worked either at York, or in clearing the land about the cottage: the necessity of adapting their wants to the means of supplying them; and the terrible anxiety when any of their number fell ill.

One of these privations, which would appear to us now as of minor importance, was the difficulty of obtaining any variety of diet. Cornmeal and milk for breakfast, milk and cornmeal for dinner, and the same for supper, day after day, became not only monotonous but nauseating. As the spring opened it occurred to Mrs. Thomson that by noticing what the cow fed upon she might find some plant that would take the place of the garden greens of her old home. Pursuing this idea, she followed the cow into the woods, and thus discovered the leek. At first it was so great a relish that they used it frequently, but soon wearied of it. A dose of warm milk in which it had been boiled, administered to Mr. Thomson while ill of an ague he had contracted at York, so disgusted him, that the leek was ever after banished from his table.

The stream supplied them with fish, some of which they salted for winter use. Doubt has been expressed as to the variety of fish caught, some affirming it to have been salmon, others that it was salmon-trout. It was undoubtedly salmon, which was then common to all our large lakes.

There are several fish stories extant. The following is vouched for by several persons still living in the township:

Andrew Thomson (who came with his brother David to Canada and settled on the adjoining lot in Scarboro) and another man, were fishing in that part of Highland Creek which flows through Springfield Farm; the former hooked and landed a fish so large that when suspended from a pole run through its gills and resting on the shoulders of the two men, its tail touched the ground. The men were about five feet nine inches in height. This fish was probably a sturgeon.

David Thomson had overcome the first difficulties of settlement in the forest when he was joined by his two brothers, Andrew and Archibald.

Andrew was born in 1770, and was twice married before he left Scotland. His second wife, Jane Henderson, and four children came with him to Canada—John, his eldest son by the first wife, and Margaret, Andrew and William, the second family.

Archibald was also born and married in Scotland, and brought a family of ten to settle near his brothers.*

* According to other accounts he came to America unmarried, some years before his brother David. After residing for a few years in the States, he reached the city of Quebec as a U.E.L. Here he was married, and subsequently removed to Detroit, which place he left for Newark on the arrival there of his brother David.

With such large families the Thomsons soon became so numerous in the township that it was necessary to designate them by the names of their farms, after a common custom followed in Scotland. Others were distinguished by local sobriquets earned by some peculiarity or some incident in which they had taken part. Hence we find "Buffalo Dave," "Stone-house Archie," "Archie's Arch," "Beardy Archie," "Squaw Village John," "Grandmother's Dave," "Russian Dave," "Springfield Jimmie," "Squire's John," "Fiddler Dick," and so on.

David Thomson took out the patent for his land, lot 24, concession 1, two hundred acres, on May 17th, 1802; Andrew, the patent for lot 23, concession 1, on the same date.

Among the records of the life of this Thomson family, during the early days of their life in Canada, is a curious account-book, in which details of work done for Andrew and Archibald Thomson are entered. A recapitulation of a few of these entries may not be uninteresting here:

"In 1796, wrought at Mr. Dickson's house for Andrew Thomson — days. Rec'd of him 2 dollars.

"1797.—Wrought to Arch'd Thomson at the jail 14 days—March 14."

Down the column of consecutive days other names appear. At May 5th it reads:

"To And'w Heron, 1 day. 6th.—At the graveyard, 1 day. 17th.—To Mr. Wilson, 1 day.

"June 23rd.—To Mr. Pilkington, 1 day.

"To plaistering the two government rooms, And'w Thomson, John Thomson, and D'd Thomson, 14 days each.

"July 26th.—Begun to wall the government brick houses—D'd Thomson."

The name of James Elliot also appears frequently in the pages which follow, the walls of the government buildings evidently taking until the end of August to build, and other work occupying the men until the 7th of October.

The account for the quantity of bricks used is also given on another page:

"53,500, at 17s. 6d. per thousand, amounting to £46 16s. 2d.; four 84-foot arches, at 1s. per foot, £4 4s. Total, £51 0 2d."

Other names prominent in Toronto and the Government are also mentioned, including those of Capt. McGill and Mr. Cameron.

An entry on one of the yellow leaves of the little book would lead us to infer that Mrs. Thomson kept her husband's accounts, as in the same handwriting there is:

"April 8th, 1798.—To sewing one shirt, 5. To hemming a handkerchief, 1."

There is no note to indicate whether she charged Samuel Heron shillings or pence for the work done. On the same page is an entry of 7¾ lbs. of beef at 11d. per lb., bought of Samuel Heron.

In course of time, as the land became cleared, there were many open glades in which comfortable log-houses and some frame farm buildings dotted the landscape. Neighbors were nearer, the population was increasing, and times were apparently growing better. The settlers could now look forward hopefully to success. Roads were being made, and traffic between the principal settlements and the markets was thus rendered less infrequent.

When war was declared by the United States against Great Britain in 1812, David Thomson was given a commission in the 3rd York Regiment of Militia, and no doubt fulfilled the attendant obligation of raising the company he was to command from the settlers in the township, so many of whom bore his own name. (Further particulars of his military career will be found in the chapter on Militia.)

After the cessation of hostilities, the settlement of the country was more rapid, a number coming over from the United States, and others from Great Britain and Ireland. Shortly after the close of the war, David Thomson built a tavern, or stopping place, on the opposite bank of the stream from that on which the first cottage stood, and on the old Markham Road, in order to accommodate the public travelling to and from the north by that route. The site is now occupied by the fine residence of his grandson, Amos Thomson. The vacated cottage was rented by Mrs. Betsy Stafford, a widow, who kept the first store in the township.

The tavern was a frame house built by one of David Thomson's sons. The roof was covered by hand-made clap-boards. In this house David Thomson and his wife lived the remainder of their days. Hospitable, kind and full of sympathy for those in trouble, they were honored and respected by all who knew them.

About a year before he died David Thomson underwent a surgical operation, having his leg amputated for some disease of the knee. When Drs. Graham and Hamilton were ready to operate, the old man, with a nerve wonderful in one of his age, mounted the table without assistance, laid himself down, and endured the amputation without flinching. He died in

1834, and was buried in the old church-yard of St. Andrew's. His wife survived him some years, dying on November 8th, 1847.

A large tombstone marks the spot where they lie. It bears the following inscription which tells its own story:

In

Memory of

Mary Thomson,

The Mother of Scarboro,
Who died the 8th November, 1847.
Aged 80 years.

Here her remains repose side by side
with those of her husband

DAVID THOMSON,

Whose gravestone tells the Land
of their Nativity and when they
settled in Scarboro, which was
then a Wilderness. On the opposite
bank of the passing Rivulet, a
little above this Burial-ground,
they built their lonely cottage,
and there they contended successfully
against the hardships of a
forest life; and there she passed
the first seven months after their
settlement without seeing a woman,
and the first was an INDIAN.
As her husband, she lived and
died respected, leaving behind her
above 100 Descendants.

As time runs on, so families pass away;
Ye living men improve the present day;
O seek that home that lies beyond the grave,
Employ all means th' immortal soul to save.

The experiences of other early settlers in the township were more or less similar to that of the Thomsons—they all had to overcome the difficulties of clearing the forest, to live in the rudely-built log-houses and to endure the like privations. In writing the history of one we have that of all. Among the names most prominent in the annals of the township in the early days of the century are Annis, Cornell, Elliot, Pherrill, Devenish, Kennedy, Smith, Post, Palmer, Paterson, Secor, Chester and Adams.

The founder of the Annis family on this continent came to Massachusetts, U.S., in 1670. His descendant, Charles Annis, attracted by the bounty offered by Lieut.-Governor Simcoe, came over into Canada in 1793. He first settled in Whitby township, but removed to Scarboro, to lots 16, concessions C and D, which he purchased in 1808.

He had not borne arms in the War of Independence, and he took the oath of allegiance to the British Crown before Robert Baldwin, J.P., on January 15th, 1801. His son Levi, with William Cornell and the early settlers in the township, cut out the timber along the route through the forest for the Kingston Road in 1800, and Charles Annis with his second son was employed by Government, in 1812, to carry the mail between York and a post half a mile east of the present town of Oshawa.

Roger Coonet (Vankoughnet?) and John Buck had come from the United States with Charles Annis, one of whose sons married a daughter of Coonet, by whom he had a large family, who all married and settled in the township.

Levi Annis's house appears to have been used as

quarters for contingents of British soldiers when on their way up from Kingston to York and Niagara. Fears of invasion and raids made by parties from the United States were a source of anxiety to the settlers. Many stories are told, although there are not sufficient data extant to render them authentic history. One in connection with Levi Annis's house is to the effect that upon an alarm being given of the approach of the enemy, the soldiers quartered there buried their money in Gates's Gully, close by. As there is no record of the money having been dug up again, belief in the story has led to many a search being made for it by the romance-loving lads in the township.

A daughter of William Fawcett, who came to Canada from Cumberland, in 1825, and bought lot 15, concession 1, married into the Annis family.

Though not as numerous as the Thomsons, the Annises married and intermarried with the families of the other early settlers, and formed an important constituency in the township.

James Elliot, who accompanied David Thomson in his original journey, was also the founder of a large family. He came to Canada in the same year, and was employed in the government works at York. He took up lot 21, concession D, and married Janet Thomson, niece of David, in 1802, their marriage being the first celebrated in the township.

He afterwards moved to lot 24, concession 3, also taking up lot 25, which, being on Clergy Reserve land, was available for pre-emption only. Three of his sons who survived him received one hundred acres each. His daughters married, and moved with their husbands into other townships. Some of his descendants still reside in Scarboro.

Stephen Pherrill is another name around which early reminiscences group themselves. Born in 1782, near the River St. John, at a point where it divides the State of Maine and New Brunswick, he married Elizabeth Russell and came to Scarboro in 1803. The route by which they travelled was a long one. He rowed his wife and child, with the small amount of baggage they possessed, in a small boat up the St. Lawrence and up the lake to York. There he was employed in Scadding's mill, on the Don River. He took up lot 24, concession B, in 1805 or 1806.

When war broke out in 1812, Stephen placed his team at the service of the Government, and was employed to convey soldiers, stores and ammunition from Kingston to Niagara. He also carried the dispatches from York to Whitby, having to swim his horse across the River Rouge. His wife shared the task, for when he reached his farm upon the return journey, weary and wet, his horse jaded and tired, she mounted the other horse and carried the dispatches on to York, while her husband took needed rest.

There is a story told of this brave woman defying a party of rude Americans who came into her house, and, with wanton violence, destroyed all they could not carry away. She was forced to desist from active protestations against the breaking of her crockery by threats of being killed if she were not quiet. Dishes were valuable things in those days—all such necessaries having to be brought from Montreal in bateaux (large flat boats), forced up the rapids by men with strong poles, and occupying many days on the journey.

Her son Adna was born in Scarboro in 1816. He died in 1892, and his son Tilmoth now lives on the farm.

William Devenish was another of the earliest settlers. Born in London, he came to Canada *via* New York, and crossed the Niagara River in 1792. He was a carpenter, and probably was also employed on the new government buildings at York. He settled in Scarboro, lot 35, concession C, in 1804, and built the first frame barn in the township in 1807. It was pulled down by D. Hough, of Medonte, in 1846. The scantling used for braces and girths were hewn from rough timber with the axe ; the boards were split from pine logs ; the material used for doors was sawn by hand ; the nails were made by a blacksmith. It is to be regretted that this building was not preserved as a monument to the industry and perseverance of the early settlers. It is supposed that the old school-house in this section was built about the same time.

The loneliness of life in the woods is graphically illustrated by a gift made by William Devenish to an incoming settler named Foglie, in 1810, whom he induced to accept a life-lease of one hundred acres of heavily wooded land, part of his own lot, for the nominal rental of one shilling a year, in order that he might secure him as a neighbor.

Foglie settled on it and married. He does not appear to have done much clearing, except to dispose of the timber. The Lewis Lumber Company, having built a large steam mill at Norway in 1822, bought a quantity of the valuable pine from Foglie. He died in 1825, but his landlord allowed his widow to remain on the lot. Mrs. Foglie was found murdered in her house about twelve years after the death of her husband. It was generally supposed that the reports of her wealth and the hope of getting possession of it had excited the cupidity of some of the men employed at the mill. The truth of this has never been ascertained. The murderer failed to find her money, as it was discovered later sewed up inside a mattress. The land then reverted to the original owner.

William Devenish was married to Jane Webster by Parson Addison, a well-known divine of that date, 1799. Her family came to Scarboro and lived on the Devenish farm. His brother-in-law and William Purdy built a carding mill on the little Don, just on the town line between York and Scarboro. This mill was run by the latter in 1820, but the date of its erection is uncertain.

William Devenish was the assessor and tax collector and commissioner for the township for twenty-seven years before the municipal laws came into force, and was a J. P. until his death, on July 29th, 1856. He had eleven children, the only one of whom surviving is Ann, married to J. P. Wheler.

William Cornell also belongs to the group of the earliest settlers, coming in next to Thomson. Descended from a Cornell, or Cornwell, who came to America and settled in Rhode Island in 1636, William Cornell was born on October 29th, 1766. He came to Scarboro and took up lots 17 and 18, concession C, on the lake front, at the end of last century. He brought his wife and family across the lake in a boat, which they anchored out from the shore and lived in until the house was built. He plied a lucrative trade across the lake, carrying grain, potatoes, etc., to

Oswego. He lost both her and her cargo of wheat in 1812. She was probably seized in Oswego as a legitimate war-prize. Having to carry his corn and wheat to Port Hope to be ground, he made an early effort to supply the need of the settlers. He built the first grist and saw-mill in the township, conveying the mill-stones for the former from Kingston on his sled, and paying for them with a span of young colts. He set out the first orchard in the township about the year 1802.

William Cornell was twice married. His first wife died in 1808. His second was Tiny, the widow of Parshall Terry. By her he had two sons and four daughters. She died in 1834.

Cornell belonged to the Society of Friends. He lived to the great age of 93 years and 6 months.

William Knowles, the ancestor of the present R. Knowles, also had an eventful journey to the township. Born in England, he came here from New Jersey with his wife and seven children in 1803. Coming by boat round the head of Lake Ontario, they were obliged to put in at the Forty Mile Creek, the site of the present town of Grimsby, where the eighth child, and father of the present R. Knowles, was born.

No details are extant as to whether the poor woman had other care than her husband could give her, or whether the child was born under the shelter of a roof or of a tent. This was probably but one more of the many instances recorded of the endurance and bravery of the women whose sons have inherited their pluck and made Canada what it is to-day

As soon as Mrs. Knowles was able to travel, they came on to Scarboro, probably by road, as the record is that William Knowles bought lot 3, concession 1, from Jesse Ketchum, paying for it with a span of horses, a set of harness, and waggon. It is reasonable to suppose that after the birth of the child it was more difficult to continue their journey by water. The Forty Mile Creek was also in the direct road from Niagara to York, and the exchange of boat for horses and waggon would not be a difficult matter to arrange.

He had been led to suppose when he purchased the lot that he would find a house ready to receive his family. He found only the roofless walls of a log shanty, and the first days of his life in Scarboro were spent under the trees.

Knowles was a blacksmith and built the first smithy, making the nails used in building the first frame barn in the township. He planted out an orchard, naming each tree after the child who dug the obstructing stump out of the spot where the tree was set. He grew his own flax, and his wife, who was of Dutch descent, carded, spun and wove all the blankets, linen and cloth required for the family. William Knowles died in May, 1825; his wife survived him till January 27th, 1842. Dying intestate, his property went to his eldest son Richard, who, however, generously divided it equally with his brothers. Daniel subsequently bought out his brothers' shares, and lived on the estate until 1861. The stone house on the lot was built in 1832, and while being the second erected in the township, is believed now to be the oldest standing. Daniel kept the first store in the section, and was part owner with James Adams of a vessel plying between Canadian and United States ports.

In 1835, Daniel Knowles was appointed one of the Commissioners for making the present Kingston Road. In 1850, he was a prominent member of the Scarboro and Pickering Wharf Company. This company did an excellent business in shipping grain, tan-bark, timber and cordwood, until the building of the Grand Trunk Railway diverted the traffic. He was elder of a sect known as the "Disciples of Christ." They held their meetings in the old school-house on his land.

His sister Anna was one of the notables of the township. She kept house for him. Rising early, she performed her own domestic duties, then saddled a horse, well known in the section as the "Old Sorrel," and rode five miles to Pickering, where her brother John lived. After baking, washing or scrubbing for him, and setting his bachelor quarters in order, she rode home again before evening, following the banks of the Rouge, making "Old Sorrel" swim across intervening creeks. She seems to have been a matter-of-fact woman, probably possessing a sense of humor, and was celebrated as one of the best soap-makers in the section. When one of her neighbors asked "in what moon" she made it, she replied to her superstitious querist, that her "soap was made in a kettle, not in the moon."

James Kennedy came from Schenectady, N.Y., in 1800, and settled on lot 28, concession 5. The names of three of his sons are prominent in the militia annals of the township. He had five sons and three daughters, most of whom married and settled here. His grandson Thomas, having sold lot 28, concession 4 (his father's property), to Mr. Eckardt, succeeded him on the old homestead, where he lived till 1847, when he bought lot 26, concession 3. Many of James Kennedy's descendants own lots in the township; others are in good positions in different parts of the country.

Isaac Chester, born in Northumberland, England, about 1785, married Elizabeth Whitfield, in 1808, and came to Canada, *via* New York, in 1819. He remained some time in York, where he was employed in building the brick house (still standing) on the corner of King and Frederick streets, Toronto, afterwards occupied by the Canada Company's offices. He moved to Scarboro about 1820, taking out a 100-acres' grant on lot 26, concession C, and bought the present homestead, lot 25, concession D, from —— Flummerfelt, another resident of Scarboro, about 1828. He died at the age of eighty-six, his wife at eighty-two. He had nine children, and has a number of descendants still resident in the township.

George, his fourth son, who lives on lot 19, concession D, keeps a general store. He was lieutenant in the Scarboro militia; postmaster from 1853 to 1858; member of the council for eight years, filling the office of Reeve for six and of Deputy-Reeve for two years. He is a member of the Church of England and a Conservative. He married Elizabeth Finlay, and has three sons and two daughters.

Thomas Adams, or, as he was better known among the settlers, "Uncle Tommy Adams," was another of the early settlers. He was said to like his sobriquet so well that he declined to be addressed by any other name. He came to Canada from Vermont, U.S., in 1808, and settled upon lots 1, concessions D and 1. He built a log-house on the bank overlooking the lake, and

SCARBORO AS IT WAS AND IS.

OLDEST LIVING RESIDENTS.

1. Andrew Young, J. Morgan, A. M. Secor, S. Phœnix, T. Ormerod, J. L. Paterson, J. Little, A. Elliot, G. Taylor, J. Lawrie.
2. A. Bell, J. Callender, H. Elliot, J. Holmes, A. Walker, D. Forfar, Jonathan Baird, J. McBeth, W. Bell, J. McGinn, J. Tingle.
3. Mrs. D. Thomson, Mrs. Green, Mrs. Clark, Mrs. Elliot, Mrs. Johnston, Mrs. Morgan, Mrs. Stephenson, Mrs. Kennedy, Mrs. Carmichael, Mrs. John Wheler, Mrs. Gordon Rennie.
4. John Dunn, A. McCreight, J. Wyper, W. Oliver, W. Helliwell, Mrs. Jackson, Mrs. Pherrill, Mrs. White, Jas. McCowan, R. Loveless.
5. D. W. Thomson, D. Martin, I. Chester, J. Buchanan, E. Wood.

later on, a brick one. The latter was struck by lightning about the year 1832, when his son William was killed. Thomas Adams was a carpenter, and captain of an American sailing-vessel during the war of 1812. He was driven for refuge into Highland Creek. There, fearing his cargo of guns, brass kettles and ammunition might be seized, he threw everything overboard, and, tradition adds, "the drowned cargo is still supposed to be lying at the bottom of the creek."

About 1834, Thomas Adams, in partnership with John Allen, built a sailing-vessel at the mouth of Highland Creek. They named her the *Mary Ann*. Adams built the first school-house in the section, in 1836. It is still standing, a cottage of planks, on the Kingston Road. Many of the first frame houses in the neighborhood were also put up by him. Adams had six sons and two daughters. One of the sons, James, was a sailor and part owner with Daniel Knowles of the *Highland Chief*, a vessel built at the Humber River about 1834. This vessel was lost in a great storm on the lakes, when all hands perished. The wreck was driven ashore at Presqu' Ile Point, overhauled, and ultimately sold to Thomas Scott.

Among the earliest names in the township is Ashbridge, a U. E. Loyalist. Around it a peculiar interest centres. Sarah Ashbridge, a widow, with her children, came from Philadelphia in 1790. She was given a grant of two hundred acres, lot 27, concession B. Her story would be interesting; her loyalty, endurance and perseverance in making the journey from Philadelphia to Canada, and at that early date taking up land in the wilds of a new township, in order to live and bring up her children under the shadow of the Union Jack, should be a narrative of no commonplace nature. It is to be regretted that this story cannot be gathered and given now to the readers of the records of a century in the township.

Mrs. Ashbridge bequeathed her land to two of her grandsons, Andrew Heron and James McClure. Her son Jonathan was granted lot 26, concession B. He gave it to his son Isaac in 1844. Isaac married Ruth, daughter of George Auburn, and his son Jonathan now owns the farm. Isaac died in 1894.

At the time of the terrible massacre of St. Bartholomew, when so many lost their lives for the Protestant faith, two brothers and a sister left their home and property. They made their escape from the shores of France in an old scow, and were taken on board a British merchant ship bound for New York. Here they landed and made a home for themselves and their descendants, accumulating a fine property in the New World. Part of this estate is the present Jerome Park, the finest race-track in America. Upon the outbreak of the Revolutionary War, their loyalty to the flag under which their ancestors had been rescued made it impossible for them to join the rebels, or take any part in the revolutionary movement. Isaac Secor, the representative of the Old French Huguenot family of De Sécor, left his property and crossed into Canada.

He came first to Kingston, and moving west, built the first stone mill at Napanee, and it is probably from this mill, and the quantity of flour ground in it that the place was named by the Indians "Napanee,"—flour or bread. In or about the year 1817, he undertook the contract to improve the Kingston Road through the township of Scarboro, a distance of about twelve miles, for the sum of $1,100. He married and left four daughters and two sons, who remained in the township. The Secors, father and sons, served in the militia (for particulars, see Militia chapter), proving their loyalty and devotion to be as great in the Scarboro branch of the family as in that settled in the Niagara peninsula, which had the fidelity and courage of Laura Secord to glorify it.

Instances of the changes made in names by their environment are common throughout the country. In the Secors the Scarboro branch had but dropped the noble prefix of "de." In Niagara it was also dropped; but the pronunciation of the name led to its being spelled with a final "d," *Secord*.

A greater alteration, however, occurs in that of Pierre le Pelletier, which, in Scarboro, is now only known and recognized as Peter Pilkey. The celebration of the centennial of Scarboro settlement might be a favorable date on which to restore the name to its original form.

Pierre le Pelletier de Scarboro was born at Three Rivers about 1775. He came to Kingston in 1800, and thence to York, in a vessel carrying a cargo of potash kettles. There being no wharf at York, the kettles were carefully lowered from the deck to the water, when, it is said, the men got into them and paddled ashore!

Thus did Pierre le Pelletier, the ancestor of the Pilkeys of to-day, arrive at York. He first located on the right bank of the Don, within the limits of the town of York, and obtained employment at the New Fort.

During 1812 he held the post of baker to the garrison, and when the capital was attacked by the Americans under Chauncey, his stone bread-trough was rendered useless by an enemy's cannon-ball.

It is stated that Le Pelletier took an active part in the war of 1812, and that his family still possess a medal given him for blowing up the fort at Detroit. Fort Detroit was not blown up—the fort at York was, either by accident or design, probably the latter; and if this French-Canadian was the man detailed to the duty, and was thus rewarded for it, a valuable item would be added to the history of that memorable day.

In the same year he was employed in the conveyance of a cannon and an anchor from Kingston to Penetanguishene. These were drawn by oxen from the Rouge to Holland Landing, by way of the Danforth and Old Ridge Roads. From Holland Landing to the head of Kempenfeldt Bay they were conveyed on a raft, thence from the site of the present town of Barrie to the Nottawasaga River by land, with the intention of completing the distance by that river to the Georgian Bay, and along its shores to Penetanguishene. But, alas! the anchor was lost in the river, where it remains to the present day.*

Pierre le Pelletier settled on lot 35, concession 1, and his family of nine sons formed a valuable company for the development of the township's resources.

Another Scarboro pioneer with an interesting record was Joseph Harrington. His father, mother,

* This anchor was of enormous weight, and the cost of its transport reached the sum of seven hundred pounds. It should be taken up and preserved as an historical relic in the County of Simcoe. It would make an excellent monument.

grandmother and one child, U. E. Loyalists, left Cleveland, Ohio, early in the spring of 1804. Driving their own horses and bringing several cows with them, they crossed the Niagara and came around the head of the lake. Owing probably to the rate of travel possible for the cattle, the party were longer on the road than they had calculated upon. When they reached the Humber River near Weston, it was necessary to make a halt. They succeeded in securing an old stable as a lodging, and there Joseph Harrington was born, on July 17, 1804. As soon as Mrs. Harrington was able to travel, they moved on to Markham. Young Joseph married Sarah Pickel, of Darlington, in 1832, and settled in the township of Scarboro, on lot 19, concession 2, seventy-five acres of which he bought from Wm. Proudfoot. This part of the township was still covered with forest, and the Harringtons had many experiences similar to those of the earliest settlers. During the first summer they lived in a frame house without either door or window, and did all their cooking on a camp fire in the open air.

Harrington built a mill-dam and mill during the first year, and although it was a great labor it was a great success, and the time spent in the work proved a good investment both for himself and his neighbors.

James Jones, a Welshman, took up his abode on lot 28, concession C, in 1811. He obtained a twenty-one years' lease of it from the Clergy Reserve, paying for the first seven years an annual rental of ten shillings, or three bushels of good wheat ; the second seven years the rental was increased to one pound (twenty shillings), or six bushels, and the last seven, one pound ten shillings, or nine bushels of good wheat, was claimed. He purchased this hundred acres in 1829, obtaining a deed from King's College.

Jonathan Gates, who settled on lots 19 and 20, concession C, in 1815, is another name familiar to early settlers. He was the proprietor of the well-known Gates's Tavern, and his name will occur frequently in what follows.

The name of Helliwell is now a prominent one in the township. In the records of the founder of the family in Canada there are several very interesting items.

Thomas Helliwell was a cotton spinner in Toughstone, Yorkshire, England. In 1818 he decided to try his fortune in the New World, but owing to some guild regulation preventing skilled workmen leaving England, he was obliged to smuggle himself on board a sailing-vessel at Sunderland, and arrived in Quebec just after the river was free of ice. He settled first at Lundy's Lane, and opened a store for general merchandise at the junction of Lundy's Lane and the Chippewa Road, now a central corner in the village of Drummondville. His family joined him in August. He also rented the building afterwards occupied as a museum at Niagara Falls. It was then a distillery, and Thomas Helliwell carried on the business in connection with his general store, exchanging goods for grain, which he made into whiskey and sold at a York-shilling a gallon.*

Thomas Helliwell bought lot 7, concession 1, from a man at the Falls in 1820, but did not settle on it.

* A York-shilling was a British sixpenny piece, and was equivalent to sevenpence halfpenny currency, or twelve and a half cents.

His son, William Helliwell, came to the township in 1847. In 1821 he bought the Don Mills, and built a brewery there. After his death in 1825 his three elder sons carried on the business, until William became of age, when he was taken into partnership and remained in the firm until he removed to Scarboro in 1847. He lived in the rough-cast cottage near the present post-office at Highland Creek. He has been twice married, and has a number of descendants living in the township and in other parts of Canada.

John Hough was another of the earlier settlers who came to Canada, crossing at Queenston in 1794. His son William, born in Albany, N.Y., in 1777, came to Scarboro before the close of the century. He settled on 200 acres of lots 28, concessions A and B, on what is now called the Kennedy Road. His father and the rest of the family followed him in 1804, and took up the 200 acres of lot 30, concession B, since known as Hough's Corners, a name it has borne for over eighty years. John built the first saw-mill on the little stream running through the east corner of lot 30, concession C, in 1816.

We get a quaint little peep of life in the bush from the records of the Walton family. John Walton, born in Cumberland, England, in 1799, emigrated to Canada, with his parents, in 1818. Having worked in the lead mines in England, he turned his knowledge to account by sinking wells. Many of those in the neighborhood of Gooderham & Worts' distillery were sunk by John Walton. In 1823 he settled in Scarboro, on lot 35, concession 2, and lot 35, concession 3, for which he paid $1 an acre. He afterwards sold the north half to Robert Oliver, and lived on the south half. He married Mary Thomson, third daughter of the first settler in Scarboro.

Mrs. Walton carried her butter and eggs to York market, a distance of ten miles, by a footpath through the woods. She received fourpence a pound for her butter, or one York-shilling for two pounds, and the same for her eggs per dozen, taking groceries and other necessaries instead of cash. One takes an interest in learning that at the end of three years the family fortunes had prospered well enough to provide the worthy daughter of a brave mother with a mare called "Kate," and a side-saddle on which she might ride to market. After two years more, the industrious couple procured a second steed, and, with ingenious fingers, fashioned for the team a set of harness, from strips of basswood bark.

Thomas Paterson, born in Kelso, Scotland, settled on lot 28, concession 3. He was a Presbyterian, and Thomas Paterson was one of the first elders ordained in St. Andrew's Church. His son William had preceded him by two years, taking out his patent in 1818. The land was uncleared, and the family endured all the hardships and privations inseparable from life in the bush. His grandson, John L., settled on lot 27, concession 3, is noted for the pride he has taken in the successful working of his farm. Other grandsons are James, Thomas and Andrew, all leading farmers on the Kennedy Road.

Between the years 1820 and 1830 we find many names still prominent in the township. Among them was John Perryman Wheler, a Devonshire man, who took an active interest in church affairs and was one of the most prominent in all agricultural matters, being for thirty years a director in one or other of the agricultural societies in the township, or in the East Riding of York, and a life member of the Agriculture and Arts Association of Ontario. He was also a member of the township council, and for eighteen years held the office of reeve. Mr. Wheler was an able man, being conversant with municipal law, and considered an authority on all questions within its scope. As president of the first regularly constituted Reform Association in the township, he took a lively part in its proceedings. He was License Inspector from the date of the Crooks Act until his death.

James Ionson is another name belonging to this date. He came from Westmoreland, England, and settled on lot 29, concession D, in 1827.

Robert Jackson, born in Yorkshire in 1803, came with his wife and four children to Canada. He bought lot 17, concession D, from J. Willmot. After living twelve years in the log-house, he desired to build a brick residence. To do so it was first necessary to make the bricks. This he did on the farm, puddling the clay by the feet of his oxen. Mr. Jackson actively assisted in the building of St. Margaret's Church, and served as churchwarden in Christ Church for eleven years. He was married twice, his second wife being a daughter of Pennock Thompson. He had eighteen children, all of whom married and settled in Canada, and his descendants would make a regiment 350 strong. His son, Thompson Jackson, was director and president of the Scarboro Agricultural Society for ten years, and representative of the township council for three.

Stephen Washington, the founder of Washington Methodist Church, built in 1842, settled on lot 22, concession C, in 1824.

James Humphrey, born in the County of Tyrone, Ireland, on May 31st, 1797, came to Canada in 1824. He purchased the two hundred acres of lot 16, concession D, for which he paid five dollars an acre to the Clergy Reserve Fund. He was a member of the Church of England, and gave the site on which Christ Church stands. He died in 1893, at the advanced age of 95 years and 11 months.

Francis Armstrong, familiarly known in the township as "Daddy Armstrong." He is a carpenter and wheelwright, and though in his eighty-third year, is still active.

The Richardson family came from Ireland, in 1823 and 1824, to lot 14, concession D. Notwithstanding the prosperity that has attended this family, its members are now widely scattered, the only representative left in the township being John, who represents East York in the Local Legislature, and who is a Commissioner in Queen's Bench. For fourteen years he was Reeve, and in 1885 he held the position of County Warden. Numerous physicians and ministers, elsewhere mentioned, have done honor to the name both in this country and the United States.

Jordan Post, a settler who has left his own and his wife's names upon two of the central business streets of Toronto, was born in Connecticut, U.S., in 1767, came to Canada, and settled in York about 1790, and did business there in after years as a watch and clock maker. He married Melinda Woodruff about 1804. Having faith in the future of the place, he invested largely in real estate, part of it being the block where Jordan and Melinda streets retain the old names. He moved to Scarboro in 1829, to five hundred acres on Highland Creek, where he built a saw-mill, and became one of the pioneer lumbermen of the district. He floated the output down the stream to a point known as Cornell's Landing, and shipped it in small sailing-vessels to various ports on the lake. He built what was known for years as the "Old Yellow House." It was burned down in 1885. It stood on the site of Mr. Tredway's present house. Here he kept a general store until his death in 1845. He left six children. His sons Jordan and Woodruff inherited the property. The latter built a second saw-mill about half a mile east of the old one, and carried on a successful business for some years. He finally sold out to his brother-in-law, Stephen Closson, and went to the United States, where he entered the Episcopal Methodist ministry, and is still living at Olean, N.Y.

John Bell came to the township in 1820, and purchased lot 29, concession C, from Captain John McGill. He kept the "Blue Bell" from 1833 until his death in 1866. The only clearing between this tavern and the Woodbine was a small patch on lot 32, concession B, on the hill south of the Danforth Road, known as McCarthy's clearing.

David Brown was a wheelwright and waggon-maker, lot 30, concession 3. He built two stationary threshing machines for the late Wm. Hood and his brother Thomas Brown, making his horsepower wheels with wooden cogs. His name is perpetuated in the township in "Brown's Corners," where the present owner of the lot is post-master.

William Oliver, lot 10, concession 3, was born in Norfolk. He was employed by Richard Beatty, contractor, for improving and straightening the Kingston Road, in 1836, and was familiarly. known as "Billy-go-the-Road," probably from having tramped some distance in search of work. He leased a point of land adjoining Highland Creek, which is still known as "Billy's Point." He was the first settler on lot 2, concession D.

Marshall Macklem, lot 24, concession 4, is spoken of as the pioneer planter of trees along the roadsides, setting an example which many have followed, to the great advantage of the township.

George Morgan took up lot 32, concession 3. His son John, who, with his wife, survive, are aged respectively, eighty-two and eighty years. He owned the first mowing machine used in the township (about 1838).

Wm. Nash, lot 20, concession 4, was for many years a well-known county constable.

William Clark, born in the parish of Beith, Renfrewshire, Scotland, settled on lot 30, concession 4, which he purchased from John Kennedy in 1838. He was a member of the Home District Council in 1842. He left seven sons and two daughters. William, jun., succeeded him, and had five sons and two daughters. The second son, John C. Clark, J.P., now occupies the homestead. Hugh, fifth son of William, sen., settled on lot 28, concession 4.

Samuel Horsey, lot 30, concession 3, located in 1835. His son Ralph now lives on the homestead. His second son, George Edward, now of Kansas City, U.S., is a musician and composer of more than local fame.

Andrew Fleming, born in Lanarkshire, Scotland, settled on lot 9, concession 3, 1834. He left a number of descendants worthy of the name to form a clan in the New World. One of them, his namesake, now occupies the homestead.

Of the other names which belong to a later date of settlement, many are treated under other chapter headings and need not be referred to more particularly here.

When this chapter was first undertaken, it was intended to give a brief account of all the families in the township, but when the material was sent in, it was found to be so incomplete, and to contain so many apparently conflicting statements, that it was decided to select only a few of the earliest families whose experiences might, in a general way, represent all.

Imperative as this decision was, it is not the less regrettable, both on account of the fact that so much valuable information has been brought together, and because of the desirability that family records of the kind in question should be compiled. The manuscript, however, is preserved, and is available for future use, should it ever be decided to prepare a Scarboro Family Book.

THE LAND OF THE BRACING NORTH.

Sing ho! for the land of the bracing north,
For the land of the maple tree,
Whose million of fields of gold extend
From the east to the western sea.
Oh, ho! for the land of a thousand lakes,
Where a myriad rivers run,
Where leaps the bold blood of a hardy race
In the heart of each sturdy son.

May the God of the nations prosper her,
May Canada's fame increase;
May the leaf of the maple proudly wave
Till time shall forever cease.

Sing ho! for the land of the northern lights,
Where they flash in the winter sky,
And shine like the deeds of heroes dead
Who were strong in the years gone by.
Then here's to the land of the brave and free,
And of women divinely fair,
Where nature is glad and the sunlight laughs
As it gleams in the buoyant air.

Sing ho! for the land of the warlike north,
For a Brock and a Lundy's Lane;
Let foeman but touch our sacred soil
And we'll show him our might again.
Sing ho! for the land of our birth and pride,
For a nation that yet shall be
As splendid, as famed, and as numberless
As the leaves of her maple tree.

—WILLIAM T. ALLISON.

CHAPTER V.

ON THE FARM.

"The first farmer was the first man, and all historic nobility rests on possession and use of land."—*Emerson.*

"In ancient times, the sacred plough employed
The kings and awful fathers of mankind."
—*Thomson.*

"Oft did the harvest to their sickle yield;
Their furrow oft the stubborn glebe has broke;
How jocund did they drive their team afield!
How bow'd the woods beneath their sturdy stroke!"
—*Gray.*

POSSESSING, as Scarboro does, almost every variety of soil, from the sandy in the south to the clay loam and heavy clay of the centre and north, the methods of tillage pursued differ accordingly, but in most cases it may be said that agriculture is intelligently followed, and the results will correspond favorably with those of any other similar area in Ontario.

Without exception the original settlers were characterized, not by industry alone, but by that strong common-sense which, while it accepts the inevitable, strives as best it may to adapt means to ends. It was, perhaps, a fortunate circumstance, that from the earliest years, those who took up land were not all, or even mainly, from any particular place. Scotsmen, Englishmen, Irishmen and natives of the United States mingled fraternally and exchanged opinions.

The social friction proved beneficial all round, and manifested its good effects, especially in the chosen occupation of the people. During the first half of the century, some of the best farming in Upper Canada was conducted in this township, and many of the farms were brought to a condition scarcely, if at all, inferior to the best in Great Britain.*

Up to this date, Scarboro has maintained its agricultural reputation, and some of the very finest farms on our continent may be found in this township. Special reference is made to one of these in the following pages, although it is but fair to state that there are other farms in Scarboro, quite equal to "Kelvin Grove" in all that goes to constitute high-class, successful treatment of the soil.

The extracts that follow from the records of the Agricultural Society tell their own tale, and a run through the township will demonstrate the correctness of all deducible inferences.

The Scarboro Agricultural Society was formed on the first day of January, A.D. 1844. The subscription for each member was five shillings. The officers were a President, Vice-President, Secretary and Treasurer, and not less than twelve Directors, to be chosen annually.

* "One of the best farms to be seen in this neighborhood is in the township of Scarboro, belonging to Mr. Gates. He keeps a splendid tavern just ten miles from the City Hall, upon the plank road in Kingston Street, and his house is surrounded on both sides of the street with his farm, which contains about 300 acres, some of which extends to the borders of the lake. He takes care that every portion of it is well manured, having a large supply made in his stables, and he grows everything upon his own farm that is consumed in his house except groceries. He catches as much fish as serves his table all the year round, and makes as much sugar from his own maple grove as he wants, and kills his own mutton, beef and pork."—W. BROWN'S "Four Years in United States and Canada," p. 86. LEEDS, 1849.

The annual meeting was fixed for the first Friday of January in each year, and the office-bearers' meeting quarterly, on the first Friday of January, April, July and October.

It was also decided to hold annually an exhibition of farm stock, produce and other articles, to be held on the first Friday of October in each year.

It was determined, too, to hold a ploughing match if the funds would admit.

The list of subscribers comprised: William Crone, J. P. Wheler, John Torrance, Thomas Brown, Arch. Malcolm, John Lee, Wm. Mason, Martin Snider, Joshua Sisley, Arch. Glendinning, John Stobo, Stephen Closson, R. D. Hamilton, Joseph Armstrong, W. H. Norris, Wm. Armstrong, Isaac Chester, Geo. Scott, Wm. March, Thos. Smith, Robert Reid, Rev. Jas. George, John Rogers, Thos. Paterson (Toronto), Jas. Finlay, Jas. Palmer, Ed. Cornell, Geo. Weir, Jas. A. Thomson, Jas. McCowan, Jas. Patton, Alex. Neilson, Geo. Monkman, Stephen Washington, Nicholas Richardson, Jonathan Gates, Geo. Bambridge, John Gibson, Joseph Johnson, Francis Muir, Wm. Devenish, David Marshall, Chas. Cornell, Wm. Fitzpatrick, David Brown, Thos. Jacques, Henry Howell, Alex. Bederact, Thos. Paterson, Jas. Carnaghan, Barbara Berwick, Thos. Whiteside, Jas. Lawrie, Benjamin Johnson, Geo. W. Post, Ed. Whitefield, Thos. Young, Thos. Davidson, John Holmes, Wm. Clark, Robert Sellers, Jas. Davidson, Wm. Weir, Robert McCowan, John Ferguson, Wm. Paterson, Geo. Auburn, Allan McLean, W. D. Thomson, Wm. Hood, Jas. Harley. Total, 71 members.

The officers elected were: President, Wm. Crone; Vice-President, J. P. Wheler; Secretary, Stephen Closson; Treasurer, Thos. Brown.

	£	S.	D.
Total received from members' subscriptions	17	15	0
Government grant	11	5	0
Total	£29	0	0

The first fair was held at Sisley's Hotel. Danforth Road, on October 18th, 1844, when the following premiums were awarded:

Brood mare	1st prize	10s.	Jas. Patton.
"	2nd "	5s.	Geo. Auburn.
Two-year-old mare colt	1st prize		Arch. Glendinning.
" " "	2nd "		Jas. McCowan.
" horse "	1st "		John Holmes.
" " "	2nd "		John Stobo.
One-year-old mare "	1st "		T. Davidson.
" " "	2nd "		John Holmes.
Aged bull	1st "		H. Howell.
One young bull	1st "		Robt. McCowan.
Milch cow	1st "		Jas. Davidson.
"	2nd "		Jas. McCowan.
Two-year-old heifer	1st "		Geo. Auburn.
" "	2nd "		John Torrance.
One-year-old "	1st "		Robt. Reid.
" "	2nd "		Robt. Reid.
Aged ram	1st "		Wm. Mason.
"	2nd "		J. P. Wheler.
Ram lamb	1st "		John Lee.
"	2nd "		Geo. Scott.
Aged ewe	1st "		J. P. Wheler.
"	2nd "		Geo. Scott.
Ewe lamb	1st "		J. P. Wheler.
"	2nd "		Geo. Scott.
Boar	1st "		John Lee.
Sow	1st "		John Lee.
"	2nd "		Geo. Weir.

GRAIN.

2 bush. fall wheat	1st prize	W. Paterson.
" " "	2nd "	John Holmes.
" spring "	1st "	John Lee.
" " "	2nd "	A. McLean.

2 bush. peas	1st prize	..	A. McLean.
" "	2nd "	..	Wm. Mason.
" oats	1st "	..	Jas. Patton.
" "	2nd "	..	J. Torrance.
" potatoes	1st "	..	Joshua Sisley.
" S. turnips	1st "	..	John Torrance.
" W. "	1st "	..	Wm. Weir.
4 lbs. butter	1st "	..	J. P. Wheler.
" "	2nd "	..	Jas. McCowan.
2 lbs. cheese	1st "	..	Jas. Patton.

For stock, the prizes were 10s. and 5s. respectively for 1st and 2nd.

For grain, potatoes, roots, butter and cheese, the prizes were 5s. and 2s. 6d. for 1st and 2nd respectively.

The total prizes awarded amounted to £13 7s. 6d.

The second fair of the Agricultural Society was held at Sisley's, on the 18th day of October, 1845.

	£	s.	d.
The total receipts were	39	10	0
The expenditure was—			
Premiums awarded	27	10	0
Ploughing match	2	10	0
Printing	0	18	9
Total	£30	18	9

Leaving a balance of £8 11s. 8d. to carry over to next account. The officers were the same as for the previous year. In addition thirty-seven directors were elected. The total number of subscribers was eighty.

Premiums were awarded—in horses, to M. Hutchinson, Jas. McCowan, Thos. Davidson, and Geo. Scott; in cattle, to John Torrance, John Bell, Arch. Forfar, M. Davidson, and James McCowan; in sheep, J. P. Wheler and A. Taylor; in hogs, John Lee, D. Thomson, and Geo. Weir; in grain, A. Glendinning, W. Clark, Alex. Neilson, Geo. Scott, John Torrance, Col. McLean, Jas. Patrick, J. P. Wheler, Thos. Brown; in roots and potatoes,

R. Reid, S. Washington, and J. P. Wheler; in butter, James McCowan and Jas. Patrick; in cheese, Jas. McCowan and G. Scott.

In 1846, the fair was again held at Joshua Sisley's, when £24 10s. was awarded in prizes. The successful competitors were: in horses, A. Forfar, A. Neilson, Wm. Mason, D. McBeath; in cattle, John Torrance, A. Taylor, Margt. Davidson, A. Forfar, E. Whitefield; in sheep, A. Taylor, G. Scott, George Miller; in hogs, Wm. Boynton, J. P. Wheler, A. Neilson, J. Donaldson; in grain, J. P. Wheler, Wm. Devenish, Thos. Brownlee, James Patton, John Torrance, D. Thomson, W. Crone; in potatoes and roots, S. Washington, J. Crawford, W. Crone; in butter and cheese, Margt. Davidson, Jas. McCowan, John Torrance, Geo. Scott.

The total amount of premiums awarded was £24 1s. The officers were the same as for 1845.

The fair in 1847 was also held at Sisley's, on Friday, the first day of October. One of the regulations was that any male animal taking a first prize was to remain in the township during the next ensuing season. The judges appointed were: For horses, John Thom, John Elliott (of Pickering), and Joseph Smith; for cattle and sheep, William Mason, John Darling (of Markham), and Robert Reid; for butter, cheese, and roots, Wm. Devenish, Thos. Dowswell, and Edward Cornell.

The successful exhibitors were: in horses, W. Miller, R. Reid, M. Hutchinson, W. Boynton, and Hugh Elliot; in cattle, A. Taylor, J. P. Wheler, G. Scott, Jas. Patton; in sheep, W. Miller, Geo. Miller, and R. Reid; in pigs, W. Boynton, G. Scott, J. Ferguson, Alex. Wilson; in potatoes, R. Reid, and J. Pilkey; in roots, J. Patton, W. Crone, S. Washington; in grain, J. P. Wheler, J. Gibson, Wm. Clark, J. Torrance, and Thos. Brownlee; in cheese, George Scott and James McCowan; in butter, Thos. Brownlee and Margt. Davidson.

The total amount awarded was £22 7s. 6d.

In 1848, a resolution was passed prohibiting any person not residing in the township from showing any description of property for competition at the annual show. The show was held at Sisley's, on October 13th, when £26 2s. 6d. was awarded in premiums.

The fair for 1850 was held at J. H. Smith's tavern, Kennedy Road, when £15 2s. 6d. was awarded in prizes.

The fair for 1851 was held at the same place, but no particulars are available.

In 1852, the total number of subscribers was 121, and the total receipts were £44 5s. 6d.

The premiums awarded at the fall fair amounted to £25 0s. 6d.

	£	S.	D.
In 1853 the receipts from subscriptions were	19	7	6
Balance from previous year	17	10	7
Grant from Government	11	2	6
Total	£48	0	7

EXPENDITURE.

	£	S.	D.
There was paid in premiums	28	2	6
Paid in printing	1	5	0
" judges' dinners	0	18	9
" balance to ploughmen	14	10	0
By balance on hand	3	4	4

The successful exhibitors were: in horses, J. P. Wheler, J. Crawford, R. Steers, George Scott, A. Glendinning and A. Forfar; in cattle, G. Scott, A. Forfar, J. P. Wheler, J. Patton, W. Wride, J. Gould; in sheep and swine, J. P. Wheler, G. Scott, J. Lawrie, William Wride; in grain, J. P. Wheler, William Paterson, William Forfar, J. Sisley, J. Patton; in roots, J. Sisley, J. Crawford, J. P. Wheler, G. Ridout; in dairy products, J. McCowan, A. Glendinning, William Hutcheson; in implements, James Gilray, J. Crowther, R. Sylvester.

Fall fair, 1854. The total number of subscribers was 101.

The fair was held at Malcolm's "Speed the Plough" Inn, Malvern, Markham Road, on October 6th, 1854.

The successful exhibitors were: in horses, J. P. Wheler, James Lawrie, James Patton, James Bowes; in cattle, J. P. Wheler, James Patton, A. Young, John Wilson, Richard Collins; in sheep, Geo. Scott, J. P. Wheler; in swine, J. P. Wheler, William Wride, John Weir; in grain, J. P. Wheler, William Paterson, John Muir, John Weir, James Patton; in roots, Joshua Sisley, A. Glendinning, J. P. Wheler, John Weir; in dairy products, James Patton, A. Young, George Ridout, John Weir; in implements, George Ley, James Bowes, R. Sylvester. The total amount awarded in prizes was £26.

The annual meeting of the Agricultural Society was held at Malcolm's Inn, Markham Road. The following were elected office-bearers:

President, J. P. Wheler; Vice-President, J. H. Smith; Secretary-Treasurer, A. Glendinning; Directors, William Paterson, James Lawrie, Robert Buchanan, William Hood, John Weir, William Mason, Robert Paterson, Thomas Crone and James Patton.

The fall fair was held at Robertson's Inn, Kennedy Road, on October 26th, 1855, when the successful exhibitors were: in horses, J. P. Wheler, William Paterson, Andrew Young, A. P. Thomson; in cattle, J. P. Wheler, James Patton, William Wride, James Lawrie, John Crawford; in sheep, J. P. Wheler, John Malcolm, George Scott, Joshua Sisley; in swine, J. P. Wheler, John Malcolm; in grain, William Paterson, William Wride, John Malcolm, William Forfar, Joshua Sisley; in roots and potatoes, J. P. Wheler, William Paterson, James Lawrie, John Malcolm, William Forfar, J. Sisley, F. Bell; in implements, etc., George Ley, George Richardson, Richard Sylvester. The total amount awarded was £25 15s.

The officers for Scarboro Agricultural Society for 1856 were: President, J. P. Wheler; Vice-President, J. H. Smith; Secretary-Treasurer, Wm. Crawford. Directors—David Brown, Andrew Fleming, R. McCowan, Wm. Wride, Jas. Purvis, J. B. Burk, J. L. Paterson, Thos. Brown.

The fair was held on October 10th, 1856.

The successful exhibitors were: in horses, Wm. Wride, John Crawford, A. P. Thomson, Joshua Sisley, Jas. Lawrie, Wm. Paterson; in cattle, J. P. Wheler, Wm. Wride, John Crawford, John Malcolm, Jas. Patton, Jas. Lawrie, Geo. Scott, Alex. Gibb; in sheep, John Malcolm, Geo. Scott, Jas. Weir; in swine, J. P. Wheler, Wm. Wride, John Malcolm; in grain, Wm. Wride, Jas. Patton, A. P. Thomson, Joshua Sisley, Andrew Fleming, Andrew Walker; in roots and potatoes, J. P. Wheler, J. Sisley, G. Ridout, Andrew Fleming; in butter and cheese, Andrew Fleming, Alex. Wallace, Jas. Russell; in implements, John Malcolm, John Brown, John Burk, John Heck.

The total amount awarded was £29 10s.

The officers of the Scarboro Agricultural Society for 1857 were: President, J. P. Wheler; Vice-President, Jas. Lawrie; Secretary-Treasurer, Wm. Crawford. Directors—A. Fleming, Thos. Whiteside, Jas. Purvis, R. Sylvester, F. Scott, D. Brown, Wm. Wride, Alex. Thomson, John Hockridge.

The fair was held at Hockridge's Inn, Kennedy Road, on Friday, October 16th, 1857.

The successful exhibitors were: in horses, Jas. Lawrie, John Crawford, Wm. Crawford, Andrew Young, Geo. Scott, Andrew Taylor, Joshua Sisley, Mark Hutchinson, Wm. Oliver, Geo. Weir, D. Thomson, Alex. Muirhead, Geo. Graham; in cattle, J. P. Wheler, Jas. Lawrie, Andrew Young, John Malcolm, John Torrance, Jas. Patton, Wm. Wride, Andrew Fleming; in sheep, J. P. Wheler, Jas. Lawrie, John Malcolm, Geo. Scott; in swine, John Malcolm, Wm. Wride; in grain, Jas. Lawrie, Geo. Scott, Joshua Sisley, Wm. Wride, Andrew Fleming, Wm. Forfar, A. Glendinning; in roots and potatoes, J. P. Wheler, John Malcolm, Wm. Irving, Wm. Paterson, John Weir; in dairy products and bread, Andrew Young, Jas. Patton, John Chester, Wm. Irving, A. Glendinning, Wm. Paterson, John Stobo; in implements, etc., J. Brown, J. Patton, J. Fowler, Joseph Bowden.

The total amount awarded was £45 12s. 6d.

The Scarboro Agricultural Society has held fairs each year since organization, and during the last twenty years the progress of the Society has been steady, while the improvement both in the number and variety of the exhibits and in the amount offered in premiums has been marked. As a consequence, Scarboro breeders have become well known to American buyers—our magnificent heavy horses especially commanding very high prices.

The fair held at Woburn, on the 27th day of September, 1895, was one of the most successful in the Society's history, there being no fewer than 1,462 entries in the various classes, and a total amount of $1,110 was offered in prizes.

There were entered for competition 139 horses, 71 cattle, 60 sheep, 19 swine, 78 poultry; 190 entries were made in dairy products, 62 in grain and seeds, 211 in roots and potatoes, 351 in fruit and garden products, 32 in implements and manufactures, 249 in ladies' work and fine arts.

The following sums were awarded in prizes: For horses, $204; cattle, $80; sheep, $52; swine, $24; poultry, $24.50: dairy products, $137.50; grain and seeds, $46.50; roots and potatoes, $62; fruit and vegetables, $104.50; implements and manufactures, $51; and for fine arts and ladies' work, $85.

The principal exhibitors were: in horses, Alf. Mason, W. Howard, Wm. Annis, W. C. Ormerod, Wm. Fisher, Thos. Hood, Jas. Maxwell, J. Chapman, J. Lawrie, A. Summerfeldt, H. Armstrong, W. A. Noble, Wm. Milliken, Jas. Torrance, Jas. McGrisken, J. Little, A. Coulson, P. Stewart, T. Jackson, J. Stobo, Wm. Mason, Wm. Loveless, G. R. Forfar, J. Ashbridge, L. Kennedy, J. Kirton, Thos. Walton and Wm. Doherty; in cattle, John Lawrie, Crawford Bros., Wm. Fisher, John Little, A. A. Forfar, W. J. Haycraft, Jas. Lawrie and J. Miller; in sheep, W. F. Pearson, J. W. Cowan, F. Wheler, J. Miller, P. Boynton and T. F. Boynton; in hogs, W. J. Haycraft and Boynton Bros.; in poultry, W. J. Haycraft, J. Lawrie, A. Martin, J. M. & Thos. Ramsey and G. Robins.

In grain, S. Rennie, U. Young and T. & J. Manderson; in roots and potatoes, W. B. Davidson, A. W. Thomson, S. Rennie, R. W. Thomson, G. McCowan, J. L. Paterson, W. White, S. Morgan, Geo. F. Morgan, P. Carroll, R. Sellers, J. McGrisken and U. Young; in fruit, etc., R. W. Thomson, A. W. Thomson,

H. T. Ormerod, J. Johnson, H. White, Alex. Baird, Wm. Patton, A. Ionson, Thos. Ionson, Alex. Neilson, D. Bean, J. Ashbridge, Wm. Loveless, Jas. Chester, J. Lawrie and J. Holmes; in dairy products, Mrs. Wm. Mason, Miss A. Davidson, Miss Jackson, Miss N. Malcolm, Mrs. Alex. Baird, Mrs. Wm. Young, Mrs. F. Weir, Mrs. R. S. Powers, Mrs. Robert Chapman, Mrs. Adam Richardson and Mrs. W. W. Walton; in ladies' work, Mrs. S. Rich, Mrs. W. J. Haycraft, Mrs. R. S. Powers, Mrs. J. Holmes, Mrs. Cousins, Misses M. and A. Paterson, Miss M. Mason, Miss J. Forfar, Mrs. M. Secor, Mrs. G. Gray, Miss M. H. Thomson, Mrs. A. W. Forfar, Miss Beldam, Mrs. A. Ionson, Miss N. Malcolm, Miss E. Hammond, Miss A. Davidson, Miss F. Chester, Mrs. J. Chapman, Mrs. G. R. Forfar, Miss M. Jackson and Mrs. A. Mason; in implements and manufactures, D. Beldam, Jas. Ley, Jas. Gibson, A. W. Forfar, Thos. Ramsey, G. D. Davies and the Speight Waggon Co.

The officers and directors of the Scarboro Agricultural Society for the present year are: President, W. H. Tredway; Vice-President, D. Beldam; Directors—Wm. Doherty, T. Jackson, T. Pherrill, W. W. Walton, G. R. Forfar, Geo. C. Chester, J. Ramsey, W. J. Haycraft and Geo. Little; Auditors—A. M. Secor and Alex. Baird; Sec'y-Treas., Alex. McCowan.

EAST RIDING OF YORK FARMERS' ASSOCIATION.

The East York Farmers' Institute, composed largely of Scarboro farmers, originated at a meeting held at Ellesmere, February 11th, 1886, called for the purpose of forming an association for mutual improvement and protection.

An association was accordingly formed, to be known as "The East Riding of York Farmers' Association."

The officers were: J. T. Brown, President; A. Richardson, 1st Vice-President; George May, 2nd Vice-President; W. D. Fitzpatrick, Secretary; W. W. Walton, Treasurer.

Various committees were appointed, and the first subject selected for discussion was, "The feeding of cattle for the production of milk."

EAST YORK FARMERS' INSTITUTE.

The former Association was continued until July, 1887, when the East York Farmers' Institute was organized at a meeting held at Ellesmere, by the election of J. T. Brown as President; A. Richardson, Vice-President; Alex. McCowan, Secretary; Thos. Whiteside, Treasurer.

The directors were: F. Armstrong, J. Leadley, George Smith, Jos. Tingle, R. Galbraith, Geo. Elliot, B. Carnaghan, D. Marshall, Frank Glendinning, and W. Glendinning.

Since organization, the Institute has held meetings regularly every second week during the winter months, principally at Ellesmere and Agincourt; and special yearly mass-meetings, addressed by delegates sent by the Department of Agriculture. At these meetings subjects connected with agriculture are discussed. Among the subjects engaging the attention of the Institute have been: "The improvement of stock;" "Breeding of Clydesdale horses;" "Rotation of crops;" "The selection and cultivation of fruit trees;" "Buying, feeding and marketing of cattle for the British market;" "Sheep-feeding and raising;" "Farm Fences;" "Statute Labor;" "Country Roads;" "Farm Insurance;" "Poultry on the Farm;" "Bees on the Farm;" "Farm Help;" "Mistakes made in Farming;" and kindred subjects.

J. T. Brown held the office of President until 1890, when Andrew Hood succeeded him, and held that office until 1892. John Leadley was President in 1892 and '93. L. Kennedy was President in 1894-95.

T. M. Whiteside was elected Secretary in 1888, and continued in that office until 1892, when J. C. Clark succeeded him.

The present officers are: A. Richardson, President; W. J. Haycraft, 1st Vice-President; Jos. Armstrong, 2nd Vice-President; J. C. Clark, Secretary; Geo. Elliot, Treasurer. Directors —S. Rennie, E. Wood, J. Elliot, Wm. Johnson, and J. Kennedy.

The membership for 1895 was seventy-seven.*

*The foregoing account of the Agricultural Societies and Farmers' Institutes was supplied by J. C. Clark.

TYPICAL BUILDINGS—OLD, AND RECENT.

1. Old Log Barn. 2. Old Log Blacksmith Shop. 3. Malvern Hall.
4. Barn (transition period). 5. Farm Steading of To-day.
6. Side-drive Barn. 7. End-drive Barn.

THOROUGHBRED STOCK.

J. P. Wheler deserves the credit of having done much to improve the stock of the township and of the Province by his enterprise in the importation, first, of Durham, and, more recently, of Ayrshire cattle, many of which secured the highest premiums awarded at local and provincial fairs.

John Torrance, sen., is also well known as an importer of Ayrshire cattle and draught horses. Mr. Torrance's efforts to improve stock have been crowned with well-merited success.

John Hockridge was one of the first importers of Leicester sheep, early in the "forties." He lived on the Kennedy Road.

Others who devoted themselves to the importation of thoroughbreds were James Lawrie, George Scott, John and William Crawford, and Simon Beattie, most of whom included horses, cattle and sheep in their enterprise; the Crawfords making a specialty of Ayrshire cattle and Clydesdale horses. Mr. Beattie, too, favored Clydesdale horses.

With so many noted importers and breeders in the township, it is little wonder that in stock, as in other departments, Scarboro stands so high at the present day.

PLOUGHING MATCHES.

From an early date in the history of the township there seems to have been a disposition, or rather a determination, to conduct farming in a manner superior to the slip-shod methods that characterized many other portions of the Province. The presence of huge pine stumps did not, however, favor "scientific" ploughing, but as soon as these provoking obstacles could be removed, a desire was evinced to emulate the accurate "rig and fur" performances of Old Country ploughmen.

Mr. Wm. Brown already quoted, wrote in the "forties": "Everything you see and hear [in Scarboro] reminds you of your English home. You will see as good ploughing and general farm management as you do in the best parts of England."

Mr. A. M. Secor, one of the oldest living natives of the township, thinks there was a ploughing match held on the farm of Mr.

R. Stobo, lot 21, concession C (Kingston Road), in 1830 or 1831, and that the ploughmen were, Messrs. J. Torrance and A. Glendinning; and J. L. Paterson states that there was a ploughing match held (he thinks, at Ed. Cornell's), about 1832 or 1833, in which the late Wm. Hood was a competitor, Abraham Torrance taking first prize.

In 1836, a ploughing match came off on the farm of David Annis, lot 16, concession C, the principal and only competitors being Jas. Patton and J. Atkinson.

Another account says the first ploughing match was held at Robert Stobo's place in 1833, when R. Stobo, R. McNair, and one of the Torrances took prizes, and that another match was held where part of Toronto now stands, in 1835, the prize-takers being John Lawrie, Archibald Thomson, and Jas. Patton, all of Scarboro. He further states that in 1836 or 1837, among those who carried off the honors were Jas. Patton, Abraham Torrance and John Lawrie. It was probably at this match (some think it was in 1838) that Walter Crone took first prize in the boys' class, his ploughing being thought the best on the field.

But most of those, and probably even some earlier trials of skill now wholly forgotten, were individual, rather than general, in their character, and it was not until the organization of the Scarboro Agricultural Society in January, 1844, that it became possible to manage such friendly contests in a regular manner. Notwithstanding the cautious nature of the Society's resolution only "to hold a ploughing match if the funds would permit," the hearty support extended to this movement warranted a competition in the following spring,* and we find accordingly that "The first ploughing match under the auspices of the Scarboro Agricultural Society was held at Arch. Muir's, Kingston Road, on April 26th, 1844, when there were eight competitors.

The first prize (£1 10s.), was awarded to John Gibson; second (£1 5s.), to Archibald Glendinning; third (£1), to Joshua Sisley; fourth (15s.), to Wm. Crone, a total of £4 10s.

* The statement following is almost word for word as written by J. C. Clark, of Agincourt.

The judges were Jas. Patton, And. Bertram and Ed. Cornell.

The second ploughing match under the auspices of the Scarboro Agricultural Society was held April, 1845, on the farm of Chas. Cornell, Kingston Road.

The judges were Jas. McCowan, Thos. Brown and Wm. Clark, jun.

In this match there were to be two classes, viz., one for Old Countrymen, and one for Canadians. The *time* of the match to be at the rate of an acre in ten hours. Only two prizes were awarded—first, to Jas. Patton (£1 10s.); second, to Alex. Wilson (£1), the rest of the competitors failing to complete their work in the time required.

The third annual ploughing match was held in April, 1846. In this there were two classes, those under, and those over seventeen years of age.

The prizes for those over seventeen were awarded: first, to John Gibson; second, to John Crone; third, to Arch. Glendinning; fourth, to Joshua Sisley.

Prizes for those under seventeen: first, to John Wakefield; second, to Wm. Wakefield; third, to J. Pilkey. At this match £7 was awarded in prizes.

The fourth ploughing match was held April 22nd, 1847, on lot 28, concession D.

The successful competitors were: In class one—first, Jas. Patton; second, John Gibson; third, John Wakefield. In second class—first, William Wakefield; second, J. Pilkey.

The fifth ploughing match was held April 22nd, 1848, at W. Buchanan's, lot 33, concession 3, in the L'Amaroux Settlement.

The successful competitors were: first, Jas. Patton; second, Wm. Hood; third, J. Sisley. Junior class: first, J. L. Paterson; second, W. Wakefield; third, J. Pilkey.

The sixth ploughing match was held in 1849, at Asa Post's, township of Pickering, when twenty premiums were awarded to the twenty best ploughmen, these to be selected to plough against an equal number from Whitby.

The following were the ploughmen for Scarboro: J. Crone, John Weir, George Evans, James Weir, William Addison, James

Patton, J. Torrance, R. Gilchrist, William Hood, John Crawford, J. Morrison, John Wakefield, J. L. Paterson, Thomas Crone, Joshua Kennedy, William Weir, Robert Addison, A. P. Thomson, A. Bertram, and James McCowan.

The Scarboro men defeated those from Whitby.

The following is an extract from the treasurer's book as to expenses incurred in connection with this competition:

	£	S.	D.
To bill for dinners at William Palmer's in Pickering	21	0	0
Pay for beer on the field	0	5	0
" Mr. Brown [Geo.?] for printing	2	15	0
" Turnpikes (tolls)	1	5	0

In 1850, a ploughing match was held at lot 31, concession D (Mr. John Martin's), at which 15s. was awarded to each of the twenty best ploughmen, these to be selected to plough a match against an equal number from Vaughan. The judges for Scarboro were John Weir, of Reach; J. Gibson, of Markham; William Crone and James Darling.

The following is extracted from the Treasurer's account:

1850.	£	S.	D.
To paid Mr. Sheppardson	20	0	0
" 200 bills	1	0	0
" Township bills	0	7	6
" Beer on the field*	0	5	0
" Turnpikes [tolls]	0	6	0
" Postage	0	1	1½
Total	£21	19	7½

1850.			
June 14th, to paid the 20 men	20	0	0
" " " expenses as above	£21	19	7½

The balance £3 0s. 4½d. was divided among the ploughmen.

* Mr. David Martin says that this does not account for all the beer, that there were three booths, that his father supplied a keg, and that he himself carried the beer around, and his brother Robert distributed the cakes.

In 1851, another ploughing match between Scarboro and Vaughan came off near Thornhill in the latter township, when Scarboro achieved even a more decisive victory."

At this point a break may be made in Mr. Clark's annals to introduce an interesting statement by Mr. David Martin, explanatory of the origin of the inter-township contests just mentioned:

" For some time previous to the period above referred to (1849 to 1851), a spirit of rivalry had existed between the townships of Whitby and Darlington, and a good deal of chaffing was indulged in with regard to the merits of their respective ploughmen. In order to bring matters to an issue and thus end the controversy, Whitby sent out a challenge, open to any township in the Province, conditions to be twenty men and $100 a side.

This was done with the expectation that Darlington would instantly take up the gauntlet thus thrown down. This, however, the latter failed to do, and the challenge remaining open for some time, was at length accepted by Scarboro. This was in the spring of 1849, and the match at which these twenty men were selected to meet Whitby, was held on lot 33, in the 3rd concession, at that time tenanted by William Buchanan. The representatives of the respective townships met each other half way, viz., on the farm of Asa Post in the township of Pickering, Scarboro winning easily. One of the conditions of the match was that the winners be bound to accept a challenge from any other township in the Province, if made within one year.

The following spring, viz., 1850, Vaughan challenged Scarboro to a trial of skill, number of men and stakes to be the same as before. The match at which the twenty were chosen to meet Vaughan took place on the farm of John Martin, lot 31, concession D, April 26th. And a few days after, the Scarboro ploughmen met their opponents on the farm of M. Welch, near Thornhill, township of Markham, the Scarboro men beating Vaughan scarcely less decisively than they had Whitby the previous year. This result was a surprise to the

Vaughan ploughmen, who attributed their defeat to every reason but the true one, viz., the superior skill of their opponents; and what rendered the defeat all the more galling was the presence of the Earl of Elgin, the first and last Governor-General to grace a ploughing match with his presence. This extreme dissatisfaction on the part of Vaughan prompted them to challenge Scarboro again in the following spring. The latter, of course, at once accepted, and twenty of her best men were again chosen at a match held on lot 28, concession D, then occupied by Mr. George Evans. Rigfoot Farm, Markham, the property of the late George Miller (the celebrated importer of Durham cattle and Leicester sheep), was chosen as the battle ground on which the question of supremacy was to be settled. The honors again remained with Scarboro, Vaughan sustaining a more signal defeat than before.

The ploughmen of the latter township were now more dissatisfied than ever, and the following spring issued a third challenge, conditions as to number of men and stakes same as on the two previous years. Scarboro, however, having now beaten Vaughan twice, refused to be bound by the former conditions, but offered to meet them with thirty men a side, the stakes to be doubled. Vaughan accepted. Scarboro held a match on the farm of James Ionson, lot 29, concession D, at which the requisite thirty were selected. Vaughan, however, now began to haggle and to demand such unreasonable changes in the conditions on which the match was to be held, that Scarboro refused to entertain them, and after a great deal of bickering the match was declared off.

These contests led to a marked improvement in what to the husbandman is a most important and necessary art. The ploughs used, it may be proper to state, were mostly imported from the celebrated makers, R. Gray and Sons, Uddingston, near Glasgow, Scotland.

Another matter may also be mentioned here. Although not having any necessary connection with ploughing, yet it serves to illustrate a great change in the social habits of the people. It was then quite common to see three or four liquor-bars in the field in full blast, the hotel-keeper holding that his license conferred the right to sell drink anywhere within the limits of the municipality. Nobody questioned it; indeed, it was thought quite a convenience to have the supply there, a state of matters which public opinion would not now tolerate for an instant.

No record of these matches having been kept, it is now difficult, if not impossible, to obtain the names of all the ploughmen who took part in them, but the following list may be taken to be correct as far as it goes; some of them ploughing in one match and some in another—those marked with an asterisk certainly in all of them:

*James Patton, *John L. Paterson, *James McCowan, *Archibald P. Thomson, *George Evans, *John Crone, *James Weir, *Thos. Crone, *John Weir, John Crawford, *Wm. Weir, Joshua Sisley, *John Wakefield, Geo. Burk, Wm. Wakefield, Archibald Browning, *Wm. Hood, Robert Gilchrist, Walter Hood, Andrew Bertram, Henry Mason, John Cash, Wm. Addison."

Proceeding with Mr. Clark's account, we find that "In 1852, at the annual meeting of the Agricultural Society, held probably on lot 28, concession D, it was moved by J. P. Wheler, and seconded by Mr. Palmer, 'that the money now lying in the hands of the Treasurer, and belonging to the Ploughmen's Society, remain in the Treasurer's hands for six months.'" Carried.

In 1854, at the annual meeting of the Agricultural Society, held at John Malcolm's Inn, Markham Road, a communication was received from Messrs. P. Paterson & Son, Toronto, placing at disposal of the Society a double-mounted iron plough as a premium to be competed for at the annual ploughing match. A vote of thanks was passed to the Messrs. Paterson for the gift.

The entrance fee was placed at 25s. for each ploughman, and the total amount was to be divided into a number of additional prizes.

The ploughing match was held at Mr. Arch. Malcolm's farm, on the 5th of May, when the following ploughmen competed: Jas. Patton, Jas. Hamilton, Thos. Mason, John Paterson, Robt.

Paterson, Geo. Evans, J. Sisley, John Weir, Chas. Curtis, Wm. Breckon, Robert Gilchrist (of Scarboro), Wm. Hood (of Markham), Geo. Strachan, Geo. Burk, Josh. Lotton, Jas. Rosson (of Pickering), Wm. Dalziel, and Henry White (of Vaughan).

The prizes were awarded as follows:

FIRST CLASS.

1st.	Jas. Patton, Scarboro	Iron plough.		
2nd.	Robt. Paterson, Scarboro	£3	5s.	0
3rd.	Joshua Lotton, Pickering	3	0	0
4th.	Chas. Curtis, Scarboro	2	15	0
5th.	Geo. Burk, Pickering	2	10	0
6th.	Thos. Mason, Scarboro	2	5	0
7th.	Wm. Hood, Markham	2	0	0
8th.	Geo. Strachan, Pickering	1	15	0
9th.	Wm. Dalziel, Vaughan	1	10	0
10th.	John Paterson, Scarboro	1	5	0
11th.	Geo. Evans, Scarboro	1	0	0
12th.	Jas. Rossen, Pickering	0	15	0
13th.	Wm. Breckon, Scarboro	0	10	0

SECOND CLASS.

Boys under eighteen years of age and residents in the township:

1st.	Geo. Breckon	£1	5s.	0
2nd.	Duncan Malcolm	1	0	0

At the first quarterly meeting of the Scarboro Agricultural Society for 1855, held at Robertson's Inn, April 6th, it was moved, seconded, and

Resolved,—That the purse of £50 * won from the ploughmen of Vaughan Township, shall be equally divided among the men who ploughed at the several matches between the townships, giving each ploughman a share in proportion to the number of matches at which he ploughed.

The ploughing match was held on the farm of Mr. James

* As £50 currency was equal to $200, the "purse" must have meant the two years' winnings.

Ionson, on the 4th day of May, 1855. This match was restricted to residents of the township, and there were two classes, those over the age of twenty years and those under that age. The successful competitors were:

FIRST CLASS.

	£	S.	D.
1st. Robert Paterson, iron plough, value	9	0	0
2nd. James Weir, cash	1	5	0
3rd. John Paterson, cash	1	0	0
4th. John Weir, cash	0	15	0

SECOND CLASS.

1st. Arch. Malcolm, cash	2	5	0
2nd. Robert Muir, cash	1	15	0
3rd. George Patton, cash.............	1	5	0
4th. George Breckon, cash	0	15	0

The ploughing match for 1856 was held at Mr. John Malcolm's farm, Clyde Bank, on Friday, the 1st day of May, when the following were the successful competitors:

First class, all ploughmen over the age of 18 years:

	£	S.	D.
1st prize, Robert Muir	1	5	0
2nd " Arch. Malcolm	1	0	0
3rd " George Patton	0	15	0
4th " James Cooper	0	10	0

Second class, boys under 18 years of age:

1st prize, Watson Wride	1	5	0
2nd " David Burk...............	1	0	0

The annual ploughing match for 1857 was held on the farm of William Bell, Kennedy Road, on Friday, April 24th. At this there were two classes, as formerly. The following prizes were awarded:

SENIOR CLASS.

	£	S.	D.
1st prize, John Bushby	2	10	0
2nd " Arch. Malcolm...............	2	5	0
3rd " George Evans	2	0	0

		£	s.	d.
4th prize,	George Walton	1	15	0
5th "	Richard Burk	1	10	0
6th "	Robert Muir	1	5	0
7th "	Wm. Thomson	1	0	0
8th "	Joseph Stark	0	15	0
9th "	George Patton	0	10	0

SECOND CLASS.

1st prize,	David Burk	1	10	0
2nd "	Simpson Rennie	1	5	0
3rd "	George Sheppard	1	2	6
4th "	Watson Wride	1	0	0
5th "	Francis Papineau	0	17	6
6th "	Robert Skelton	0	15	0
7th "	George Morgan	0	12	6
8th "	John Wride	0	10	0
9th "	John Brown	0	7	6

A special prize was awarded to William Sylvester of £1 2s. 6d.

From 1857 the progress of ploughing in the township was rapid, and it may be said that the next twenty years saw the development and culmination of this art, bringing to the front the Rennies, Hoods, Morgans, Patersons, Malcolms, Pattons, Weirs, Kennedys, and Stewart, of the first class, and Ormerods, Vradenburg, Ley, Pickering, Telfer, Masons, Burk, Keats, Yeomans, Wood, Dix, Littles, Shadlock, Steers, and others of the second class.

It may be doubted whether their acknowledged superiority could have been attained by Scarboro ploughmen had they not had the services of a skilful mechanic in the constructing and adjusting of their ploughs. Thus the artisan at the forge, and the ploughman in the field were enabled to evolve an implement constructed on scientific principles, thoroughly adapted to the work of moulding and placing the upturned soil in the position required by judges of what constitutes perfect ploughing.

The right kind of mechanic was found in James Ley, whose shop, for weeks before an important match took place, was thronged with ploughmen from near and far, while the glow of the forge and the merry ring of the anvil could be seen and heard far into the night. Mr. Ley's iron ploughs have still a reputation in the Province second only, if indeed, second, to that of the Grays, of Uddingston, Scotland.

Charles White, of Milliken (who, though not a resident of the township, had a shop located so near the border as to be under the influence of the prevailing ploughing sentiment), also contributed to the success of Scarboro ploughmen, and was considered by many to be quite as skilful as Mr. Ley.

At a ploughing match held near London in the fall of 1865, S. Rennie took third place among eighty-three competitors. The judges, moreover, paid a high compliment to Mr. Rennie's work by saying it was done more in accordance with scientific principles than that of any of his competitors, and they regretted that he had been assigned to a field the soil of which was such that high-class work was impossible.

At another match, under the auspices of the Agriculture and Arts Association, held near Hamilton in the following year, Andrew Hood took second prize, and another Scarboro-taught ploughman, in the person of his brother, Walter Hood, of Ancaster, was awarded first.

At Brooklin, in 1868, over sixty ploughmen competed. In the first class, of five prizes awarded, four came to Scarboro, viz.: S. Rennie, first; Adam Hood, second; Wm. Hood, third; and Andrew Hood, fifth. In the second class, a Scarboro ploughman, William Patton, took first prize. At this match the time allowed was twelve hours to an acre, while the length of the lots was under twenty rods. The time taken up in turning was thus increased. The field abounded in stones, and in the hurry and excitement of a close finish an enthusiastic Scarboro ploughman did not notice that he had lost a portion of his ploughshare, which loss, however, did not prevent his taking a first place.

October 21st, 1875, was a red-letter day in the history of Scarboro ploughing, as the provincial match under the auspices of the Agriculture and Arts Association was held on that date on the farm of Hugh Clark, lot 29, concession 4, near where Agincourt station now stands.

The committee in charge was composed of Messrs. Wilmot, Aylesworth and Graham, representing the Agriculture and Arts Association; Messrs. Tran, Wheler, Crawford, Speight and Rennie, representing the East York Agricultural Society, and John Little, representing the Scarboro Agricultural Society. John Crawford was appointed Secretary of Committee, and $558 was awarded in prizes. The judges were James Borland (Darlington), James Weir and George Burk (Scarboro), for the first class; Wm. Foley (Darlington), James McCowan and Jas. Weir, for the second class; Geo. Shaw (Darlington), Peter Bristol (Bath), and John Coxworth, for the third, fourth and fifth classes. Among the 1,500 spectators was Wm. Hood, sen., than whom there is none more deserving of a niche in the history of the agricultural-development of the township. Mr. Hood had three sons competing in this match, and each of them obtained a first prize.

The Markham *Economist* said of this gathering: "The committee, judges, ploughmen, and many of the visitors were very generously entertained by Mr. Clark, who, with his good lady and family, were untiring in their efforts to promote the comfort of their guests, and their hospitality will be long remembered by the numerous participants."

Mr. S. Rennie was equally generous; in fact, all the farmers residing within a radius of two miles made visitors welcome.

The judges said they had never seen such uniformly good ploughing, nor so much done in one day, while no dissatisfaction was apparent.

In the first class there were twelve entries and five prizes. Of these, three were won by Scarboro ploughmen, viz.: first, Andrew Hood; second, John Morgan, and the fifth, Jas. G. Paterson.

In the second class there were twenty-five entries, and the first five prizes were secured by Scarboro men, viz.: first, Thos. Hood; second, Thos. Keats; third, A. Smith; fourth, Wesley Ormerod, and fifth, Alex. Stewart.

PRIZE PLOUGHMEN.

In the third class, Adam Hood took first prize.

In the fourth class the Scarboro winners were: J. P. Mason, who took third prize; J. Thomson, who took fourth, and Norman Malcolm, who won fifth.

In the fifth class the Scarboro prize-takers were: J. R. Secor, who won first; W. Ormerod, who won third; Wm. Ferguson, fourth, and Arch. Paterson, sixth.

At a provincial match held at Eglinton in 1878, Thos. Hood took first prize in first class.

Adam Hood took first in third class, with Jas. Patton second.

In 1888, at a ploughing match held near Montreal under the auspices of the Quebec Provincial Association of Agriculture and Arts, Andrew Hood won the first prize in the first class, a very handsome gold medal, valued at $75, and his brother-in-law, Wm. Milliken (Markham), took second prize.

In 1890, the East York Ploughmen's Association was formed. The officers were: A. Quantz, President; John Little, of Scarboro, Vice-President, and Thomas Hood, of Scarboro, Secretary-Treasurer. The Directors were: Wm. Hunter, Wm. Milliken, Wm. Hood, W. T. Hood, S. Ritter, D. C. Steele, F. W. Jackes, J. B. Gould and George Gormley, of Markham; S. Rennie, Robt. Petch, J. G. Paterson, J. L. Paterson, Alex. Doherty, Andrew Hood and J. Morgan, of Scarboro.

This association has held a ploughing match each year since its organization.

In 1894, they received the Provincial grant, and held their match on the farm of Wm. Milliken, Markham. In the various classes there were sixty-two entries. In the first class the Scarboro winners were: F. Weir, who took second prize, and Thos. Little, who won sixth prize. In the second class R. Rennie took first prize; Alex. Sterling, second; Thos. Shadlock, fifth, and W. Bennett, sixth. In the third class Walter Pilkey took third prize. In the fourth class A. Thomson took second prize, and in the fifth class Jos. Nash took first prize; Thos. Craig, second; John Loveless, fifth, and Wm. Doherty, sixth. In the sixth class A. Bennett took first prize; Thos. Bell, second; John Monk, third; Albert Mason, fourth; R. Chapman, fifth; Thos. Jackson, sixth; F. Collins, seventh, and Geo. Beare, eighth.

The last match was held on October 31st, 1895, on the farm of John Lawrie, near Malvern, Scarboro, when there were thirty-nine entries. The Scarboro winners were: In the first class, George Little, who won fourth prize, and Thos. Little, who won fifth. In the second class R. Rennie took first; Thos. Shadlock, second; Alex. Stirling, third, and Alex. Weir, fifth. In the third class Wm. Fisher won first prize; Jos. Teeson, second; S. Pickering, third; W. E. Bennett, fourth, and L. Thomson, sixth. In the fifth class Thos. Bell took second prize; Albert Mason, third, Thos. Craig, fourth, and F. Collins, sixth. In the sixth class, John Malcolm took first prize, and C. Mason, second."

IMPLEMENTS.

For many years the implements used on the farm were primitive in design and rude in construction, but well adapted for the work they had to perform. Settlers from Britain quickly perceived that they must modify their views regarding such things by adapting themselves to the circumstances of a new country, as well as by philosophically accepting the inevitable. But as the clearings increased in size and the stumps disappeared, the demand grew for implements and machinery to take the place of the old "No. 4," or even less elegant and less efficient plough; the "Wild Goose" or ʌ-shaped drag; the reaping-hook and scythe; the flail and the ancient methods of winnowing. When oxen became despised as aids on the farm, and horses came into general use, iron ploughs were imported from Scotland, and counterparts of them were produced here. Blacksmiths began to vie with each other in turning out the lightest, most wide-spreading, and most serviceable harrows; the cradle displaced the hook, while lighter waggons and more comfortable sleighs took the places of the cumbrous vehicles that had done duty in pioneer days. No longer were the sleighs shod with strips of beech; and the erstwhile spring-pole waggon-seat was supplanted by one supported on elastic steel. Then the day of machinery dawned.

The first reaper, the "Hussey," was brought into the township by Martin Snider in 1851, from Albany, N.Y. In the following year someone imbued with old fogy ideas, and inspired by diabolism, ruined this machine, upon which Mr. Snider immediately proceeded to Albany and procured another.

Self-rakers were brought from Rochester in 1854. On the occasion of their introduction, on the 17th July in that year, a procession of seventeen waggons was formed, each carrying a reaper, and a parade was made along King Street, from the city to Scarboro. As self-rakers, these machines were not a success, and in most instances the rakes were removed and the bundles thrown off by hand.

The Hussey reaping machine had to be drawn at a trot to make it work at all satisfactorily, especially when the grain stalks were a little damp; and so exhausting was this work on horses that two teams had to be kept in the field for needful changes. The original reapers had no reels, but this defect was soon remedied, and improvements rendered the draught considerably lighter than it was at first. Some of the machines delivered the grain at the side so that cutting could be done without waiting for the sheaves to be made, but in most cases these were pushed off by a man on the rear of the machine, the binders following. Self-rakers came next, and after them the self-binder (about 1883), the latter performing its work, at first with wire, but afterwards with twine.

John Morgan was the pioneer in the introduction of the mower, he having purchased a machine known as the "Kirby," and made by Massey in Newcastle in 1851.

The six-horsepower "buzzer" followed the flail, but as it did not thoroughly separate the grain from the straw and chaff, the newer threshing machine took its place, and latterly, steam has been employed as the motive power instead of horses.

Hugh Elliot and Peter Pilkey were among the first to run buzzers in this township.

The first separators were imported from Rochester.

At the other end in the line of development, it is stated that the steam threshing engine was introduced July 31, 1879, by David Beldam, who paid $1,216 for a Woodbridge machine. Mowing machines, too, have been considerably improved, and in connection with hay-making we have also the sulky-rake and the "tedder," all saving much labor and time.

Even the sowing is not now performed by hand, broadcast and drill machines being employed for this purpose.

Tillage is no longer confined to the old single plough and the harrow. In addition to innumerable improved forms of both of these, we have sulky and gang-ploughs and cultivators in great variety, which largely answer the purpose of both plough and harrow.

Spades, shovels, hoes, manure-forks and hay-forks, as we have them to-day, are fully fifty per cent. lighter than those in use at the beginning of the nineteenth century, and the same may be said regarding almost every other farm implement in which steel has taken the place of iron. Hand-tools, like those just mentioned, must ever retain a place on the farm, although they are not now employed to anything like the extent of their old-time application. Modern devices have largely displaced them all, except on the very smallest plots of ground, and every year decreases the amount of labor formerly done with such tools, the best illustration of which may be found in the present-day methods of loading and unloading hay by means of horse-power, which is also utilized to carry the material to the most distant part of the mow. Roots are no longer chopped with a cleaver, or slowly sliced with a knife; a windy day is not now required to separate the chaff from the wheat; it is not now necessary to lose a day by going to mill for the purpose of having a few bags of coarse grain ground for feed; even the pumping of water by hand has ceased on many farms, and in all the above instances machines of one kind and another, whatever their motive power may be, have rendered obsolete the older and simpler, but more laborious methods.

In the dairy, too, it would astonish our grandmothers if they could have but a peep or two at the way things are managed where there *is* a dairy; but on many farms this department has become most modest in its proportions and equally so in its aims, for the milk, when not sent to a joint-stock company's creamery or cheese factory, is usually dispatched in large cans to supply the wants of Toronto's population.

The vast improvement that has taken place in implements has enabled the farmer to dispense with the employment of so many extra "hands" as were formerly required during busy seasons, and has not only rendered it necessary for him to provide special accommodation for the housing of his machines, but has laid upon him the obligation to become, in considerable measure, a mechanic.

His wife, too, has profited not a little from the nowadays order of things. Of course, she is still kept busy, or, rather, she keeps herself busy. She has convinced herself that "woman's work is never done," and she is determined to live up to this creed or perish in the attempt; but when all her old-fashioned and ever-necessary daily dusting, and sweeping, and cooking have been performed, she has now much more leisure to knit a little, to "piece and patch" a little, to read a little, and even to exchange confidences with her neighbor.

The results consequent on the development of electrical science during the twentieth century, now almost within hailing distance, are certain to revolutionize agricultural methods in a still more marked degree than has yet been effected, and in no way will the change be more noticeable than in the variety and structure of farm implements. Through the windmill, and by other agencies (until the time is reached when solar heat itself shall be cheaply transformed into electrical energy), batteries will be charged as motors for the plough, the harrow, the reaping and all other machines that now require the use of horses. Even weeds may be exterminated and plant-growth regulated by the same mysterious means, while scarcely anything can be more certain that not only will heat and light for domestic purposes be similarly supplied, but that the farmer of the future will market his produce and ride to church in electrically propelled vehicles.

KELVIN GROVE FARM.

It can be said of the township of Scarboro that it occupies the proud position of having the farm that won the gold medal and the sweepstakes prize awarded by the Provincial Government in 1883 and 1886, respectively.

When the instructions given to the judges, and the number of farms entered upon the list of competition are known, the distinction gained and the honors won are all the more gratifying.

The instructions to the judges were in the following terms: "In addition to any other points that may be thought desirable by the judges, the following shall be taken into consideration in estimating what is 'the best-managed farm':

1. The competing farm to be not less than one hundred acres, two-thirds of which must be under cultivation.

2. The nature of the farming—whether mixed dairy, or any other mode—to be the most suitable under conditions effected by local circumstances.

3. The proper position of the buildings in relation to the whole farm.

4. The attention paid to the preservation of timber, and shelter, by planting of trees.

5. The condition of any private roads.

6. The character, sufficiency and condition of fences, and the manner in which the farm is subdivided into fields.

7. Improvements by removal of obstacles to cultivation, including drainage.

8. General condition of buildings, including dwelling-house, and their adaptability to the wants of the farm and family.

9. The management, character, suitability, condition and number of live-stock kept.

10. The number, condition and suitability of implements and machinery.

11. State of the garden and orchard.

12. Management of farm-yard manure.

13. The cultivation of crops, to embrace manuring, cleaning, produce per acre in relation to management, and character of soil and climate.

14. General order, economy and water supply.

15. Cost of production and relative profits."

In 1883 the group comprised the counties of Cardwell, Peel, York, Ontario, Durham, Simcoe, Muskoka and Algoma. The gold medal was won by Scarboro.

In 1886 there were eighteen entries, comprising farms in the counties of Middlesex, Oxford, Kent, Brant, Simcoe, Wellington, York, Norfolk, Renfrew, Carleton, Frontenac, Victoria, Huron, Halton, and Bruce.

These included all the gold medal farms of previous years, nearly all the silver medallists, and a number of the bronze medallists. Here again the same township and the same farm won the sweepstakes prize.

This farm is situated in concession 5, lot 30, township of Scarboro. It was deeded by Mrs. James Fenwick to Joshua L'Amaroux, on January 16th, 1832, for £75. On February 17th, 1838, it was sold to Robert Rennie for £175, and on June 5th, 1867, it was deeded to Simpson Rennie, its present owner.

Probably no better history could be given of this farm than that to be found in the "Reports of the Council of the Agriculture and Arts Association of Ontario" for the years 1883 and 1886, as follows:

"The casual observer, in passing Kelvin Grove, owned by Mr. Simpson Rennie, township of Scarboro, might easily be oblivious of the fact that on his right and left lay the different compartments of a farm that for some years hence shall be regarded as the most famous in Ontario, and which will live in the story of Canadian agriculture in all time. This farm, consisting of about one hundred acres, lies principally in the 5th concession of Scarboro, extending from side-road to side-road, with twenty-two and a half acres across the highway. . . . The country around it is plain and level. There is almost a total absence of the romantic in nature, either on the farm or the surroundings, as the running brook, the tree-clad hill, or the shady dell, with its witchery of attractions. The buildings are plain, and so are the fences. There is no attempt at display, and yet there is a perfection of neatness about everything belonging to the place, and everything that is done upon it, such as we never saw at any other farm.

"When the farming that is usually done at our Agricultural Colleges equals that of Kelvin Grove, either in its essence or upon its surface, then shall students crowd in from all quarters to get lessons in this first and noblest of the sciences. . . . The farm could not be better divided into fields. . . . No better site could have been chosen for the buildings, and the bush is in the most convenient location. The plan of the yards and the site of the orchard could not be improved upon, so that in all these particulars we assign to Kelvin Grove the full number of marks. The orchard, comprising two and a half acres, is in a flourishing condition, and is surrounded by one of the most perfect Norway spruce hedges to be found anywhere. It resembles a high fortification, sloping inwards toward the top, so dense that the blasts of winter cannot penetrate it, and so high that the winds which scale it blow above the tops of the trees within. No limb in all its length protrudes beyond another, and although but some twelve years planted, it is now more than twelve feet high. . . . The soil of this farm, a clay loam, blackish in its texture, and resting on a not over retentive sub-soil of clay, is most thoroughly underdrained.

"The obstacles of cultivation were absolutely lacking. They had all been removed, not a stick or stone was to be seen disfiguring the garden-like surface of this farm, nor is there a prong of a stump on the place to jar the plough, or disturb the equilibrium of the ploughman. The cultivation was simply perfect, if perfection is attainable in this line. . . .

"The system of husbandry is mixed, though in a modified form. . . .

"The fences were the neatest of the kind that we have ever seen, without any exception. They consist mainly of the straight rail, post, stake and wire; but the rails are all fitted at the ends, and perfectly level on the top and even with the posts, and the stakes were sawn. The posts are sunk four feet in the ground. You might look along the top of a line of this fence the full extent of the length and breadth of the farm, without detecting the slightest variation in the construction. . . .

"The singular neatness about every detail of this farm was one of its unique features; even in the most trifling details it is everywhere manifest. . . .

"A word to our young men before we leave the description of this sweepstakes farm. Kelvin Grove has not attained its present proud distinction by accident, or as the result of a happy combination of circumstances. In several respects others of the competing farms had by nature a most decided advantage, as in natural beauty, water supply, and in other ways. It has been made what it is by the unflinching determination of its owner. The sweepstakes prize for the best farm in Ontario is not the first prize he has won, but the last of a long line, each one of which has been the direct result of a personal effort."

MILK.

The most recent industry, and one which is rapidly developing year by year to the advantage of the Scarboro farmer, is the production of milk for consumption in Toronto.

Joseph Gray, of Toronto, is said to have begun the Scarboro trade in May, 1877, but on account of the difficulty in keeping the milk sweet, his venture did not prove a success.

On the 1st of May, in the following year, two farmers, James Taylor and David W. Thompson, determined to establish dairies and handle their own product without the aid of any middleman. They also purchased milk from their neighbors, and so successfully did they carry on this business that others have devoted their attention to it, and the consequence is that from seventeen eight-gallon cans per day taken into the city in 1878, there are now upwards of three hundred. The principal concerns and their daily product are here given:

Loudon Dairy	27 cans.
Hillside "	27 "
Wexford "	27 "
Elm "	27 "
Bendale "	25 "

Lake Shore Dairy	25	cans.
Highland Creek Dairy	25	"
Danforth Dairy	27	"
Woburn "	65	"
Agincourt "	25	"
	300	"
Individual dealers, say	50	"
Total........................	350	"

As each can contains eight gallons, the daily average quantity delivered in Toronto is about 2,800 gallons, and as the producer is paid at the rate of 85 cents per can, the cash returns amount to fully $100,000 per annum to the farmers.

The development of this industry has not been without a very perceptible effect on the methods of farming. Indian corn, hay, and forage crops of various kinds have largely displaced grain. Many milk*-cows are kept in stalls during part of the summer, and supplied with green food and meal, or chopped grain. Farmers who formerly depended mainly on wheat and other grains, now rely chiefly, or altogether on dairy products, especially milk.

LOGGING AND RAISING BEES.

Bees of many kinds are a necessity in every new settlement, where it frequently happens that the united labor of numerous hands is required.

First, in point of time, if not in importance, came the logging-bee. Usually, during fall, the portion of forest to be cleared would be "underbrushed," or freed from all saplings and low growths that might interfere with one's freedom of motion from place to place, or with the swing of the axe. Winter-time was devoted to the real chopping, which consisted not only in felling the trees, but in cutting them into lengths of from twelve to fifteen or sixteen feet. The most skilful choppers succeeded best in making as many trees as possible fall with their tops

* The ugly and useless word *milch* is purposely avoided here, as there seems to be no more reason for speaking of a milch-cow than of a milch-maid, a milch-pail, or a milch-sop.

together, thus saving much labor in disposing of the "brush," a matter of very considerable importance.

So far, one man might carry on the work alone, but as soon as the logs were cut, co-operation became necessary. Neighbors arrived at the "chopping" by invitation, many bringing their oxen with them, and the work of forming immense log-heaps began. In Scarboro it was customary to divide the "chopping" into portions about four rods wide, and forty long, containing an acre, for seven or eight men, and a yoke of oxen. Such a portion was called a "through." The gangs of men vied with each other as to which should first accomplish the task of arranging the logs in great piles, so constructed as to burn freely, and on the completion of the work festivity and rollicking mirth followed in due course.

Sometimes logging-bees were carried on during the early hours of summer mornings, chiefly, perhaps, for the sake of the oxen, which frequently succumbed to the effects of noon-day heat.

After a good "burn" the clearance could be rendered fit for receiving seed during the fall.

Raising-bees, or, simply, "raisings," as they were usually called, demanded skill of a different order. Gatherings of this kind were not of such frequent occurrence as those for logging purposes, but from the first they were of great importance. The putting up of the simplest log shanty required the united labor of several men; barns of this description demanded a score or more, and when frame structures took the place of the log ones, large numbers of hands were needed to place the timbers in position after the framer had done his work. The raising of a big barn was a matter of no small consequence. All the neighbors for miles around were invited, the women being required to prepare and serve the immense quantities of food used on such occasions. As time and opportunity served, individuals in every section or settlement developed special aptitude in handling the huge "sticks" and placing them in position. Two good men were always chosen as "captains," and they, in turn, selected their assistants from the crowd of willing workers, young and old. The right of first choice was settled by one of the captains tossing up a piece of bark, or chip, marked on one side, the opposing captain guessing white or black, wet or dry, before it reached the ground. Naturally enough, the men first selected felt the honor, and looked forward with no small degree of ambition to the time when they themselves would be chosen captains and have the choice of men, for it must be borne in mind that, in connection with these "bees," there was frequently much rivalry among the young men, because, in pioneer communities, bone and muscle, added to skill in the execution of manual labor, stand deservedly high in popular estimation. The captains, having decided by another toss which end of the building each gang should tackle, the contest (and it was a real one) takes place between the twenty, forty or fifty men engaged on each side. All is commotion and apparent confusion, but only apparent, for every stick is numbered. The race begins for who shall first get one of the bents together, and next as to which side shall have it first up. The excitement becomes more intense; the grog-boss moves about discreetly, dispensing his favors; the men's clothing is now no more than trousers and shirt—some have even dispensed with boots and stockings, that they may skip freely along the uplifted bents and purline plates when the proper time arrives. The clamor of gruff voices is deafening, and the stentor-tones of "Yoh, heave!" may be heard easily half a mile away. But long before sundown every brace is in its place, the last pin has been driven, and all the rafters are in position. If no serious accident has happened, the raising may be regarded as a success, for it is extremely dangerous work. Bumped heads, "barked" shins and jammed fingers may be numerous, but they are not taken into account. The frame is up, the job is well done, and our side came out ahead. Hurrah!

Of late years, when a barn is finished, it has been the custom for the farmer to invite the young people of the neighborhood to a dance on the spacious floor of the new building. In 1894 about four hundred young folks gathered in the large barn of Mr. J. Mason. In 1892 a similar celebration was held at Mr. T. Jackson's.

THE CANADIAN BACKWOODSMAN.

WM. CLARK, JUN., AGINCOURT (1840).

Away in the bush on my stump-studded clearance,
  I fret na' for kintra' nor kin;
Here a body's no' fashed* wi' a laird's interference,
  Though a livin's gey fashious† to win.
I dinna forget the green haunts o' my childhood,
  Loved spots in the lands far away,
Which memory will cherish while leaves deck the wildwood,
  Or plants woo the freshness o' May.
But oh, in yon islands how aft did it grieve me
  The poor man's condition to see,
And sometimes to feel too wi' nane to relieve me:
  Now here I hae little to dree.‡
I hae sax score guid acres, tho' rough to be sure,
  Wi' houses and cattle to fit,
And though cash binna plenty, I'll no' say I'm poor
  (There's a thing they ca' "trade" gangs for it).
Wi' chopping and logging and ploughing and reaping
  I've mair aye to do than I can.
O' a' places else, there's least time here for sleeping,
  It's labor, no' rank, mak's the man.
To plough my ain land is nae sma' consolation,
  Though the rigs§ binna straight to a line;
In ilk molehill o' life there's aye some dislocation,‖
  And so there, of course, is in mine.
'Tis cheery to look on the trees waving yellow
  And think there's nae rent day at han'.
The taxes at hame are the bane of a fallow,
  Wha hasna a mine at comman'.
I hear o' rebellion, distress and commotion
  In the lands I hae left far ahin,¶
And rejoice, there's a soil on this side o' the ocean
  Where the willin' a livin' may win.
Even kings noo a days are na free frae adverses,
  Where the tide o' convulsion has flown;
Here peace is the crown o' a' man's ither mercies,—
  A shanty's mair sure than a throne!

* *Fashed*, annoyed, worried.
† *Fashious*, difficult, troublesome.
‡ *Dree*, to endure or suffer.
§ *Rigs*, ridges (the ploughing).
‖ *Dislocation*. The word here is obliterated in the MS., and the reader may supply a better one than we have succeeded in doing.
¶ *Ahin*, behind.

CHAPTER VI.

DOMESTIC LIFE.

> "At night returning, every labor sped,
> He sits him down, the monarch of a shed;
> Smiles by his cheerful fire, and round surveys
> His children's looks that brighten at the blaze;
> While his loved partner, boastful of her hoard,
> Displays her cleanly platter on the board."
>
> —*Goldsmith.*

THE "father" and "mother" of Scarboro were not left long in the absolute loneliness referred to elsewhere. Members of his and her families settled around them, but the difficulties of life in the bush were not easily overcome. Perhaps the greatest inconvenience was the absence of mills. Many a makeshift had to be resorted to, of which remembrances still linger. A corn-mill (for Indian corn) in common use is thus described: A long pole was balanced on a forked upright post, well sunk in the ground; to one end of the pole was attached a rope, by which it could be worked up and down; to the other end of the pole was affixed an elongated block of wood, which had its lower end rounded to fit into a hollow in a large and heavy block standing on the ground. In this hollow the corn was put, and the pole, by means of the rope, was worked up and down so that the descent of the upper block crushed the corn in the hollow of the lower.

Roads not being opened up in the township, and the difficulty of travelling the mere ox-trails and bridle-paths being great, stores were few. Yet industries flourished, and, necessarily, they were such as have always been common to new, or secluded communities in the Old, as well as the New World.

Straw-working was carried on to a considerable extent, for men and women wanted light covering for their heads, and the bees required hives. The early crops of cereals were but large enough to little more than supply the necessities of the farmers themselves, and much of the straw was converted into hats. Many a wet day and spare hour were usefully filled by the young folk in preparing and plaiting the straw for head-wear. Rye, wheat and oat straw were all used for the purpose, but rye was the favorite. The hats being sewed, they were bleached by exposure to the fumes of sulphur in a close box. The best rye hats sold for four York-shillings (fifty cents), those of wheat straw for half that price, and a large number were sent to market.

The women of Scarboro were also famous spinners. Four skeins of fourteen knots each was considered a good day's work, but some of the maidens, in their desire to outdo their rivals, reached as high as eight, and produced that number day after day. The latter skeins appear to have been of the size containing eight knots, and this would give them a supremacy of eight knots in the day's work.

This, of course, was with the large wheel. But the small wheel had its honors, too, and one loves to imagine the bright, healthy girl of those early days as she lilted her happy song while she drew the fine thread, perhaps to be woven into her bridal outfit, from the humming wheel, and gaily smiling to herself as the tones of her lover's voice fell upon her ear from the distant field or the full barn, as he pursued his day's employment.

Nor can we forget the mother, full of cares and projects for the welfare of her dear ones, whose thoughts would run in a quieter strain, yet who sang to her toddling bairns, or to the babe in the cradle, the words of some homely old ditty.

As far as can be ascertained, David Thomson had the first flock of sheep in his section of the township, but he had great difficulty in keeping his lambs from the wolf, that would attack the flock even in daylight.

Before the introduction of carding mills, all work in preparing wool for cloth was done by hand. Picking, dyeing, carding, spinning, and weaving were part of the thrifty housewife's work. Nor were her colors aniline dyes either; she procured the plants that grew around. For brown she took butternut; for yellow, onion skins or wax-wood, and golden-rod; sumach came in for her purpose also, and a dozen other color-sources that the Indian had found out long before.

When carding mills were introduced, wool was taken to the mill to be made into rolls, then spun, dyed and woven at home. Here, too, the good wife made her husband's clothing as well as her own and her children's. How she did so much in a day of twenty-four hours only is a present-day puzzle. It is true, neither housekeeping nor cooking in those days was very elaborate. There were no drawing-rooms—the open-hearthed, hospitable kitchen, with its blazing fire, served all purposes.

Stoves of any kind did not find their way to Scarboro for a good many years. An amusing story is still told of one of the old settlers, evidently an oddity, who has left behind him the legend of a fire called the "koonet," or "coonet," or, as was probably the correct word, the "Vankoughnet" fire. Mr. Vankoughnet's idea of comfort and convenience savored of the rough plenty of the time, and is wholly inapplicable to a date when wood is worth six dollars a cord. Near the middle of his one-roomed house he constructed a fire-bed by digging a shallow pit about six inches deep and three or four feet across, the edges of which were flanked with stones set in clay mortar. He made a door on each side of his cabin, through which he drew the logs with an ox. Having taken in sufficient fuel for the night he closed his doors, rolled the logs at full length across the fire-pit, and sat down to read, to meditate, or perhaps chat with a friendly neighbor.

But the ordinary settler's fire, large as it was, was not on so liberal a scale. The place which the stove now holds in the farm kitchen was well filled in past days by the bake-kettle and Dutch oven, in which both bread and meat could be nicely prepared for table. Indeed, for the baking of bread the iron kettle, covered by a lid, and buried beneath the live coals, is said to have surpassed the stove appliances of to-day.

Various other methods of preparing food were resorted to in the kitchen before the advent of stoves. Meat was sometimes hung to roast, suspended on a hook before the fire, or, as the Indian used to carry out the same idea, by holding the meat on a forked stick close to the red-hot coals on the hearth. Nor were the resources of the housewife exhausted by these methods. Did she wish to prepare bacon or pancakes? Then she used the long-handled frying-pan, and it was quite a feat for the cook to turn the pancake by a toss without letting it fall into the fire. Her camp-kettle or pot, hung upon the "crane," could be swung off, or over, the fire as required.

The clay, or brick oven was also an adjunct of the kitchen, that was considered indispensable, and was used for the various purposes which the more pretentious arrangement serves to-day; and what batches of bread—salt-rising or hop-yeast—it would hold! And what an array of saleratus-raised cakes! And as for pies! well, ask grandfather about them.

The first stoves—all for burning wood, of course,—great generous things that took half a cordwood stick at once, were the Burr, the King, the ever-famous Davy Crockett, and the Lion Air-tight. In the early part of the century a single stove called Dr. Nott's was actually imported from England, as well as anthracite or "Kilkenny" coal for its fuel!

Soap-making was another domestic economy every housewife practised. Hard-soap, soft-soap, lye and leach-barrel, what a history is hidden in the world-old word soap! The men were economical, too, and carefully burning their fallow, produced from the clean hardwood ashes a valuable article of commerce—potash. How good the God of nature is to His creatures we never know, until we are deprived of outside assistance. No stores! then where did our ancestors get their rope and string, harness for their oxen, and cordage for all other purposes?

Long before the white man's appearance, the Indian

had found out the toughness of the young bark of the moose-wood, and used it for loose handles to his baskets; this the earliest settlers of Scarboro also used. The bark of the elm, and of the bass-wood (used for the same purpose in Russia), made strong ropes and was in great demand. Elm bark, too, was much used for chair-bottoms, and some of these primitive seats are still kept as relics in the township. For this purpose black-ash was, however, preferred, because it did not stretch. The wood was split into slabs about an inch and a half in thickness, and then pounded with a mallet, when it could be readily split into thin ribbons and woven, basket-fashion, into the chair-bottoms. It is hardly likely that rush-bottomed chairs would be unknown, as they were the common chairs of the Old World, and every countryman knew how to prepare the rushes. For ropes, also, flax was sparsely grown; it was used, besides, for grain-bags and coarse ticking, at an early date. Some years ago a flax mill was built by the Milnes on the River Rouge, but did not prove financially successful, because after the civil war in the United States, cotton became so cheap as to make flax-working unprofitable.

There are few places where the sweets that our nature craves are not to be found, and Canada has her splendid maple trees for a supply. Sugar-making was largely carried on in Scarboro for many years. Happy memories of those by-gone times still linger among the older people. They had their "sugaring-off" and "taffy-pulls," when the young people met for an evening's enjoyment, including the invariable dance which followed.

In the sugar-bush would be found the large trough,

made from a section of a pine-tree dug out with an axe. It was big enough to hold several barrels of sap as it was collected from the trees. There, also, were large kettles, or caldrons, in which the sap was boiled down, and the "camp," in which was stored the necessary utensils used in the process. Sugar, syrup, and vinegar, in sufficient quantities for family use, were made by each household. Corn-cakes and buckwheat pancakes, with maple syrup, was, and remains, a favorite Canadian dish.

Nor were sugaring frolics the only fun that our forefathers indulged in. Logging, husking and paring bees, and barn-raisings were seasons of great enjoyment as well as of industry. Logging-bees and raisings have already been referred to at length in the chapter, "On the Farm."

Husking-bees employed the united industry of both sexes, and were a favorite source of amusement with the early settlers. The farmer having gathered his crop of Indian corn into his threshing floor, or upon the open field, invited the young people to husk it; or, rather to unhusk it, and the merriment on such occasions was most hilarious; but, alas! the monster and insatiate silo has come with its friend the cutting-box, and the happy husking-days have gone never to return!

When the orchards of the first settlers began to bear, and the beautiful fruit was garnered, all the apples that were not sold, or would not keep through the long winter, were pared, cut into eighths, strung on cords and hung up to the kitchen ceiling to dry, with a view to future pies. The young folk gathered in the farmer's ample kitchen and took the work in hand.

Generally a certain quantity was made the task of the evening, and after this was done a supper was served and dancing followed.

Every country community in the new, as well as in the old lands had its violinist. Among Scarboro's early sons who swung the bow gracefully were, notably, "Fiddler Will," "Fiddler Andrew" and "Fiddler Dick," and one of these worthies having been given a comfortable place, reels, strathspeys, hornpipes, and country dances begun, and merriment reigned supreme.

"New times, new manners," so to-day many of the old amusements have fallen into disuse, and new ones have come in. One anniversary, the royal birthday, remains, however, and is always a season of recreation. On this day the loyal militia of Scarboro used to meet for annual drill, and it was called "training day." Since then George IV. and William IV. have reigned for short periods, and each birthday has been right royally celebrated.

For the last fifty-nine years all loyal subjects have kept the 24th of May, the birthday of our present beloved sovereign, Her Majesty Queen Victoria. For twenty-eight years another occasion of public rejoicing and recreation has been added to our national holidays in Canada, namely, Dominion Day, the 1st of July. On this day picnics, socials, or social tea-parties, lawn parties, or excursions by rail or steamboat, are the usual forms of pleasure. Sunday Schools avail themselves freely of the opportunities for a little outing to some point, generally on the lake shore, which the simple form of the picnic affords. Gates's Grove in early times, and at present

Victoria Park and many other convenient points are selected for these gatherings.

The story of domestic and social life in Scarboro would be incomplete without some reference to its mental food. Books, though few, by reason of many causes, were not entirely absent, even in the humblest families of early Scarboro. Beyond the cherished Bible and prayer-book, or, as in the case of the Presbyterian Church, the paraphrases of the Psalms of David, other highly-valued volumes were to be found: "Baxter's Saints' Rest," "The Imitation of Christ," "Bunyan's Pilgrim's Progress," with perhaps also an odd copy of "Defoe's Plague of London," or his "Robinson Crusoe." Among the remains of the old Thomson library we find such works as "*Spectacle de la Nature*, or Nature Delineated," an excellent work preparatory to the fuller study of natural history, translated from the French by Dr. Bellamy and others in 1743. On the shelves were also "Pinnock's Catechism of Mental Philosophy," and his "Catechism of the History of Greece." With these were "The Complete English Farmer," "Mechanickal Dialing," "The Marrow of Modern Divinity," as well as several volumes of Sermons, and works on the Shorter Catechism.

In the old Walton library we find "The Complete Body of Practical Divinity," by John Gill, 1796, and on the Brownlie bookshelves were "Ebenezer Erskine's Works," "Matthew Henry's Commentary," and quite a large number of other works of value.

Of newspapers read in the township in very early times, people in the Old Country furnished their friends in the New with such as they could afford, but it must be remembered that this was before the daily press possibilities were dreamt of. There were also *The Colonial Advocate*, first issued in Toronto in 1824; *The Courier*, *The Mercury*, *The Upper Canada Gazette*, the first newspapers published in the Province, and undoubtedly others, for the period between 1824 and 1834 was one of great activity in the public press. *The Montreal Witness* has been read in Scarboro from its first issue in 1844 or 1845.

The Scarboro and Highland Creek Public Libraries are fully described in another chapter, but special reference may be made here to the books now supplied to Sunday School scholars, such books being immensely superior to the namby-pamby stuff that used to be doled out to *us*.

The house furnishings of to-day correspond with the rest of the internal fittings. The dinner-horn or conch-shell of old time has given place to the more melodious bell on the kitchen roof, and the "spread" for a meal nowadays is in striking contrast with the humbler fare that constituted one in the early days. City folk are prone to regard the farmer's table as one that is set out, substantially it may be, but coarsely and uninvitingly. The sight of a Scarboro *menu* would speedily dispel this notion, in view of the snowy linen, the excellence and variety of the dishes, and the tasteful manner of serving.

It is claimed for the wives and daughters of this township, that if they could only enter into competition with outsiders as the husbands and fathers have done in *their* lines, Scarboro would bear the palm in all that pertains to housekeeping, as it confessedly does already in so many other departments, industrial as well as social.

How different, not only in appearance, but also in comfort and convenience of its internal arrangements, is the Scarboro farm-house of to-day from that which sheltered our grandfathers and grandmothers in the beginning of the century.

Other pages in this history give a description of the material used in, and method of constructing, the old-time farm-house.

The interior of early houses comprised only one room, with the clay and stone-built fire-place—or, as at first, clay and wood—at the one end, and beds at the other, while, to economize room, the children's bed was pushed underneath the larger one. The bunk was used as a seat by day and a bed at night. At one side of the fire-place, and at an angle of 60 degrees, there was a narrow staircase, or a ladder, leading to the garret, which in some cases had to be used as a sleeping apartment. The recess formed by the angle of the stairs and the outer wall of the fire-place, was known as the "pot-hole." The furniture of the room consisted of beds, table, chairs and cupboard, all home-made. Nails, or pins, driven into the wall held the various pans, etc., used in kitchen. The fire-place, in the earliest times, supplied the only light. Next was introduced the saucer with oil, or melted tallow, in which was placed a cotton wick. The days of the tallow candle followed, and these in turn were succeeded by the kerosene lamp. The modern farm-house is designed in all its arrangements with a view to comfort and convenience. There are parlor, private sitting-room, dining-room, and from three to five bedrooms with clothes-room off each, wide halls, and, in some instances, hoists from the cellar to the dining-room. Many houses are heated by means of coal furnaces, and where there is no furnace, coal stoves are used. The large kitchen is always convenient to the dining-room; a supply of soft-water is kept in underground cisterns, the pump being not unfrequently placed in a corner of the kitchen, while the hard-water pump is equally handy.

In the modern house the sleeping apartments are chiefly upstairs, the aim being to have only one on the ground floor, which is used in case of sickness. A hanging-lamp in each supplies light in dining-room and parlor, hand-lamps being used in bedrooms. In most houses of to-day all the rooms are carpeted, with the exception of the kitchen, which is in some instances covered with oilcloth or linoleum. Musical instruments are found in nearly every house, and in many a Scarboro home may be heard the sweet strains of organ or piano produced by no unskilful fingers.

CHAPTER VII.

ROADS.

"It is one thing to see your road, another to cut it."—*George Eliot.*

"Who can answer where any road leads to?"—*Lytton.*

IT is not unusual to find that the first roads in lake-shore (or first opened) townships followed tortuous Indian trails, as these always led along routes presenting fewest difficulties and most advantages. In many instances the surveyors' work is regardless of deviations, but it is probable that the Kingston, Danforth and other old roads in this township were laid out on the lines pursued by ancient paths.

Danforth Road.—Governor Simcoe being duly impressed with the value of good roads, contemplated the opening of one from Burlington Bay to Kingston, to be known as Dundas Street (in honor of Henry Dundas, Lord Melville, at that time Secretary of State for the Colonies), a name retained by that portion of the road extending westwards from Toronto.

"The road eastwards towards Kingston was to be constructed in course of time by the settlers. Meanwhile the communication with Montreal was to be made by water. . . . In 1799, it is recorded that the road from York to the Bay of Quinte was 'contracted out by Government to Mr. Danforth,* to be cut and completed, forty feet wide, by the first of

* His name is said to have been in full, Asa Danforth.

July next.* Mr. Danforth had already made forty miles of excellent road.' The *Gazette* of December 14th, 1799, says: 'The road from York to the Midland District is completed as far as the township of Hope, about sixty miles, so that sleighs, waggons, etc., may travel it with safety.'"†

During the war of 1812 military stores are said to have been landed at the mouth of Highland Creek, and carried over the Danforth and Old Ridge Roads to York, on their way to Penetanguishene. A large anchor that had been taken by this route and the Old Ridge Road was lost in the Nottawasaga River, by the wreck of the raft on which it was carried. (See p. 52.)

For many years a toll-gate stood on the Danforth Road, on lot 31, concession B.

It was evidently in following this as a mere trail from the lake-shore that David Thomson reached the spot he chose as his home in 1796.

Portions of the Danforth Road are closed to allow of some lots being squared.

Kingston Road.—This road connecting Kingston and York, was first known as Kingston Street. It was made in 1800, but for many years was little better than a wide path through the woods, there having been scarcely any attempt to make it what we now call a good road, at all seasons. An old resident describes it as he remembers it sixty years ago, when its course was nearer the lake than it is at present. He says: "Passing through this section from east to west, it ran

* A correspondent says the contract price was $100 per mile, and Danforth was to run the road to suit himself.

† From a very excellent summary of the history of York, by Dr. Wm. Canniff, in Miles' "Historical Atlas of the County." Toronto, 1878.

between Old St. Margaret's Church and the present parsonage, entering the north corner of lot 13, concession D. Near this point was the first (Elliot) hotel after passing Highland Creek. On the opposite side of the road was a log-house occupied by a shoemaker named Small. Crossing lot 14 near the house of J. Richardson, M.P.P., it ran into lot 15 about four rods north of the present road. A log school-house stood here, in which Miss Closson taught. About twenty rods west of the Grand Trunk Railway crossing, it crossed the present road, and began the ascent of Scarboro Heights, keeping near the brow of the hill, and passing the old home of J. Humphrey to lot 16, the Annis homestead, on which stood a hotel kept by John Muir. This place was known as the William Wallace Inn, the front of which was decorated with what was, no doubt (?) a striking oil-painted portrait of the redoubtable warrior himself. Passing south of the Methodist cemetery it crossed 'Dolway's Swale' over a log bridge to lot 17, concession C, keeping close to the top of the hill to the centre of lot 18. Near this it is said that a still earlier road ran down to the flats,* and that the first stage coaches between York and Kingston used this branch for some years.

The route of the main road over lot 19 is still marked by a row of pine-trees on the farm of Levi Annis on the south side of which stood the old Burton homestead, and farther on the frame hotel kept by Mr. Gates. It crossed the present road to the north side near Bambridge's blacksmith shop to lot 21, the old Stobo farm, where there was a toll-gate, after which it

* J. G. Cornell writes that "before this, the road ran down the hill to the flats on lots 17 and 18, concession C."

ran about thirty rods north of the present road past the homes of John Stobo, Stephen Washington, John Thoms and Stephen Pherrill to Toronto."

In 1817, the route of Kingston Street was changed by being made to take a course generally somewhat farther to the north, where more favorable grades were obtainable, the work being done by Joseph Secor for $11,000 under the superintendence of Commissioners Peter Secor, Dan Knowles, Arch. Glendinning and Wm. Helliwell. The owners of the land through which the new road ran received no compensation beyond getting the old road allowance. At one time the road was planked from Norway to Highland Creek.

Toll-gates were placed on it about 1839. In 1850 the road was taken over by James Beatty.

Markham Plank Road.—The Markham and Scarboro Plank Road Co. was incorporated under an Act of the Canadian Parliament in 1852, the President being Joseph Tomlinson, and the Treasurer, John Reesor.

Planking was laid down from the Kingston Road to Stouffville. Shares were issued at £6 5s. each. This road was considerably frequented while it remained in good repair, but to keep it in this condition cost more than was warranted by the returns.

Toll-gates were placed at Scarboro village and at the corner of the second concession.

An informant states that this road "was opened as far south as Mr. Purvis's, lot 18, concession 2, in 1830. From there it struck across lots to James Chester's, in concession D."

Old Ridge Road.—Even the memory of this old highway is almost forgotten, as it has long since been enclosed in the various lots through which it passed, on the watershed between the two main branches of Highland Creek. Following this course, it extended in a general southerly and south-easterly direction, until a little south of Bendale it met the Danforth Road, both forming, no doubt, part of the original Indian trail, one branch of which extended to Toronto, while the other led to Lake Simcoe by the Holland River.

It is referred to as "The first road, running in a south-easterly direction and crossing concession 3, in lots 26 and 27; concession 2, in lots 24 and 25, until it struck the Danforth Road."

First Markham Road.—The oldest road to Markham extended from the Old Ridge Road at a point near the south end of lot 24, concession 2, until by a somewhat devious course it reached concession 4, after which it followed a tolerably straight line between lots 17 and 18, where it entered the township of Markham.

J. C. Cornell states that "a road from the present site of Scarboro post-office, ran in an almost straight line to St. Andrew's Church."

Other particulars relating to roads will be found in the following chapter.

OLD COUNCILLORS.

1. J. P. Wheler. 2. Peter Secor. 3. J. Crawford. 4. J. Torrance. 5. Wm. Clark, sen. 6. J. Moyle.

CHAPTER VIII.

COUNCILS AND COUNCILLORS.

"Order is heaven's first law; and this confest,
Some are, and must be, greater than the rest."
—*Pope.*

THE history of municipal institutions in Ontario, however interesting, would be out of place here. Suffice it to state, broadly, that we have succeeded in elaborating what is perhaps the most perfect system of local self-government to be found in any country at the present day. If we except those offices in the gift of the Dominion and Provincial Governments, and which are usually bestowed as political favors, there is not a position from that of poundkeeper or pathmaster to that of member of the Legislature or of Parliament, beyond the attainment of any ambitious and even moderately intelligent man; our school section, township and county boards affording admirable means for the training of those who are desirous of becoming public servants.

When the first parliament met at Newark in 1792, the organized portion of Upper Canada was laid out in immense districts, the areas of which became less and less as population increased. The limits of these districts were first shown in Chewitt's map, prepared in 1795, and, with more details, in that of D. W. Smith, Acting Surveyor-General, in 1798.* At this time the

* A beautiful copy of this map accompanies the report, for 1891, of Dr. Douglas Brymner, Dominion Archivist.

Home District, of which Scarboro formed a part, extended from the head of the Bay of Quinte, on the east, to the present County of Perth, on the west. All to the east of York was included in the counties of Durham and Northumberland, and while all to the west was called the West Riding, what now constitutes York and Ontario formed the East Riding of York.

When the first Home District Council met in Toronto on the 8th of February, 1842,* the boundaries of the district were greatly restricted. The following list of townships then included will enable anyone to trace the limits of the territory on a map: Adjala, Albion, Brock, Caledon, Chinguacousy, Essa, Etobicoke, Georgina, Gwillimbury (East, West and North), Innisfil, King, Mara and Rama, Markham, Mulmur and Tossorontio, Medonte and Flos, Orillia (North and South), Oro, Pickering, Reach, Scarboro, Tecumseth, Thorah, Tiny and Tay, Toronto, Toronto Gore, Uxbridge and Scott, Vaughan, Vespra, Whitby, Whitchurch, and York.

At this time there were no township councils, and all municipal business was transacted through the District Council, in which each township was represented by one or two members, according to population, the number of members in the Home District Council being fifty-one; but in 1849 the number of townships in the district had fallen from forty to twenty-four, and the councillors had decreased from fifty-one to forty.

In the records of the Home District Municipal

* The division of the Province into districts, and the representation of each township in the District Council, was the beginning of municipal government in Upper Canada. The scheme was formulated by Lord Durham.

Council (1842 to 1849), we find that Wm. Clark and John Torrance represented Scarboro in 1842 and 1843. In 1844, the councillors were Messrs. Torrance and Secor; in 1845, '46 and '47, Messrs. Secor and Paterson; in 1848 and '49, Messrs. Secor and A. Glendinning.

During this period most of the municipal legislation affecting Scarboro related to schools, and that of but little importance.

From the minutes we find that in August, 1845, on the petition of James Jones to the Home District Council, a road was opened between lots 28 and 29 "from the Dunford* Road to the Plank Road," and on the 29th June, 1848, "Thos. Rogers, Joseph Beek and others" petitioned "that a road be established between B and C broken front in the township of Scarboro," but no action seems to have been taken pursuant to this request; and on the same day A. H. McLean prayed "that the old line of road between 18 and 19 be abandoned, and side-line first concession be adopted," with a similar result.

At this meeting, too, John Skelton asked payment "for some bridge alleged to have been built by him about twenty-three years ago"—to use the language of the Committee on Roads and Bridges—but "your committee do not recommend the prayer of the petition." This must have proved aggravating to Mr. Skelton, as it was not a recommendation of his prayer he asked for, but a recommendation of payment.

At the first half-yearly meeting of the Home District Council in 1849, a by-law was passed appropriating

* Evidently meant for Danforth.

the sum of £5,000 for the improvement of roads and bridges. Of this amount £203 came to Scarboro, "the sum of £30 to be expended in building a bridge over the Highland Creek, at Arvinston's saw-mill, on the Markham Road, and in draining and otherwise improving the same road northward to Mape's Inn; and that Peter Secor, Edward Cornell and James Purvis be Commissioners.

"The sum of £173 to be expended by John McCreight, Jordan Post, William Brown, Daniel Knowles, Wm. Helliwell, Lewis Secor, Joshua Sisley, James Lawrie, Edward Cornell, James Purvis, John P. Wheler, James A. Thomson, John Elliot, John Fitzgibbon, Joseph Smith, William Paterson, William Clark, sen., Joseph Pilkey, Robert Buchanan, Chris. Thomson, John Tingle, and William Devenish, together with the two councillors of the township, upon such roads and bridges as they, or a majority of them, may deem expedient."

The first local municipal records relate to a town meeting held on the 3rd of January, 1848, at Thomas Dowswell's Inn, J. P. Wheler in the chair, when Arch. Glendinning was elected councillor, and Wm. Chamberlain, clerk, assessor and collector. It has already been mentioned that Mr. Glendinning was a councillor for that year, but this record enables us to understand the simple methods of election, and brings out that while a councillor was chosen to hold office for two years, only one councillor was elected each year.

The first township council met at Dowswell's tavern, 21st of January, 1850. It consisted of Peter Secor, Reeve; J. P. Wheler, Deputy Reeve; Wm. Helliwell,

Christopher Thomson and Edward Cornell, all of whom took the oath of qualification before Wm. Clark, J.P., a former representative in the Home District Council.

A list of the members that have composed succeeding councils will be found appended, but reference should here be made to the fact that John Crawford, who served as Deputy Reeve from 1859 until 1865, has continued most worthily to fill the position of township clerk from 1865 to the present time.

The township records go no farther back than 1848, when a declaration was made and signed by Joseph Pilkey, Isaac C. ———, George Snider, Adam Walton, Wm. Kennedy, Wm. Fawcett, sen., Wm. Mason, Thos. Kennedy, Wedley Robinson, Daniel Kennedy, George Galway, John Palmer, John Warren, Isaac Christie, Timothy Devenish, John Richardson, Alex. Wilson, Geo. Stephenson, Abraham Stoner, Wm. Young, Wm. Richardson, Wm. Westney, Wm. Anthony, Jas. Law, Isaac Stoner, Thos. Adams, Thos. Booth, King Parkes, James Peters, Wm. Chamberlain, Marshal Macklin, Thomas Adams, jun., Isaac Secor, Wm. A. Thomson, Jas. A. Thomson, James Johnson, John Sherburn, Jas. Spring, Thomas Brown, Jas. Wilson, John Law, Wm. Nelson, Robert Jackson, Andrew Potter, Thos. Demma.

In 1850 district councils were abolished, and county councils introduced, and the words Reeve and Deputy Reeve were used to designate the chairman and vice-chairman of the township council. Up to 1867 the councillors chose their own reeves, but since that time these officers have been elected at the polls.

MEMBERS OF THE TOWNSHIP COUNCIL AND THE PRINCIPAL TOWNSHIP OFFICIALS OF THE TOWNSHIP OF SCARBORO, FROM THE YEAR 1850 TO THE YEAR 1896 INCLUSIVE.

YEAR.	REEVE.	DEPUTY REEVE.	COUNCILLORS.	TREASURER.	CLERK.
1850	Peter Secor	J. P. Wheler....	Wm. Helliwell ... Chris. Thomson .. Ed. Cornell	Jos. H. Smith.	W. Chamberlain
1851	J. P. Wheler......	Thos. Brown	Chris. Thomson Jas. Purvis ...... Wm. Helliwell ..	Jos. H. Smith.	Stephen Closson
1852	J. P. Wheler......	Chris. Thomson..	John Heron...... Geo. Stephenson Thos. Dowswell ..	Jos. H. Smith.	Stephen Closson
1853	J. P. Wheler......	G. Stephenson ...	Isaac Ashbridge .. Jos. Secor........ Wm. Clark	Jos. H. Smith.	Stephen Closson
1854	John Torrance	Wm. Clark......	Geo. Stephenson.. Wm. H. Norris .. Thos. Kennedy. .	Wm. Helliwell.	Stephen Closson
1855	J. P. Wheler......	Wm. Clark......	Jos. H. Smith.... Jordan Post...... Jas. Humphrey...	James Moyle .	James Moyle.
1856	J. P. Wheler......	Wm. Clark......	Jos. H. Smith.... Jordan Post...... John Crawford ...	James Moyle..	James Moyle.
1857	J. P. Wheler......	Wm. Clark......	Thos. Brown ..... Geo. Stephenson.. John Crawford ...	James Moyle..	James Moyle.
1858	J. P. Wheler......	Wm. Clark......	Thos. Brown .... Wm. Helliwell ... Wm. H. Norris ..	James Moyle .	James Moyle.
1859	J. P. Wheler......	John Crawford ..	Isaac Ashbridge .. Wm. Helliwell .. Edwin Snider	James Moyle..	James Moyle.

	REEVE.	DEPUTY REEVE	COUNCILLORS.	TREASURER.	CLERK.
0	J. P. Wheler......	John Crawford ..	Jas. Palmer...... Wm. Helliwell ... Edwin Snider	James Moyle..	James Moyle.
1	J. P. Wheler	John Crawford ..	Jas. Palmer . .. Daniel Knowles .. Edwin Snider	James Moyle..	James Moyle.
2	J. P. Wheler......	John Crawford ..	Thos. Brown .... Wm. Helliwell ... Edwin Snider	James Moyle..	James Moyle.
3	J. P. Wheler......	John Crawford ..	Thos. Brown .... D. G. Stephenson. Edwin Snider	James Moyle..	James Moyle.
4	J. P. Wheler......	John Crawford ..	Thos. Brown .... D. G. Stephenson. Wm. Clark	James Moyle..	James Moyle.
5	D. G. Stephenson..	Geo. Chester	John Taylor...... J. P. Wheler .... Wm. Clark	John Crawford	John Crawford.
6	Thos. Brown......	Geo. Chester	D. G. Stephenson. Thos. Kennedy... Thos. Whiteside..	John Crawford	John Crawford.
7	Geo. Chester	D. G. Stephenson.	James McCowan.. Thos. Whiteside.. John Wilson	John Crawford	John Crawford.
8	Geo. Chester	D. G. Stephenson.	James McCowan.. Thos. Whiteside.. John S. Palmer...	John Crawford	John Crawford.
9	Geo. Chester	D. G. Stephenson.	James McCowan.. Simon Miller .... M. Macklin......	John Crawford	John Crawford.
0	Geo. Chester	D. G. Stephenson.	James McCowan.. Simon Miller .... John S. Palmer ..	John Crawford	John Crawford.
1	J. P. Wheler......	D. G. Stephenson.	James McCowan. Simon Miller .... John S. Palmer ..	John Crawford	John Crawford.
2	J. P. Wheler......	D. G. Stephenson.	James McCowan.. Simon Miller ... Jas. Humphrey ..	John Crawford	John Crawford.
3	J. P. Wheler......	D. G. Stephenson.	Simon Miller .... James McCowan.. Jeremiah Annis ..	John Crawford	John Crawford.

YEAR.	REEVE.	DEPUTY REEVE.	COUNCILLORS.	TREASURER.	CLERK.
1874	J. P. Wheler......	Simon Miller	Wm. Tredway ... Thos. Whiteside.. Jas. Chester	John Crawford	John Crawford.
1875	J. P. Wheler......	D. G. Stephenson.	Jas. Chester ..... Wm. Tredway ... James Lawrie	John Crawford	John Crawford.
1876	Geo. Chester	D. G. Stephenson.. James Chester	Wm. Tredway ... John Richardson..	John Crawford	John Crawford.
1877	D. G. Stephenson	Wm. Tredway .... James Chester ...	John Richardson.. Geo. Morgan. . .	John Crawford	John Crawford.
1878	D. G. Stephenson	Wm. Tredway .... James Chester ...	Geo. Morgan..... John Richardson..	John Crawford	John Crawford.
1879	D. G. Stephenson	A. M. Secor. .. John Richardson ..	Jas. Humphrey, jr. Geo. Morgan.....	John Crawford	John Crawford.
1880	D. G. Stephenson	A. M. Secor....... John Richardson ..	Jas. Humphrey, jr. Geo Morgan...	John Crawford	John Crawford.
1881	John Richardson.	A. M. Secor....... James Chester	Alfred Mason .... Rich'd Knowles ..	John Crawford	John Crawford.
1882	John Richardson.	A. M. Secor....... Geo. Morgan	Alfred Mason .... Rich'd Knowles .	John Crawford	John Crawford.
1883	John Richardson.	A. M. Secor....... Geo. Morgan......	Rich'd Knowles .. W. W. Walton ..	John Crawford	John Crawford.
1884	John Richardson.	A. M. Secor....... Geo. Morgan......	Rich'd Knowles .. W. W. Walton. .	John Crawford	John Crawford.
1885	John Richardson.	A. M. Secor....... Geo. Morgan	Rich'd Knowles . . W. W. Walton...	John Crawford	John Crawford.
1886	John Richardson.	A. M. Secor....... Geo. Morgan......	Rich'd Knowles .. W. W. Walton...	G. M. Jacques.	Thos. Crawford.
1887	John Richardson.	A. M. Secor. .... Geo. Morgan......	Rich'd Knowles .. David Brown.....	G. M. Jacques.	Thos. Crawford.
1888	John Richardson.	A. M. Secor....... Richard Knowles..	David Brown..... Alex. Baird	G. M. Jacques.	Thos. Crawford.
1889	John Richardson.	A. M. Secor....... Richard Knowles..	Alex. Baird ...... Levi E. Annis....	G. M. Jacques.	Thos. Crawford.
1890	John Richardson.	A. M. Secor....... Richard Knowles..	Alex. Baird ...... Levi E. Annis....	G. M. Jacques.	Thos. Crawford.
1891	John Richardson.	James Chester .... Alex. Baird	Levi E. Annis.... Lyman Kennedy..	G. M. Jacques.	Thos. Crawford.

MUNICIPAL.

J. Chester.
R. Crawford. W. A. Heron. T. Crawford. J. H. Richardson.
T. Jackson. J. Ley. L. Kennedy. R. Cowan. A. Young.

	REEVE.	DEPUTY REEVE.	COUNCILLORS.	TREASURER.	CLERK.
2	John Richardson	James Chester..... Alex. Baird	Levi E. Annis.... Lyman Kennedy..	A. M. Secor ..	Thos. Crawford.
3	John Richardson	James Chester..... Alex. Baird	Lyman Kennedy.. Robert Cowan....	A. M. Secor...	Thos. Crawford.
4	John Richardson	James Chester..... Lyman Kennedy ..	Robert Cowan.... Thompson Jackson	A. M. Secor...	Thos. Crawford.
5	James Chester...	Alex. Baird .... Robert Cowan	Thompson Jackson Andrew Young ..	A. M. Secor...	Thos. Crawford.
6	Lyman Kennedy.	James Ley .... Robert Cowan.....	Thompson Jackson Andrew Young ..	J.H.Richardson	Thos. Crawford.

ODDS AND ENDS.

"Fat" pine knots were the first sources of light, the original spark having been produced by means of flint and steel to ignite a piece of "punk" or dried fungus, usually found in the hearts of decayed beech and maple trees. A good knot would yield a flickering flame for fully half-an-hour.

In course of time shallow vessels containing oil and cotton wick came in. These were succeeded by dip candles, formed by repeated dipping of wicks into melted tallow; and these again by moulded candles made by the half-dozen or more at a time. Next came the kerosene lamp.

Splints, both ends of which were dipped in sulphur, were the forerunners of the present lucifer matches.

Nearly every man, and many women, carried appliances for striking a light, consisting of the flint and steel, and punk, or prepared cotton or paper. The box in which these were contained was called the tinder-box.

CHAPTER IX.

TRADES AND TRADESMEN.

"All true work is sacred; in all true work, were it but hand-labor, there is a something of divineness."—*Carlyle.*

WOODCRAFT.

IN all early settlements, the individual was thrown to a great extent on his own resources. The mother of the family was not only cook and house-keeper, but dairy-maid, laundry-maid, and seamstress (as is yet too frequently the case); and the head of the house acted in the capacity, not of husbandman alone, but of carpenter, mason, harness-maker, shoemaker, blacksmith, and occasionally miller.

The house of the first settler was a marvel of wood-craft. His furniture consisted wholly of the product of the axe and the auger. Seats were either solid sections of trees, or slabs in which three legs had been inserted in one-and-a-half, or two-inch holes; tables were similarly put together, and bedsteads were made by means of long pins inserted in holes bored in the logs forming the wall, and supported at their outer extremities on blocks; chimneys were constructed of wooden bars crossing each other at the ends in the form of a square, the interstices being filled up with clay; floors consisted of slabs split from logs, and roughly faced with the axe; hinges and latches were of wood, and the doors themselves were indebted mainly to the axe for their existence. Locks were seldom thought of, and when a fastening of this kind was considered necessary, a wooden pin passing into the door-jamb inside was sufficient; other pins round the walls or in the joists served to support shelves or to suspend articles of various kinds; birch-bark, when procurable, was made into excellent substitutes for boxes, when sections of hollow logs were not so employed; even household vessels of large size were scooped from suitable pieces of timber; and in a general way it may be said that the Canadian pioneer lived in the Wood Age. In Scarboro he had a great variety of material, including magnificent white pine, growing two hundred feet in height; Norway pine; maples of several species; red, blue, and white beech; slippery and swamp elm; black and white ash; oak of the varieties known as white, red and scrub; red, black, and silver, or white birch; black, pigeon and choke cherry; three kinds of thorn, two of spruce, besides balsam, cedar, hemlock, tamarack, poplar, basswood, balm of Gilead, ironwood, hickory, butternut, hazel, two kinds of willow, dogwood, stinkwood (moosewood, or leatherwood), sassafras, and numerous shrubs bearing no local names.

One naturally concludes that if woodcraft did not flourish here it would be a wonder. At first, as a matter of course, the trees had to be got rid of regardless of every other consideration but the clearing of sufficient space for a crop, and it was some years before much demand sprung up for forest products of any kind in this locality. Hardwood ashes, and subsequently crude potash, were perhaps among the first of industries to yield the settler any income. These were carried in schooners from the mouths of the Rouge and Highland Creek across the lake, the return cargoes, if any, consisting mainly of salt, flour, and simple articles of household furniture. With the increase of business these trading vessels added smuggling to their enterprise, and it is said that the hollows and ravines of the cliffs were the hiding places of contraband goods as long as the illicit traffic was carried on.

This trade flourished for many years, and large quantities of tea, leather goods, and general merchandise were landed night after night at the mouth of Gates's Gully, as recently as 1838. When opportunity served, the contraband goods were delivered in Toronto, Whitby, and other places. A farmer, delivering tea on one occasion, narrowly escaped capture by hiding his two bushel bagful in the manger where his horse was feeding.

With the more rapid disappearance of the forest immediately around York, and the steady growth of the village itself, the Scarboro farmer in course of time found it worth his while, with the assistance of "Buck and Bright," to haul fuel in the shape of cordwood to the seat of government beyond the Don. But this could be done in winter only, for during the rest of the year the roads were not too good, even when they could be called roads at all. In more recent years this industry has proved a most profitable one, wood selling at one time as high as $7.50 per cord, and even now with coal in competition, it will bring from $4.50 to $5.00 a cord. While the hey-day of this trade continued, hundreds of teams entered Toronto from Scarboro every morning, and it has been stated that upwards of one million dollars must have accrued to the township from this source alone.

MILLS.

At an early date the value of the pine and oak was recognized, and as soon as possible after the settlement of the township, saw-mills of a primitive kind were erected on the numerous branches of Highland Creek and the Rouge. In some instances the machinery was also used to drive a pair of stones for gristing purposes. D. W. Thomson, of Ellesmere, supplies the following list of those owning mills that have at one time and another been running in the township, viz.: On Highland Creek, Messrs. David and William Thomson (three on one site), J. A. Thomson, J. P. Wheler, Peter Secor, Col. McLean, Wilson, Stephenson, Helliwell, Post and Closson—those of Messrs. Wheler, Secor* and Helliwell being also grist mills.

On the Big Rouge mills were owned by Messrs. Brown, Milne, Lawrie, Eaton, Knox (grist), Aikens, Smith and Burr. Mr. Aikens also made oatmeal, and Mr. Burr added carding to his sawing industry.

On the Little Rouge the owners were Messrs. Hetherington, Patton, Thomson and Gates; Mr. Thomson also made flour.

On Wilcott Creek, Messrs. Harrington, sen., Harrington, jun., Chapman and R. D. Thomson.

On the Little Don the sawyers were Messrs. Hough and Heron.

Mr. J. Law gives the date of the first saw-mill at Highland Creek as 1804. It was built by W. Cornell,

* Secor's mill was destroyed by fire in January, 1833, but was rebuilt the following year.

and rented for some years to Mr. Law's father. It was probably in connection with this mill that Thomas Adams, "an American Dutchman," told Mr. Helliwell he helped to build a dam in 1805, where the Helliwell Cider Mill stands at the present day.

Mr. A. W. Forfar says Archibald Thomson erected his saw-mill on lot 27, concession 2, about 1808, but owing to unsuitableness of situation it was removed to lot 26; and that David Thomson built a mill on lot 25, concession 1, about 1811.

A mill was erected by Simeon Tomlinson on lot 21, concession 4, in 1848, which was the first, or one of the first, driven by steam in Scarboro.

What was known as Arvinston's saw-mill stood on Highland Creek in 1849.

In 1852 John Chapman put up a steam one on lot 25, concession 3, and there was another on lot 30, concession C, on the farm now owned by Mr. Job Jones, a native of Oxford, England, who came here in 1835.

Archibald Elliot built one on lot 24, concession 3, in 1854. In 1856 it passed into the hands of John Milne. This mill is still in use, and a pair of stones having been added, grain for feeding purposes is here ground.

This list is no doubt imperfect, for it is certain that other mills existed that are now forgotten.

Twenty-four or twenty-five saw-mills have been in operation in the township at one time.

With so many mills, running even but one saw each, the limited area of timber soon became depleted, and their occupation fell away.

A few small steam-mills eventually took the place of the numerous old water ones, chiefly to supply local demands. Grist-mills were established at a few places.

Helliwell's did an extensive business for some years, but it was destroyed by fire; Stephenson's was built on the site of an old saw-mill; and the only mill in this part of the township now is one for chopping and cider-making, belonging to William Helliwell, on the south side of the Kingston Road, near Highland Creek Bridge.

About 1830 a flour-mill was erected on lot 19, concession D, and, more recently, J. P. Wheler built one on lot 21, concession D. It was burned down about 1864. Badgerow's woollen mill stood on lot 16, con. 2.

A big freshet in 1850 carried away all the old dams.

For a long time there was no mill nearer than Port Hope, and, more recently, Markham, where the grists were carried on horseback. But even this was an improvement on the earlier condition of affairs, when the settlers were compelled to carry supplies of flour on their own backs from Toronto.

Primitive methods of grinding were sometimes resorted to. Mr. Levi Annis says one plan was to burn a hollow in the upper end of a short hardwood log; into this hollow was fitted a flat stone, on which the grain was placed, to be pounded by means of a weight suspended from a spring-pole.

BLACKSMITHS AND WAGGON-MAKERS.

In the early days of pure woodcraft the want of a blacksmith is not severely felt, unless when a mishap befalls the logging-chain, or repairs are required to the plough. But the son of Vulcan becomes a necessity within a few years after settlement. Among the early mechanics of this class we find John Smith (very appropriately), on lot 19, concession 3; John Holmes, lot 26, concession 2; David Forfar, lot 28, concession 2; Peter Lyttle and A. Taylor, both in school section No. 9; Robert Brown, Chas. McGarry (who was an axe-maker), lot 27, concession 5. Thomas Ionson, father of John Ionson, had a shop on the Kennedy Road, on the north side of the Danforth Road. A log blacksmith shop, still occupied by A. McPherson, was built on lot 35, concession 4, in 1839. Guy Pollock was a blacksmith, whose name was adopted as a *nom de plume* by Dr. Hamilton.

Waggon and plough makers included Messrs. John Brown, Urquhart, Bambridge, Colgrove (school section No. 9), James Taylor, George Richardson, and Jacob Brooks. David Brown, a wheelwright, lived on the north side of the Danforth Road, nearly opposite his brother Thomas's residence. A waggon shop is now carried on at Ellesmere by the Forfars.

SHOEMAKERS.

As one correspondent says, "The first shoemakers were nearly all the first settlers, who made their own boots at night, mostly from buckskin, after chopping all day." The professional knights of St. Crispin, however, were represented by Henry Hogarth, who settled here in 1836; Homer Newell, about 1840, on lot 26, concession 4; Richard Skelton, who settled in 1851 on lot 31, concession 4, where he still resides; Joseph Hall, on lot 22, concession 4, in 1857; and Michael and Richard Crow, two brothers, who opened a shop about 1837, on Harrington's Hill, Markham Road.

OTHER TRADESMEN.

Among weavers, the names we find are those of Robert Hamilton in 1834, on lot 25, concession 3, and Messrs. Hoshel and Horn, school section No. 9, no date. Other weavers were John Brownlie, Frank Cavender and Hector Douglas.

Harness was made and repaired in school section No. 9 by T. Dowswell, and another similar business was carried on by R. Malcolm (now of Toronto). Jos. Wyper, now doing business at Malvern, has been there since 1860, and A. Walker has a shop in the same place.

The only tailors mentioned are Messrs. Rose and Lauder, and Alex. McKenzie, who "whipped the cat" in the township for several years previous to 1840, when, in modern phraseology, the tailor "made garments from gents' own material," which at that time was "homespun."

About the same time John Underwood carried on his trade in a similar way, near the front road.

Wm. Ferguson made pumps on lot 19, concession 3, as early as 1855, and Wm. Macklin, on lot 24, concession 4, was engaged about 1833, and for some years subsequently, in the manufacture of fanning mills.

Early in the century bricks were made on lot 18, concession C, and several other places. The earliest brickmaker mentioned is James Stonehouse, lot 19, concession 5, but there were, no doubt, some before his time (1830).

Immense quantities of magnificent square timber, of stave bolts and shingles were for many years shipped from the township. R. Stobo was prominent in the timber business. Norman Milligan made a specialty of getting out masts for the Quebec market.

The first tanner is said to have been Joseph Pilkey. Henry Auburn operated a tannery on lot 29, concession B, near the Kingston Road.

At the village of Highland Creek there was for some time an attempt made to manufacture artificial stone, and at the same place there was a small boot and shoe factory.

In this village Messrs. William H. and Benjamin F. Closson, sons of the late Stephen Closson, have established a business, the specialty of which is to grow potatoes for seed. They have in stock upwards of 130 new and standard varieties of potatoes, consignments of which they make between Maine on the east and Manitoba on the west. The Closson Bros. deserve success, and they have achieved it.

Many local industries were successfully prosecuted by the settlers, whose proximity to Toronto afforded them facilities of great value, which they were not slow to turn to the best advantage.

SHIP-BUILDING.

The small, but excellent harbors at the mouths of Highland Creek and the Rouge, coupled with the existence close by of the very best kinds of timber in great abundance, induced several persons to select these places during the first half of the century as ship-building yards.

In 1820 a Captain Hadley built on the Rouge a handsome schooner named the *Duke of York.* The Captain was evidently somewhat of a naval architect, for his vessel is said to have been constructed on beautiful lines and to have been the most rapid sailer on Lake Ontario, making the trip from Oswego to York in from two to five hours less than the time required by any United States craft.

During the winter of 1825-26, Joseph Dennis here built for Captain Richardson a fine steamer, called the

Canada. Alex. Secor and a few others yet living remember numerous events connected with the building of this boat, which was successfully launched on the 3rd of June, 1826, after which she was towed to Toronto, where she received the engines made for her in Montreal. She was a vessel of fine appearance, good sailing qualities, and in every way worthy of her builder and her owner.

In 1834 a vessel was put on the stocks at the mouth of Highland Creek by John Allen and "Uncle Tommy Adams," also familiarly known as "the American Dutchman." This vessel, named the *Mary Ann*, was engaged in local trade for many years, and proved of great service to the farmers in carrying ashes, grain and shingles away, and in bringing back flour, salt, lime, etc.; but her sailing qualities were such that her owners were frequently quizzed, on their return to port, about the condition of things in Liverpool, Calcutta and other distant places! The *Mary Ann* was, in all probability, constructed on some Noachian or "stone-hooker" model.

This year, also, another sailing vessel was built by William Quick, west of the ridge called the "Hogsback," on the Rouge. "Bill" Quick named his craft the *Charlotte of Pickering*, but this is all that is known regarding her.

In 1843, Messrs. Scripture and Matthews laid the keel of a schooner at Hunter's Hole, on the Rouge, and this appears to have been the last of the vessels built in Scarboro, or in connection with the township, for it should be noted that although the Rouge has the main portion of its course in this township, it empties into Lake Ontario through the township of Pickering.

CHAPTER X.

CHURCHES AND MINISTERS.

> "No silver saints, by dying misers giv'n,
> Here brib'd the rage of ill-requited heaven;
> But such plain roofs as Piety could raise,
> And only vocal with the Maker's praise."
>
> —*Pope.*

> "As pleasant songs, at morning sung,
> The words that dropped from his sweet tongue
> Strengthened our hearts: or heard at night,
> Made all our slumbers soft and light."
>
> —*Longfellow.*

ST. ANDREW'S PRESBYTERIAN CHURCH.

IN the infancy of Scarboro the only altar was that of the family. There was neither church nor minister, yet prayer and praise were not wanting; the days of the patriarchs were renewed.

But the settlement grew, numbers increased, and it became possible to organize meetings for public worship. Still, it remained impossible to build a church, and gatherings were held in barns, workshops, private houses and taverns, or, as they were more properly termed at that period, inns or public-houses. The old David Thomson tavern furnished such convenience, and there, as seems eminently appropriate to the earliest records we have of that good man, the first communion of the Church to which he belonged was administered. It was probably owing to the heterogeneous places of gathering for worship in the early

MINISTERS.

EPISCOPAL : METHODIST :

1. Rev. John Fletcher. 2. Rev. Canon Belt. 3. Rev. Wm. Briggs, D.D. 4. Rev. M. B. Conron.

ROMAN CATHOLIC : 7. Rev. E. F. Gallagher.

PRESBYTERIAN :

5. Rev. Dr. J. George. 6. Rev. Dr. Jas. Bain. 8. Rev. J. Mackay, B.A. 9. Rev. T. Wightman.

settlements that the terms "meeting" and "meeting-house" came to be used.

As far as is known, the first Presbyterian missionary or minister who visited Scarboro was the Rev. Robert McDowall, though it appears from records extant that both Baptist and Methodist preachers had also ministered to the spiritual wants of the people.

Mr. McDowall was sent to Canada by the Dutch Reformed Church of the United States in 1798, and was settled at Adolphustown, an active centre of the United Empire Loyalist immigration in 1784, and source of religious activities in the various churches.

Mr. McDowall's duties led him to visit the settlements as far west as York, and it was during these travels that he ministered to the pioneers of Scarboro.

His visits about 1805, are mentioned in the records of St. Andrew's Church.

In 1810, the Rev. John Beattie, also a minister of the Dutch Reformed Church, preached in Scarboro during his tour of eighteen weeks along the north shore of Lake Ontario.

For several years, dating from 1812 or 1813, services were held in the old log building known as "the haunted school-house," near the Springfield Farm.

The year 1818 marks a new era in the history of Presbyterianism in Scarboro. In that year the Rev. William Jenkins, who came to Canada from the United States in 1817, and was settled at Richmond Hill, began to minister regularly to the Presbyterians of Scarboro, and at once entered upon the organization of a congregation under the name of "The Presbyterian Church in Scarboro." The records state that on the 26th December, 1818, the Rev. William Jenkins and

Mr. John Stirrat, who was an elder from Whitby, met in Scarboro and took under examination the following men nominated by the congregation for the office of elder, viz., Andrew Thomson, Robert Johnston, and James Kennedy. These men were approved, and were ordained to the office of Ruling Elder in the new congregation, and the first duty assigned them was to inquire into the method of communicating religious instruction to the children of the neighborhood.

Mr. Jenkins continued his ministry in Scarboro for about twelve years, giving one-third of his time to this charge, for which the people paid him $100 per annum. In 1819 the congregation of St. Andrew's erected the first church building in the township. The land on which it was built was the gift of David Thomson, the first settler. The building was 30 x 40, frame, and is thus described by Mrs. Ross, a daughter of Rev. Jas. George, who succeeded Mr. Jenkins: "The first church as I remember it was frame, with a stair built on the outside to give access to a gallery, added when the congregation grew too large for the ground floor. The church was seated with wooden pews.* A long narrow table extended from before the pulpit nearly to the door, a long pew on each side of it; a shorter table and pews were placed across the end of the church on each side of the pulpit. These were the communion tables and pews. The pulpit, a high enclosed place, was reached by a stair. The precentor's desk, directly in front of and lower than the pulpit, was also enclosed."

It would be a pleasure to quote from this excellent account the description given of the manner of conducting the ordinary Sabbath service, and also the

*This, no doubt, means that the pews were made of plain deals or boards.

communion service, but space forbids. For some years the people of all denominations met in this building and joined in the Presbyterian service, and in the church-yard near by they buried their dead, as the tombstones show.

Mr. Jenkins is described as an excellent scholar, an able preacher, keen in sarcasm, and yet guileless as a child. He died on September 25th, 1843, exactly a quarter of a century after having organized the first Presbyterian Church in Scarboro.

In 1823, other Ruling Elders were added to the church session. They were David Elliot and Adam Bell. Two years later Thomas Paterson was added to the roll. The first session clerks were William Cassels and William Elliot.

On August 22nd, 1833, a call was given to the Rev. Jas. George. Mr. George was a Perthshire man, a graduate of Dollar Academy, and of St. Andrew's and Glasgow universities. Reaching the United States in 1829, he held several charges, and was highly thought of by his people in each place; but the then prevailing unfriendly sentiment to Great Britain was so painful to him that he preferred to live and work under the old flag, even in the woods of Canada. His Scarboro people soon built him a manse, upon land given by James A. Thomson, of Springfield Farm, and here his wife died within the year, leaving him a grieved and lonely man.

At the time of Mr. George's induction the number of communicants on the roll of St. Andrew's was seventy. At the same period the following names were added to the session roll, viz., Robert Stobo, William Paterson, John Skelton, George Thomson, and George Telford. The latter had been an elder in the Old Country.

Under Mr. George the membership rapidly increased, two hundred and fifty names being added within a few years of his ministry. In him the cause of education ever had a staunch friend. He was the founder of the first temperance society in Scarboro, and actively supported the movement to establish a public library, which for many years has afforded the chief supply of reading matter in the township.

In his time the method of conducting the Presbyterian worship in Scarboro, as elsewhere, followed much more closely than it does now the usage of the "Auld Kirk" in Scotland. The service began at ten in the morning, and with a short intermission lasted until three in the afternoon. In winter the whole service was conducted without any cessation, and generally lasted four hours. The sermon preached in the afternoon often reached an hour and a half in length. Most of the people walked to church in those days, some of them, as the Hoods and Gibsons, coming a distance of six or eight miles on foot.

Mr. George remained in Scarboro for twenty years, with the exception of a seven months' settlement in Belleville. In 1853 he was appointed Professor of Mental and Moral Philosophy and Logic, in Queen's College, Kingston. In 1855 he received the degree of Doctor of Divinity from the University of Glasgow. He remained for nine years in Kingston, then accepted a call to Stratford, and remained there until his death in August, 1870. He is buried in St. Andrew's church-yard, where a fine monument was erected to his memory by a loving people. A mural tablet to his memory was also placed in the church at Stratford.

The following persons were ordained and received into the Session of St. Andrew's by Mr. George, in 1841, viz., Andrew Telfer (or Telford), James A. Thomson, Thomas Brown, Robert Hamilton, and Wm. Clark, who, with Mr. Telfer, afterwards became elder in Knox Church. The session-clerks during this ministry were George Thomson and William Clark.

In 1849, a new church building was erected, which was then considered the finest in that part of the country. In 1893, it was put in thorough repair, at a cost of $1,550, and is the St. Andrew's Church, Scarboro, of to-day.

A relic of Rev. Dr. George remains in an old, discolored copy of a sermon preached by him in St. Andrew's Church, for the day of public thanksgiving, appointed by the Government, for the restoration of our national peace in 1838. The sermon is entitled, "The Duties of Subjects to their Rulers, with a Special View to the Present Times." It was printed "By request of the Congregation," and signed, "In the name of the Congregation," by William Paterson, Chairman, and James Whiteside, Secretary *pro tem.* The pamphlet contains thirty-two pages, and was printed at the office of "W. J. Coates, 146 King Street, Toronto."

The vacancy caused by the translation of Dr. George to the Chair of Logic at Queen's University, was not of long duration. In December, 1853, the Rev. James Bain took up the work at St. Andrew's, and, having served the congregation ten months as stated supply, was inducted to the charge in October, 1854.

Like his predecessor, Mr. Bain was a native of Perthshire, Scotland, and was for twenty-seven years pastor of the United Presbyterian congregation at

Kirkaldy. He came to Canada in 1853, and was at once sent to Scarboro, where he continued for twenty years as pastor of St. Andrew's. In 1864, a part of St. Andrew's was formed into a separate congregation, and a fine frame church, known as St. John's, was built about seven and a half miles distant. Both churches were served by the same pastor. This union was very harmonious, and lasted for twenty-five years, when a separation took place. St. John's, being within the lines of Markham township, then became part of a new charge. During this ministry Mr. Alex. Stirling was ordained elder.

In 1874 Mr. Bain demitted his charge, and retiring from the active work of the ministry, settled in Markham village, where he died on the 9th of December, 1885, in the eighty-fourth year of his age. His body was laid to rest in St. Andrew's Cemetery, where a handsome granite monument was erected to his memory.

Mr. Bain was in many respects a remarkable man. Possessed of a clear intellect, he was a vigorous thinker, had a wide range of knowledge, debating power of a high order, great fluency of speech and a magnificent voice. Few were his superiors on the platform. He was a man of good business ability, of a genial and kindly disposition, and ever ready to help, so that when he resigned his charge he had many firm friends.

The ministers who followed Mr. Bain at St. Andrew's are still living, and their work has been done so recently that it will be unnecessary to do much more than mention their names. Rev. Malcolm McGillivray, a graduate of Queen's College, Kingston, succeeded

Mr. Bain in 1875. He remained about five years, demitting his charge in 1881. Mr. McGillivray was very highly respected by his people. Under him the congregation greatly increased, and the seating capacity of the church was fully taxed. During his time also, the Sabbath School was built, and a good beginning made towards beautifying the grounds. Too much credit cannot be given to the successive Boards of Management in the congregation for the energy and taste they have displayed in making, not only the interior of the church, but all its surroundings, so attractive. During Mr. McGillivray's ministry the membership roll showed 323 names.

Rev. Charles A. Tanner, who succeeded Mr. Bain as pastor, began his ministry in St. Andrew's in the year 1882. He had been in Scarboro only a little over four years, when he was called by the congregation of Levis, Quebec. This call he accepted, and left Scarboro in 1887. During the vacancy which followed, steps were taken to effect the afore-mentioned separation between St. Andrew's and St. John's. This change was made before the present pastor was called.

In 1888 Rev. D. Barclay Macdonald, who graduated at Knox College, Toronto, in 1882, accepted the pastorate of St. Andrew's, and is still in charge. The equipment of the congregation is now complete, and the work is very prosperous. An organ was introduced into the church in 1889, and the service of praise is conducted by a very excellent choir under the leadership of T. A. Paterson, with Miss Mary Glendinning as organist. There is also a Young People's Christian Association.

In 1856 a Ladies' Missionary Association was formed with the following officers :

Directress, - - - - Mrs. Davidson.

BOARD OF MANAGEMENT :

Mrs. Bain.	Miss Chester.
Mrs. Elliot.	Miss Whiteside.
Mrs. D. Brown.	Miss Loveless.

COLLECTORS :

Eastern District,	-	Misses M. Brown and J. Thomson.
Western "	-	Misses M. A. Loveless and M. Patton.
Northern "	-	Misses A. and M. Paterson.
Southern "	-	Misses M. Brown and I. Brownlie.
Home "	-	Misses B. and A. Thomson.

This society was formed for the purpose of deepening the interest in, and collecting funds for, the education and support of female orphans in India. The first orphan thus assisted was named Mary Thomson Scarboro, in memory of Mary Thomson, *née* Glendinning, the "Mother of Scarboro." Another of these orphans was named Margaret Bain, commemorating a daughter of the manse. During its first year the Society collected for this work nearly fifty-seven dollars.

We find that the following persons have taken an active interest in the Society's work at various periods, viz., the Misses J. Glendinning, I. Gibson, Mary Weir, Margaret Lawrie, Agnes Marshall, Margaret Tingle, Janet Bain, Mary Purdie, Jane Frame, Isa. Walton.

In 1880 Mrs. Geo. Elliot resigned the treasurership, and Miss Marshall was appointed in her place. The Society continued its work until 1888, when it was merged into the Women's Foreign Missionary Society, which is now an active missionary society within the congregation. The present officers are:

Hon. President, - -	Mrs. Macdonald.
President, - - -	Miss E. Brown.
1st Vice-President, -	Mrs. W. Green.
2nd Vice-President, -	Mrs. Geo. McCowan.
Secretary, - - -	Miss Ida Carnaghan.
Treasurer, - - -	Miss Jennie A. Thomson.

Last year about $116 was sent into the General Fund, and $55 in clothing for the Indians of the Canadian North-West.

Mr. Adam Bell teaches the Bible-class in St. Andrew's Church, and the Sabbath School teachers are:

Mrs. Carmichael.	Miss Elizabeth Brown.
Mrs. Martin.	Miss I. Carnaghan.
Mrs. Green.	Miss I. Bell.
Mrs. A. Thomson.	Miss M. Glendinning.

The Secretary-Treasurer is Mr. W. Carmichael.

ZION CHURCH (PRESBYTERIAN).

In 1889 Parsonage Church, Primitive Methodist, withdrew from the Methodist body, accepted Presbyterianism, and was united with St. Andrew's in one pastoral charge. It chose Zion for its new name. This congregation has a fine brick edifice, is in a flourishing condition, and the united charge makes one of the strongest country congregations in Canada.

The officers elected at the time of the union were Messrs. David Martin, George Fitzpatrick, and Leslie Armstrong, as members of session. On the Board of

Management have been such men as Adam Richardson, John Tingle, W. W. Thomson, Thomas Pilkey, George Coulson, Joseph Tingle, James McBeth, and Joseph Armstrong.

The church has an efficient choir under the leadership of Miss Minnie Fitzpatrick. This congregation has an active Auxiliary of the Women's Missionary Society, which is doing excellent work. Its officers are :

President, - - -	Mrs. Armstrong.
Vice-President, - -	Mrs. T. Ionson
Secretary, - - -	Mrs. Fitzpatrick.
Treasurers, - - -	Mesdames A. Ionson and A. Richardson.

The latest statistics to hand for the united charge show:

Scholars on Sabbath School roll	149
Teachers	18
Present membership on communion roll	307
Contributions for all purposes	$3,079
" missionary and benevolent work	891
Gifts of clothing for Indians of the Canadian North-West....	92
Cost of manse built in 1887	2,500

The following figures show growth in the material welfare of these congregations: When Mr. Jenkins began his work in St. Andrew's in 1818, he received $100 per annum; in 1833, when Mr. George assumed charge, he received $500, with manse and firewood. Mr. Bain received about the same amount until St. John's was opened, when his stipend was increased. In 1875, when Rev. Mr. McGillivray took charge, he received $1,000 with manse and glebe. The stipend now paid by the whole charge is $1,400, with free manse and glebe.

John T. Brown was session clerk in 1888, and most faithfully did he discharge the duties of his office. He was always whole-hearted and enthusiastic in his work; a man of kindly disposition, of an ardent temperament, always hopeful, and ever ready to give both time and money to the cause he loved. He was very much missed when he withdrew from this congregation to reside in Vancouver, B.C.

The senior member of session was James Russell, a man full of faith and of the Holy Spirit. Mr. Russell was a graduate of the University of Edinburgh, and spent many years in teaching in the early days of Scarboro. For a long period he walked over six miles, night and morning, to and from his school. He was humorously dubbed, "Knight of the Birch Rod at Squaw Village."

Mr. Russell was a man of ripe scholarship, was widely read in history, science and literature, and thoroughly conversant with theology. After his retirement from the active duties of life, he spent hours each day reading alternately the Hebrew, Greek and English Bibles. He died in July, 1890, having been a member of St. Andrew's Church for forty-seven years, and a member of session for twenty of these. He was a man very highly esteemed by his brethren of the session.

Besides Messrs. Brown and Russell, there were Messrs. James Stirling, John A. Paterson, David Martin, Adam Bell, William Carmichael, Beebe Carnaghan and William Green, all men of ability, piety, sound judgment, and excellent scholarship. Of the session as it then existed, only the last four names remain on the roll of to-day. William Heron has since been added. William Green acts as session-clerk.

KNOX CHURCH (PRESBYTERIAN).

The agitation that took place in Scotland (leading to the formation of what is designated "The Free Church"), in 1843, disturbed the Presbyterian brethren in Canada, and about 1848 Scarboro was so far affected by it as to cause a break-off from St. Andrew's congregation, and the formation of Knox Church. The history is communicated to us as follows:

Previous to a congregational organization, the meetings of this body were held in the school-house, lot 29, concession 2, and at the first communion twelve persons partook. At the meeting of the Presbytery of Toronto, held on the 7th of June, 1848, steps were taken to organize Knox Church, Scarboro. The Rev. Dr. Burns, according to appointment of Presbytery, visited Scarboro on the 13th of June, examined, and enrolled forty members. Arrangements were made for dispensing communion on Sabbath, June 25th.

York Mills* and Knox Church were erected into one pastoral charge, and the first minister inducted was the Rev. Thos. Wightman. The induction took place on the 25th of November, 1848. The Rev. Dr. Willis preached, taking as his text Hebrews x. 19-22. Dr. Willis addressed the minister, and the Rev. Mr. Rintoul, the congregation. The members of Presbytery present at this induction were Rev. Dr. Willis, Moderator; Rev. Messrs. Rintoul, Harris and Boyd, and

* Then and still popularly known as "Hogg's Hollow."

PRESBYTERIAN CHURCHES.

1. Melville. 2. St. Andrew's (1817). 3. Present St. Andrew's (Erected 1849).
4. Zion. 5. Knox.

James Armour, Elder. Knox's share of the annual stipend, at that date, was $200.

Mr. Wightman was a Scotsman, having been born in Dumfriesshire. He received his literary and theological education in Edinburgh. In 1844 he came to Canada, and was settled at York Mills, which, as already stated, was afterwards joined with Knox Church. In 1848 Mr. Wightman was inducted to the Knox part of the charge. He continued to serve the united congregation for four years, and, after the separation of Knox Church from York Mills, he ministered to the latter congregation for two years longer. His death took place on March 30th, 1871.

On December 1st, 1852, the union between York Mills and Knox Church was, by action of Presbytery, dissolved, and the latter was united with Melville Church, Highland Creek.

In 1883 this union was dissolved, Melville being united with Dunbarton, Knox Church becoming a separate charge.

The first elders of Knox Church were Wm. Clark, sen., who had been ordained an elder in Scotland in 1830; Andrew Telfer, ordained in 1839 (both Mr. Clark and Mr. Telfer served in the eldership of St. Andrew's for several years, but withdrew on the Free Church question); Wm. Young, ordained in 1842, and Messrs. Wm. Ferguson, John McLevin, and Wm. Clark, jun., ordained June 28th, 1849.

The Rev. Mr. Macdonald, of St. Andrew's Church, Scarboro, has kindly supplied the following notices of the several ministers of Knox Church:

Rev. John Laing, now Dr. Laing, of Dundas, Ont., was ordained and inducted to the pastorate of Knox

Church, Scarboro, in June, 1854. The church at that time was small, but there was room for growth, and within two years the building was enlarged to double its original size.

This was Mr. Laing's first charge, and he being full of youthful vigor and earnest zeal, did not spare himself in his work. Regular services were held in Knox and Melville churches; in addition to this, services were held in various school-houses, and for two years open-air meetings were held near the Rouge. Through the instrumentality of his young men's class, Sabbath Schools were established in various sections, a preaching station was opened by him, and a church built near the York town-line, and another at Cedar Grove. In the village of Markham, too, a station was opened. Frequent visits were made to Pickering and Whitby on the east, and to Georgina and Yonge Street on the north and west. The demands of the work became so great that an assistant had to be employed for the last two years of his ministry. Dr. Laing is a graduate in Theology of Knox College, Toronto, and in Arts, of Victoria University. He has done good service for the Church, notably on the Home Mission Committee, and in connection with Knox College. He held the highest position in the gift of the Church, Moderator of the General Assembly, in 1890, and has been Clerk of the Presbytery of Hamilton for twenty-one years.

Dr. Laing was succeeded in the pastorate of Knox Church by Mr. D. H. Fletcher, who possessed in a marked degree those qualities which rendered the ministry of his predecessor so successful. It may be truly said that these two early ministers gave Knox its missionary bent; that, humanly speaking, Laing planted, and Fletcher and the Mackays watered that missionary spirit which is so vigorous to-day.

Mr. Fletcher's studies were begun in Scotland and continued in Toronto, where he attended classes in the University. Taking up the study of theology in Knox College he graduated in that institution, receiving his diploma in 1860. In November of that year he was ordained and inducted into the pastorate of Knox Church, where he continued to labor for nearly twelve years. In 1872, he was called to McNab Street, Hamilton, where he still serves. He is now Dr. Fletcher, having received the degree of D.D. from his *Alma Mater* a few years ago. Dr. Fletcher has been Moderator of the Synod of Hamilton and London, and has rendered good service to the Church as examiner in Knox College, and on the Board of Management, of which he is still a member. Messrs. Laing and Fletcher each served in Scarboro as Local Superintendent of Education.

A vacancy of more than a year's duration, caused by the removal of Mr. Fletcher to Hamilton, was terminated by the induction of Rev. George Burnfield. Mr. Burnfield received both his literary and theological education in Canada, being a graduate of Toronto University and Knox College. He came to Scarboro in 1873, and remained about four years, when he accepted a call to the First Presbyterian Church, Brockville. Mr. Burnfield was a man of wide and ripe scholarship, and was gifted with extraordinary oratorical powers; herein, indeed, lay the chief strength of his ministry. After leaving Brockville Mr. Burnfield held a charge in Toronto, whence he removed to Philadelphia, U.S.

R. P. MacKay was next in the succession. He too, is a Canadian by birth and education, the Public schools of Zorra, Woodstock High School, and Toronto University supplying his literary equipment, Knox College being his theological *Alma Mater.* In 1877, Mr. MacKay was ordained and inducted to the pastorate of Knox Church. His ministry there, which covered a period of seven years, was strong and spiritually fruitful, the missionary spirit of the congregation being perceptibly broadened and deepened. In 1884 he was translated to Dunn Avenue Church, Parkdale, from which position, after a pastorate of seven years, he was called by the General Assembly to the secretaryship of the Foreign Mission Committee.

John MacKay, also a Canadian and a Zorra man, succeeded his namesake in Knox Church. Mr. MacKay's ministry was brief, but not too brief to have done good work, and greatly endeared himself to his people. His ministry in Knox practically closed in 1890, although he did not resign his charge till 1891. After a lingering illness he died in 1894. Mr. MacKay's education was wholly received in Canadian colleges. He served for some time on the Board of Examiners of Knox College, of which institution he was a distinguished graduate.

The present pastor, Rev. James A. Brown, was inducted by the Presbytery of Toronto in November, 1891. He is Canadian-born and trained, being a graduate of Queen's College, Kingston. As may be seen by reference to the following statements, Knox Church continues in the enjoyment of uninterrupted peace and prosperity under the ministry of Mr. Brown:

Knox Church is built on lot 26, concession 3, Scarboro. A more beautiful and central site could scarcely be found anywhere. The first parcel of land, consisting of one acre, was presented to the congregation by the late Thos. Kennedy. An additional acre has since been purchased by the congregation.

The first building, erected in 1848, was a frame structure. A few years later an addition was made, giving the building the form of a T. The old church has been converted into two private residences, and a new one of brick was erected in 1872. It has a seating capacity of 450, and cost over $7,000. The sheds can accommodate upwards of a hundred vehicles. The church stands in the midst of the cemetery, where the sacred dust of many of the early and sainted members of the congregation rests, and numerous beautiful monuments mark their graves.

Compared with the small stipend that Knox Church could contribute in 1848, the present stipend of $1,000, together with a manse and six acres glebe, manifests an advance in material prosperity which is a proper subject of thankfulness.

Knox Church is widely known throughout the Presbyterian body as a liberal contributor to missions and other schemes of the Church—a Woman's Foreign Missionary Society, a Mission Band, and a Young Men's Home Missionary Society testifying to its activity in that direction. In the early history of the congregation, its Sabbath School was for many years conducted by William Clark, jun., and Wm. Crawford. At present, 140 scholars are on the roll, with seventeen teachers.

The temporal affairs of the congregation are entrusted to a board of five trustees, who are elected annually. From the year, 1880 to 1895, Knox Church has contributed to ordinary revenue and for benevolent purposes above $22,250, and for missionary purposes in the neighborhood of $12,500, a sum total of $34,750 —an average of over $2,000 per annum.

The membership of Knox Church in 1895 was 267. Of the forty members enrolled in 1848, but three remain, viz., Mr. and Mrs. Hugh Elliot and Mrs. Wm. Clark, jun.

MELVILLE CHURCH (PRESBYTERIAN).

In comparison with St. Andrew's, the parent of Presbyterianism in Scarboro, Melville Church is recent. Knox congregation, established in the north-west section of the township in 1848, took a warm interest in the foundation of another in the south-east, where the adherents of the Presbyterian Church were then, and are still, fewer than in any other section of Scarboro. It was at first proposed to erect the church on the Markham Road, where it is intersected by the first concession; but the gift of a building site, and a liberal donation of money by the late George Stephenson, influenced those concerned to erect the building on the more suitable spot where it now stands. Its position is thus described by a loving hand:

"Charmingly situated on the crown of a high hill, encircled with pines, firs, and cedars, stands Melville Church, overlooking the beautiful valley to the east through which Highland Creek meanderingly finds its way to the blue waters of Lake Ontario, which can be seen in the distance. Immediately in front of its sacred threshold passes the Kingston Road, always thronged with industrious farmers and others on their way to the markets of the Queen City, thirteen miles distant."

Melville Church, like Zion of old, is therefore "beautiful for situation."

In December, 1850, Mr. Telfer, Representative Elder for Knox congregation, appeared before the Toronto Presbytery, asking for ministerial supply, which was cheerfully granted for every alternate Sabbath. On the 19th December, 1851, the church was opened and dedicated to the service of God by the venerable Dr. Willis. The fortnightly supply from Toronto Presbytery ceased in December, 1852, when the congregations of Melville and Knox churches united as one pastoral charge. On this occasion the first "sacrament" was observed by nine communicants, two of whom are still living—Mr. Jonathan Baird and Mrs. Stephenson. The Rev. Thomas Wightman was the officiating minister at this memorable service, and Messrs. W. Young and Wm. Ferguson acted as elders.

In 1854 the Rev. John Laing was ordained and inducted. Shortly after his advent several families connected with the "Auld Kirk" (among whom were the Neilsons and Cowans) joined the infant congregation, and brought hope and strength with them. Mr. Laing remained until 1860, when, greatly to the regret of his people, he accepted a call to Cobourg.

In the same year he was succeeded by the Rev. Mr. Fletcher, who labored most indefatigably and with great success, until his removal to Hamilton in 1872.

In 1873 the Rev. George Burnfield, B.D., was called and inducted, and for over three years filled the pulpit with unusual brilliance and ability.

The Rev. R. P. MacKay was ordained and inducted

over the congregation in 1877, and labored faithfully until 1882, when the connection with Knox Church was severed, and a union consummated with Dunbarton Church, in the township of Pickering.

A call was then accepted by Rev. R. N. Craig. During his pastorate a new church was erected on the old site, and dedicated on the 4th September, 1887, by the Rev. Dr. Fletcher, of Hamilton, one of its former pastors. Mr. Craig did excellent work, but in 1889, to the regret of his congregation, 'he resigned. The minister at present is Rev. John Chisholm, who was called and inducted in 1890.

The growth of the congregation of Melville Church has been slow but steady, its most active growth having taken place within the last six years.

The number of members on the roll this year (1896) is one hundred and forty-five.

The amount given as share of minister's stipend in 1890 was $350; at present it is $500. The total amount given in 1889 to the schemes of the Church was $119; in 1895 it was $310.

William Cowan is the present superintendent of the Sabbath School, the condition of which is in every way satisfactory.

The Women's Foreign Missionary Society, presided over by Mrs. H. Westney, is in excellent working order, and annually raises large contributions in money, besides supplying clothing for the Indians of the Canadian North-West.

The elders of the congregation at present are Wm. Cowan, sen., George Scott, Wm. Stephenson, John McIntosh, Alex. Neilson and Robert Cowan.

Nec Tamen Consumebatur.

EPISCOPALIAN CHURCHES.

1. Christ Church. 2. St. Margaret's. 3. St. Jude's. 4. St. Paul's.

ROMAN CATHOLIC.

ST. MARGARET'S, WEST HILL (EPISCOPALIAN).

The mother Church of England in Scarboro, and the second of any denomination built in the township, was St. Margaret's. There seems to remain no record of the time the building was begun, but it is told that Robert Jackson, the father of T. Jackson, was out shooting in the woods in 1828 or 1830, and came upon it in an unfinished state. He at once took steps toward its completion; subscriptions were raised, and about 1830 St. Margaret's Church was opened. It is unfortunate that the records of the Church of England in Scarboro are apparently lost. Many particulars, therefore, that would have been invaluable in a history of the township are not at our service. Previous to 1830, it is certain that the Church of England had adherents in Scarboro, and that clergymen from York ministered to the wants of the scattered people. The late Archdeacon McMurray, of Niagara, at this period a young man, used to hold service in private houses in the township, and it is related that in riding to his appointments, his feet were often in the mud, he being a tall man, and the roads in many places bad.

St. Margaret's Church owes its name to Mrs. Margaret Washburn, whose husband, the Hon. Simon Washburn, contributed largely to its construction. Mrs. Washburn was a sister of Lieut.-Col. FitzGibbon of Beaver Dams fame. The Hon. Simon Washburn owned much land in and about Scarboro township, and more than once contested the county against William Lyon Mackenzie. At the time of its erection St. Margaret's Church stood close to the road between Kingston and York, but the straightening of this highway threw the church some distance north of what is now the Kingston Road.

The first interments in the grave-yard were the bodies of some persons named Fisher, who died of the cholera epidemic in 1832.

With regard to the furniture of the church, the following extract from a contribution by the Rev. Dr. Scadding, of Toronto, will be interesting: "I remem- "ber very well the sounding-board, pulpit and reading- "desk in St. Margaret's, West Hill, as the place is "now designated, so I am informed. I have more "than once taken duty there; but that church being "somewhat farther east on the Kingston Road was "rather out of my beat. I used to see the same "sounding-board, pulpit and reading-desk in St. James' "Church, Toronto, not then a Cathedral Church at "all. In 1818, on the establishment of peace, Dr. "Strachan, the incumbent, enlarged the old primitive "church building at York, and improved its appear- "ance by adding to it a belfry and spire. Hon. Francis "Gore, the Lieutenant-Governor of the period, fur- "nished the renovated interior with the sounding- "board, pulpit and reading-desk at his own expense. "When the first St. James' Church, constructed in "stone, replaced the wooden structure about the "year 1838, and all the interior fittings were changed, "the sounding-board, pulpit and reading-desk which "Governor Gore had so generously presented were "donated as a charitable gift to the Church on the "south [since the change of line, now on the north] "side of the Kingston Road, some way below the "Four-Mile Tree. The original cost of the gift was "$100." This furniture was removed five years ago.

It is believed that the Rev. Mr. Dade was the first regular incumbent of St. Margaret's. In 1840 Rev. W. H. Norris, LL.D., was appointed, and was succeeded by Rev. W. S. Darling. The following incumbents have since held the charge: Rev. W. Belt, M.A., Rev. John Fletcher, M.A., Rev. C. R. Bell, Rev. Henry Owen, Rev. E. Horace Musson, Rev. F. Burt, and the Rev. Thaddeus Walker, the present incumbent, who took charge in 1891.

The first incumbent received a stipend of six hundred dollars a year, and the present has eight hundred.

The early records being lost, the first name on the existing register of baptism is that of Stephen Westney, now of Pickering, about the date of 1843; but a correspondent, T. Jackson, says the first baptisms were those of two children, one of Mrs. George Bambridge, and the other of Mrs. Burton, and that at that time the floor of the church was not wholly laid, so that it must have been about 1830. The first marriage, which was solemnized, it is said, by Rev. Mr. Fletcher, was that of John Law to Miss Caroline Bell.

The church seats about two hundred, is now in excellent repair, and shows but little trace of sixty-eight years' wear and waste. The church-yard surrounding St. Margaret's is well cared for, and is by far the most beautifully situated of the many burial-grounds of Scarboro. Among its earliest interments was a member of the Booth family.

Bishop Strachan seems to have administered confirmation in this church, and at one time over a hundred candidates were presented. Even in later times seventy was no uncommon number. Confirmation-cards used to be given to the young communicants on these occasions, a commendable practice that has fallen much into disuse.

CHRIST CHURCH (EPISCOPALIAN).

The second Episcopalian place of worship erected in Scarboro was Christ Church. It was built in 1845-6, the funds being collected largely through the efforts of the Rev. W. S. Darling, then incumbent of Scarboro. The land was the gift of the late James Humphrey,* and the building committee was composed of some of the leading members of St. Margaret's Church. Among these were Messrs. William Westney, Robert Jackson, James Humphrey, John Taber, and Henry Galloway.

The contract was let to Wm. Harris, carpenter, and the plastering to the late John Baxter, of Toronto. The building was first covered with cement, laid off in squares to imitate stone, but this soon came off, and it was boarded, as at present.

The bell, which has a very fine tone, was hung about 1860, and cost $160, which was defrayed by the Ladies' Sewing Society.

The church was opened on the 15th of June, 1846, Rev. W. S. Darling conducting the morning service, and the Rev. Mr. Winstanley that in the afternoon.

Rev. Mr. Darling was incumbent of Scarboro for ten years, and was very active in promoting the interests of Christ Church. In all good deeds he was aided by his wife, who was an indefatigable worker both in church and Sunday School.

The Rev. Wm. Belt (now Canon Belt, of Burlington) was incumbent for sixteen years. Under his direction the Church was very prosperous, and at that time had

* Some say J. Hopper gave part of lot 33, concession 3, Scarboro.

one of the largest English Church congregations in the township. Too much praise cannot be given to Mr. Belt and his family. He was very popular with all denominations, and took a great interest in the Militia and the Public schools.

In 1887, during the incumbency of Rev. Mr. Burt, Christ Church was remodelled inside; the old-fashioned pulpit and reading-desk were taken down and new desks put in their places. One of these was the gift of the late Mr. Cheape, and the other of Wm. Rolf, of Markham. The stained glass window was put in at the same time.

The reopening on Sunday, November 6th, 1887, was conducted by Rev. Canon Belt and Rev. Prof. Clark, of Trinity College, Toronto. Many of the congregation who had left the parish attended the service.

Scarboro has other Church of England congregations beside St. Margaret's and Christ Church. At L'Amaroux is St. Paul's, about the same age as Christ Church, and at the town-line between Scarboro and York, St. Jude's was erected in 1848, the site of it being taken from St. Saviour's at East York, and St. John's at Norway.

In the early days our venerable friend Dr. Scadding conducted services with considerable regularity in the L'Amaroux settlement.

Christ Church Sunday School is one of the oldest in the township; its history is to be traced back to 1831, when Adam Anderson taught in the old St. Margaret's Church. For some time prior to the building of the present church, Mr. Anderson conducted the classes in an old log school-house on lot 14, concession D, and when Christ Church was finished they were held there.

Edward Galloway assisted Mr. Anderson, and taught for a number of years in St. Margaret's.

Among the many workers and teachers in the school in the past may be mentioned Rev. W. Belt, Mrs. Belt, Misses Matilda Humphrey, Ellen Jackson and Margaret Thompson, Rev. C. R. Bell, Rev. H. Musson, Mrs. Musson, Wm. Humphrey, Misses Anne Knight and Maggie Humphrey, and Rev. Wm. Burt.

The present officers of the school are: Albert Chester, superintendent; Misses M. Secor, M. Jackson,* M. Cornell and L. Dodd, teachers, and James G. Cornell, librarian.

The library is a good one, and although the newer plan of selling or passing on to other schools, collections of the books purchased, is now the rule, there remain on hand some of the volumes which constituted the first library. They are standard works of the time, and become increasingly valuable.

METHODIST CHURCHES.

In the year 1820 the Methodist circuits in Upper Canada were seven, viz., Detroit, Thames, Westminster, Ancaster, Yonge Street, Duffin's Creek, Niagara.

It was from Yonge Street that Scarboro was served, and when it is understood that in 1805, this Circuit "included the townships on both sides of 'the street' from the Bay of Toronto to Lake Simcoe; as Scarboro, York, Etobicoke, Vaughan, Markham, King, Whitchurch and East and West Gwillimbury," some idea of its area may be formed. It is possible that it also included the hamlets of Toronto township, namely, Trafalgar and Nelson, of "The New Purchase."

* Died since MS. was prepared.

Itinerancy was a distinguishing feature of Methodism in those early days as now, but then it was an itinerancy that meant everything the word implies in a newly opened country of forest, lake, and stream, in winter as well as in summer; in the rains and mud of autumn, and the mire and slush of spring.

"The opening of Methodist activity in Canada," says Carroll, "began with the entrance into the Province of the *Unity of the Empire Loyalists* in 1784," and in his "Case and his Cotemporaries," Vol. I., p. 3, a very graphic account of early Methodism and of the United Empire Loyalists in Canada is to be found; but these pages are too few to allow us to enter into more than the local history of the great movement.

As far back as 1803, itinerant ministers came into the township and preached wherever they could get a house. One of the chief meeting places was at the home of Levi Annis, who kept a public-house. Meetings were also held in barns, waggon-shops, school-houses, or wherever a congregation could be gathered.

There was no station or circuit nearer than Yonge Street. Very few individual members of the Methodist Church came from the Old Country to Scarboro, but the persistency of the travelling Methodist preacher won many adherents. Levi Annis was a very warm friend to the ministers, who had to travel many miles over bad roads and through the woods in those days from one "preaching place" to another. They invariably rode on horseback in summer, and sometimes on a "bung"—a small sleigh with a pole and neckyoke for one horse—in winter. They were compelled to carry with them their books, horse-provender, and food for themselves, the latter often including tea, then considered a great luxury, and, probably too, a treat for the good wives who entertained them on their way.

When the preacher arrived in a neighborhood the day before "meeting," messengers were sent in all directions, and the entire community for miles around came to the service. The stipends in those days were very moderate, single men receiving $80 per annum, and married men $160. This the preacher had to collect for himself as he went, and not seldom it would be paid him "in kind," while in bad times he might have to content himself with less than his due.

Annis's was the chief centre of Methodism in the township for many years, and among the earliest families identifying themselves with the body were also the Richardsons, Proctors, Howells, Washingtons, McGinnises, Pilkeys, Fawcetts, and Thompsons.

Some of the travelling preachers who helped to mould the character of the people, and preached at least once every two months at McGinnis's or Annis's, sometimes at other farm-houses, were, in 1803, Seth Crowell, Wm. Anson, Dr. Bangs; 1805, Robt. Corson; 1808, Mr. Pickett; 1809, John Reynolds; 1810, Joseph Lockwood, who hunted coons in the north of the township till he got enough skins to make himself a coat; 1811, Andrew Prindle; 1812, Jos. Gatchel; 1813, Thos. Harmon, who fought alongside of General Brock on Queenston Heights, and who preached powerful sermons, dramatic, passionate and emotional; 1815, John Rhodes; 1817, David Culp; and in 1818, James Jackson and W. W. Rundle.

At this period Messrs. McGinnis and Pilkey often went all the way to York to attend the preaching there, driving an ox-sleigh in winter and a lumber waggon in summer. From the year 1818 to 1827 the following pioneer itinerants preached more regularly in various parts of the township than did their predecessors : Revs. David Yeomans, David Culp (who exchanged at times with the preacher at Duffin's Creek), Daniel Shepherdson, John Ryerson, Wm. Slater, Wm. H. Williams, Jos. Atwood, Jas. Richardson, Egerton Ryerson, Cornelius Flummerfeldt, John Carroll.

In 1828 the Methodist Episcopal Church of Canada separated from the Methodist Episcopal Church of the United States; but the separation had not much effect on the cause in Scarboro, as no church had yet been built. A very notable conference in Canadian Methodism was that at Hallowell, held in 1833. At this conference it was decided to unite with the parent body in England, and from that date Methodism in Scarboro progressed with great rapidity, and numerous church buildings were erected. Scarboro was still supplied from the Yonge Street Circuit; but among later developments and necessary rearrangements, Markham was set off as a circuit and Scarboro included as one of its stations.

From 1828 to 1850 the following names of ministers laboring in the township are given as well-remembered and faithful men: Revs. David Wright, Mr. Corson, Edmund Stoney, John Beatty, Thomas Bevitt, James Hutchinson—nearly all of them Canadians, the fruit of the labors of the first Methodist preachers from the other side.

In connection with Markham Circuit are mentioned Rev. Messrs. McFadden, Campbell, Madden, John Potts, Graham, Norris, Haight, John N. Lake; and the following families, among others, as helping in the formation of societies: J. P. Wheler, Wm. Bambridge, Peter Secor, the Swallows, William Heron, Isaac Brumwell, the Duncans, and Richard Staunton.

If space would permit, a most instructive and interesting chapter dealing with the *personnel* of the earliest Methodist ministers who served the township could be given, but we must refer the reader to Rev. Dr. Carroll's exceedingly valuable work, from which we have already quoted, namely, "Case and his Cotemporaries," and proceed at once to the churches.

The Wesleyans seem to have built the first Methodist church, or, as it was then called, "meeting-house," in Scarboro, in 1838. It was named after Stephen Washington, a respected member and liberal donor, and about 1865 two other churches, Wexford and Highland Creek, were joined with it in one circuit, called the Wesleyan Methodist Scarboro Circuit, with the Rev. J. P. Lewis—now rector of Grace Church (Anglican), Toronto—as first pastor. His successors up to date of the union of all Methodist bodies, were Revs. D. L. Brethour, J. H. Harris, J. H. Robinson, J. E. Smith, C. V. Lake, J. F. Medcalf, J. W. Annis, M. Fawcett. To the latter is due the commencement of the Ladies' Aid Society, in 1884, Mrs. Fawcett being President, and the membership twenty-six. The ministers since the union have been Revs. T. R. Read, M. B. Conron (who has lain these four years by the side of his beautiful young wife, *née* Annie Wilson, in Mount Pleasant Cemetery, Toronto), J. J. Redditt, F. C. Keam, G. W. Stephenson.

In 1875 a parsonage was built by the Wesleyans in Scarboro village, at a cost of $2,000. It was enlarged in 1893, and belongs to the united body, the Primitive

METHODIST CHURCHES.

1. Malvern. 2. Christie's. 3. Scarboro Junction. 4. Free Methodist. 5. Hillside. 6. Centennial. 7. Ebenezer. 8. Washington. 9. Wexford.

Methodists and Bible Christians having paid their share towards it.

The amount of money raised annually by the Washington Church congregation for all purposes is $800.

The Sunday School is a flourishing institution, and has 110 scholars on its roll. William A. Heron is the superintendent, Harvey Dix the secretary, and Joseph Sparks the treasurer. The teachers are L. E. Annis, Hattie Wilson, Mrs. W. A. Heron, Mr. Wilkins, Mrs. Baker, and Sarah Heron, the latter being also librarian. Since 1865 the following have been superintendents of the school: Joseph Richardson, James Montgomery, John Ross, Wm. Dark, John P. Wheler, and Wm. A. Heron, the latter having acted from 1875 to the present date.

The pastor of Washington Church is Rev. G. W. Stephenson.

In 1875 Christie's Church was joined to the Scarboro Circuit. It first belonged to Yonge Street South Circuit, and was built in 1846. In 1888 this church was joined to the Unionville Circuit, to which it still belongs.

Ministers who have been appointed to this church were Rev. T. Turner, who was in charge when the church was built; Revs. Wm. McFadden, Thos. Jones, Wm. Wilkinson, J. W. McCallum, and John Hunt. According to Methodist practice, married ministers remain three years on a circuit; the young, or unmarried men, one.

The Primitive Methodists began to preach in Scarboro about 1840. They first met in a school-house near where Zion Presbyterian Church now stands. In a short time they built a hewed log meeting-house, lathed and plastered inside, and clapboarded on the outside, and this was used for worship until 1874 or 1875.

The Primitive Methodist church on Kennedy Road, known as Sewell's, and also as Bethel, was built on a site presented by Thomas Walton in 1842. The deed of the Bethel site was signed by the following representing the Primitive Methodist Church: Joseph Sewell, Wallis Walton, Joseph Pilkey, Isaac Chester, Jas. Palmer, John Atkinson, and Charles D. Maginn.

It was witnessed by the minister then on the circuit, Rev. Wm. Lyle, and by John Sewell.

This church was built of brick burned on the ground by John Atkinson, now of Toronto. He also did the masonry of the church; and the carpenter work was done by a son of Isaac Chester, whose name appears on the deed. The whole cost of the unpretentious edifice was £100. A plan of the Circuit in 1844 is preserved; it contains the names of twenty-seven preachers and three exhorters. Revs. John Lacy and M. Nicholls were the itinerant ministers, the others being local preachers. The Circuit at that date embraced Toronto and several stations outside, as well as Sewell's, or Bethel, Twaddle's* Chapel, now Zion Presbyterian Church, and Markham Road Chapel. Services were held in Bethel every Sunday afternoon up to 1881. The membership numbered about forty.

Providence, another Primitive Methodist appointment in the Scarboro Circuit, was built on the Kingston Road in 1859. Services were continued in this place until 1890, when the present Methodist Church

* Spelled in the baptismal certificate of Mrs. Jas. Ionson, *Tweedle*.

was dedicated. After Bethel was closed, the two societies united and met only at Providence.

This congregation built a new church at Scarboro Junction after the union, about 1891. It is a frame structure and cost $1,000.

Some of the leading members at the time were John Everest, John Heal, and G. F. Stephenson. They have a flourishing society, with an aggressive Christian Endeavor organization, which contributes to support a foreign missionary. It was organized in 1890, with William Oliphant as President. Wm. Dark is the superintendent of the Sunday School.

The Primitive Methodists also organized a society and built a church at Malvern about 1855.

These three churches, forming part of a circuit, had as ministers Rev. Messrs. Markham Sims, William Thornley, R. J. Stillwell, Eli Middleton, C. O. Johnston (now of Toronto), Wm. Avison, and R. McKee, who was the last pastor before the union, the pastor residing at the Parsonage Church.

Another Primitive Methodist church was at Milliken's Corners. The society was first organized in a dwelling-house (some say Brookes's waggon-shop, lot 26, concession 5, Scarboro), where it met for two years. Its first ministers were Rev. Messrs. Lyle and Jolly. A frame church was then built, and called "Ebenezer." The trustees were Thos. Harding, John Turner, Wm. Stonehouse, and John Stonehouse. Thos. Harding gave the land, on lot 24, concession 5, Scarboro. The building cost $300.

The travelling minister for the new church was the Rev. Matthew Nicholls, the "young man" being Rev. J. Edgar. The senior or married minister received

$300 per annum, and the younger or unmarried, $150. In 1853 a flourishing Sabbath School was organized, the superintendent being Mr. Waters.

In course of time, the building becoming inadequate to the wants of an increasing congregation, a new brick church was erected in 1877, on the other side of the town-line, the Rev. J. W. Robinson being the pastor in charge. In order to get the deed for his own land back from the Conference, the former donor, Thomas Harding, bought an acre of land from Wm. Morgan, at a cost of $200. It was situated on the south-east corner of lot 1, concession 6, Markham. The church is a fine structure of brick, with a full-sized basement, and cost $7,000. The trustees at present are Thos. O. Harding, R. H. Mills, and M. Risbrough, the ministers in charge being Revs. R. J. Fallis and A. J. Paul, with a membership of forty persons. The amount raised for church and school purposes per annum is $310. The married minister's salary is $700, the unmarried $350. There are eighty children on the Sunday School roll.

The cemetery grounds are pleasantly laid out in plots, with gravel walks, and a beautiful row of evergreens and maples surrounds them.

The Free Methodist Church at Armadale was the result of a revival in 1879 under Valtina A. M. Brown and Arlette E. Eddy, who were sent by the Canada Conference of the Free Methodist Church. The outcome was the organization of a society of thirty members. The first class-leaders were Silas Phœnix and Robert Loveless, the Rev. Thomas Carveth taking charge as pastor. A place of worship was built and dedicated free of debt in November, 1880.

The building is frame, and has seating for 250; the cost, with shed, being $1,100. The site, consisting of half an acre on lot 19, concession 5, was given by Francis Underwood. The dedicatory sermon was preached by the Rev. B. T. Roberts, M.A., of North Chili, N.Y.

The following pastors have had charge up to the present, viz., Revs. Thomas Carveth, John Adams, James Craig, D. Marston, Wesley C. Walls, Wm. H. Wilson, Stewart Walker and James Clink. The salary paid is $300 per annum.

The Discipline of this Church requires members to renounce the use of tobacco and spirituous liquors, and forbids connection with secret societies. The members are most conscientious in these particulars, and the missionary spirit of the Church is manifest from the fact that they have sent out three preachers and three evangelists. They have held five camp-meetings in the neighborhood.

The Sabbath School numbers thirty-five scholars and four teachers, Elijah Loveless being the present superintendent.

The total amount of money raised in 1895 was $500, thus disbursed: Preacher's salary, $300; District Elder, $48; Sabbath School supplies, $20; Incidentals, $50; the balance, $92, being devoted to missionary purposes.

Of the Bible Christian Methodists, who were among the bodies that united to form a grand Methodist whole, the congregation which used to worship on lot 3, concession 1, Kingston Road, in turn with the other denominations, bought a site, in 1863, for a church of their own. Their pastor at the time was Rev. H. J.

Stevens. The lot they purchased from Thos. Adams was the north quarter lot 1, concession 1, upon which they built a stone church, 27 x 30, at a cost of $300. The congregation was in connection with Pickering Circuit. In 1867 a Sunday School was opened, with Andrew J. Courtice as superintendent, a position he held for fourteen years, when he was succeeded by Richard Collins. This was a "union" Sunday School up to the date of amalgamation with the Methodist body in 1883.

After the union, the "Stone Church" congregation was joined to Highland Creek Methodist Church, and was placed on the Scarboro Circuit. At the time of the union, Rev. Mr. Read was appointed on the Circuit, and services were held alternately in the Stone Church and at Highland Creek. This pastor endeavored to bring the two congregations together by building a new church, but failed. The late Rev. M. B. Conron, his successor, organized a Ladies' Aid Society to raise funds for the same purpose, but it was reserved for his successor, Rev. J. J. Redditt, to further the project by the appointment of a building committee, which purchased a site on lot 3, concession 1, north of Kingston Road, from R. Knowles.

Under the pastorate of Mr. Redditt's successor, Rev. F. C. Keam, tenders were called for by the Building Committee for the erection of a church, and the contract was awarded to Messrs. A. Gray and A. W. Secor. The price for the building proper was agreed on at $2,500, and on November 7th, 1891, the whole was completed at a cost for site, building, furnishings, sheds, fence, etc., of $3,420, of which $1,000 towards the church building was contributed by the Ladies'

Aid. This is known as Centennial Methodist Church. A good Sunday School is held in the basement of the church. W. H. Closson is the superintendent.

An Epworth League holds meetings every Sunday evening at 7 p.m., the members taking turn as leaders, the subject to be considered being prescribed by the League.

THE ROMAN CATHOLIC CHURCH.

As the first form of the Christian religion presented to the Indian nations who occupied Canada at the time of the French settlement; as the religion of the government then set up, and of the colonists themselves with very few exceptions; as the centre of education in the colony, and the heart of a most vigorous missionary effort on behalf of the savages, the Roman Catholic Church in Canada must ever engage the careful attention of the historian.

In the Province of Ontario, then an unknown region of the great west, ineffaceable traces remain of the labors of great French missionary priests as early as the beginning of the seventeenth century. Lalemant, Breboeuf, Daniel, Jogues, are names the poet still delights to honor. They were men of learning whose observations have been invaluable to science; men of piety whose lives were not dear to them. Later days have kept up the record of able priests of the Roman Catholic Church who gave their best to the building up of their faith and the country of their birth or choice. Laval, Macdonell, LaSalle, Charbonnel, Power, are names honored and revered not alone in their own Church.

As settlements grew in number and extent throughout this province, it was deemed desirable that a more exact oversight of their people should be established, and certain new dioceses were set off. In 1826, when that of Kingston was organized, there were but seven stationed priests in the Province, and Roman Catholics in the back settlements were, like their Protestant neighbors, often without the ministration of their Church for lengthened periods. Scarboro, therefore, only shared the common lot in having no settled priest. At York, however, Father Crowley was stationed, and as often as possible he visited his little flock at Scarboro, they honoring his teaching by travelling into York as often as wind and weather permitted, to receive the Sacraments of the Church for themselves and children.

In 1843 the parish of Oshawa was established, and the Church in Scarboro received the ministrations of the priest stationed there. This was Rev. Father Proulx, whose stately figure and noble bearing are still remembered.

Father J. B. Proulx was born at Lachine in 1808, was ordained at Montreal, July 26th, 1835, and was first stationed at Laprairie, opposite Montreal. On coming to Upper Canada he was sent by Bishop Macdonell to work among the Indians at Penetanguishene, and afterwards on Manitoulin Island. In 1846 he was given charge of the parish of Oshawa, and in 1858 went to Toronto.

On his visits to Scarboro, Father Proulx said mass at the houses of Mr. McHenry and Mr. Nash, now included in Markham township; and at Highland Creek at the house of Mr. Walsh, where the travelling priest always found a warm welcome and a home.

In 1854 Father Proulx earned the gratitude of his scattered little flock at Scarboro by building for them a church, their present place of worship, St. Joseph's, at Highland Creek, and leaving it to them free of debt as a gift of his love and good-will.

In 1860 the parish of Pickering was erected, and Scarboro was included therein. The present priest in charge is the Rev. C. F. Gallagher. This gentleman studied classics and philosophy at St. Macarten Seminary, County Monaghan, Ireland, and theology at the Grand Seminary, Montreal. He was ordained by Archbishop Lynch on the 21st September, 1877.

Since his ordination he has held charges at Niagara, Caledon, and Schomberg, and came to his present parish in October, 1892.

MENNONITES.

Any account of the religious denominations of the township would be incomplete without a special reference to the Mennonites, who, though comparatively weak in numbers, are strong in moral influence.

Unpretending and unaggressive as these people are, they pursue the even tenor of their way most consistently. Owing to their system of government, without a clerical body of any kind, mention can be made of no leading members.

In Markham the Mennonites are considerably more numerous, and excellent accommodation has there been provided for worshippers, those of Scarboro uniting for this purpose with their brethren in the former township.

BIBLE SOCIETY.

The Scarboro Branch Bible Society was organized on the 11th of November, 1856, within St. Andrew's Church. Rev. James Bain, President; Wm. Clark, Robt. Hamilton, J. P. Wheler, John D. Thomson, Vice-Presidents; Rev. John Laing, Secretary; James A. Thomson, Treasurer; Archibald Glendinning, David Brown, Depositaries.

Present officers: W. A. Heron, President; Alex. Neilson, Vice-President; Amos Thomson, Treasurer; R. M. Loveless, Secretary.

Total contributions since organization, over $5,300.

As an illustration of the pranks performed by the whirligig of Time, the following may be taken:

In the early part of this century Mormon missionaries invaded the township and secured a number of converts among whom was John Taylor, a Methodist preacher (some say he was also a teacher), who "forsook all and followed" the disciples of Joseph Smith. He was imprisoned with the Smiths in 1844, and on the occasion of the attack made upon them in jail he was severely wounded. In 1880 he became head of the Church of Latter Day Saints, as successor to Brigham Young, and died in exile, July 23rd, 1880. He was born in England in 1808.

OLD TEACHERS.

1. E. R. Jacques. 2. Mrs. Thompson. 3. James Russell. 5. W. D. Fitzpatrick.

OLD DOCTORS.

4. Dr. Pollock. 6. Dr. Closson.

CHAPTER XI.

SCHOOLS AND TEACHERS.

"There is no teaching until the pupil is brought into the same state or principle in which you are; a transfusion takes place; he is you, and you are he; there is a teaching: and by no unfriendly chance or bad company can he ever quite lose the benefit."—*Emerson.*

THE occupation of teacher in the early days was not in every respect a happy one. In nearly every instance the teacher was a man—no one else was thought able to rule the rough-and-ready youngsters of pioneer days. At an early age the boys of the farm were initiated into the mysteries of "hunting" the cow, "branding" and "niggering" in the new clearings, "minding gaps," driving oxen, blazing away with old flint-locks at predacious crows and hawks, and of numerous other employments, many of which are now rendered unnecessary by the march of events. The associations connected with some of these experiences, coupled with the lack of home comforts and conveniences, and the general extremely natural condition of society, did not tend to foster in the young people of those days what we call refinement. The parents had neither time nor inclination to concern themselves about manners, and, as a consequence of these and other factors, discipline was frequently very lax. Given, therefore, from a dozen to a score or more of precocious backwoods boys and girls, crowded into a small log building, in nowise characterized by commodiousness within, any more than by architectural beauty without, we may well cease to wonder why the grandparents, and great-grandparents were less amenable to discipline than are the young folk of our own day.

But this was not all. The old-time preceptor had no knowledge of educational principles; he entered the school and left it, a tyrant, in the worst sense of that word. His professional creed was summed up in the easily understood and easily applied dogma, "No larnin' without lickin'." An old soldier, a decayed tailor, an otherwise unsuccessful anybody, was good enough for a school-master, if only he could prove his claim to be a master after the approved manner of his day and generation. All things considered, his pay was not bad—it was not, at any rate, much worse than salaries paid to-day, when qualifications are taken into account. Indeed, if we gauge the scale of payment in early days by the ability on the part of parents to pay it, it was very high. Consider, also, the delights of the erstwhile dominie when he "boarded 'round!"—a week here, two or three weeks there, in proportion to the number of young rebels from one family over whom he had to raise his rod, aye, and let it fall, too! What splendid opportunities were afforded him to gain a varied experience of sleeping quarters, of cookery, of domestic etiquette, of the home influences brought to bear on his pupils—to display his own erudition and exalt his attainments before the old folk, to increase his stock of knowledge from the recitals of others, and to become familiar in every sense with "the people of the parish."

School fittings were extremely simple in character—long backless benches, sometimes so high that when the children were seated, their feet did not reach the floor; equally long desks ranged round the walls, or when double-sided, standing in the middle of the floor; a chair and table, perhaps, for the teacher, and we have the furniture of the old-time school-house, unless we add the stove, which in its time superseded the big fire-place with roaring chimney. Yes, this was all. The first school-rooms were innocent of pictures, of maps and charts, of globes, of blackboards, and of the numerous appliances that are now to be found even in the poorest schools. But changes came in due course, and as the circumstances of the people improved, comforts and conveniences were added for the benefit of pupils.

It must not, however, be supposed that these details were in every instance applicable to our township, the pioneers of which had in most cases received the benefits of parish school education,* including, it need hardly be said, a thorough grounding in Christian doctrine, both directly from the Bible, which was the text-book for reading purposes, and from the pages of the Shorter Catechism. These people were, therefore, not likely to overlook the amenities of every-day life either in the domestic, or in their somewhat restricted social relations, and when children appeared in the clearings of Scarboro, they were brought up with nearly as much rigidity of discipline as if they had been in the "land of brown heath and shaggy wood." English, Irish and American settlers were also of an intelligent class,

* Receipts and accounts kept by the Thomsons in 1796 are well written and accurately spelled.

with clearly defined ideas regarding the respective duties of parents and children, and the advantages pertaining to common school education. We may therefore readily understand that in settlements so constituted, much interest would be displayed in providing for the young people as good schools and school-masters as were possible at the time. Notwithstanding this, it is evident that the circumstances of the settlers necessarily implied the existence of conditions which, while they were not by any means approved of, had to be tolerated, and there is no lack of proof that the backwoods seminaries in Scarboro at the beginning of the nineteenth century, and even somewhat more recently, were not of a type greatly superior to those of other districts.

The following from the pen of David Martin, who himself received his education under Scarboro schoolmasters, is an excellent epitome of educational affairs in his day, but it must be remembered that the genuine old-time school had by this time been considerably improved upon, although he makes some reference to the condition of things preceding his own experience. Mr. Martin says:

"For many years, indeed during the first half of the century, the school-houses were of the most primitive kind. The forest furnished the readiest and cheapest material. The logs, if of pine, were flattened on two sides; if of hardwood, they were generally left round, dovetailed in the usual way at the corners, the interstices between the logs being chinked and plastered. In size, the buildings seldom exceeded 18 x 24 feet, and were never too high. The fire-place usually occupied one end, and desks facing the wall ran round the other three sides. The seats consisted of long forms without backs. Similar forms or benches placed crosswise in the centre of the room furnished seats for the smaller children. The limited space forbade anything in the shape of desks, those luxuries being reserved for pupils in arithmetic and writing. Light was admitted through long windows similar to those common in blacksmith and carpenter shops, and were usually two panes high and ten or twelve panes long, the sashes sliding past each other horizontally, for purposes of ventilation. In winter, fuel was supplied by the parents, who were required to bring a quarter of a cord per pupil. The teacher was promised no stated salary, but received a rate per pupil (commonly 3s. 9d., or 75 cents per quarter), taking his chances of emolument,—the more pupils, of course, the more pay. In the early part of the century it was not uncommon for the teacher to receive his board gratis, staying a few weeks with one and another of the families represented at the school. If unmarried, which was often the case, he sometimes lived in the school, keeping 'bachelor's hall.' The number of teaching hours was alternately thirty and thirty-six per week, each alternate Saturday being a holiday. About 1860 a change was made, the time of teaching being reduced to five days per week.

"It will readily be seen that as long as the teacher was paid as described above, the schools were situated without regard to any kind of system, the first consideration being the desirability of a large attendance. Indeed, this was the chief factor in determining where a school should be placed. This method of locating school-houses continued until 1847, at which date a change took place. The township was then regularly divided into sections, almost exactly as they are at present, new schools being erected in the centre of each section. For the building and maintenance of these schools, trustees were empowered to levy a rate on the section. Among other advantages, this enabled the trustees to engage a teacher at a certain fixed salary. A rate bill, commonly twenty-five cents per month, per pupil, was charged, and if the amount so collected failed to pay the stipulated salary, a tax was levied on the ratable property of the section to supply the deficiency. All the expenses of conducting the school—fuel, repairs, etc.—were provided for by general taxation.

"For a long time great difference of opinion prevailed as to the relative merits of free schools *versus* rate-bill schools, and as the matter was for a number of years entirely optional with the ratepayers, the question as to which should be adopted, recurred regularly at the annual meeting, and very heated discussions sometimes took place. A poll frequently being opened, adherents of the respective systems drummed up votes with as much enthusiasm as at a parliamentary or municipal election. Opinion, however, gradually settled down to the conviction that on the whole, the free system was the preferable one; opposition to which having almost entirely ceased, the schools were finally declared free, by law. In those early days very high qualifications on the part of teachers were not demanded, and were seldom secured, ability to teach the three 'R's' fairly well being considered sufficient. The method of teaching differed widely from what it is now. The younger children were taught individually until sufficiently advanced to read and spell words of one or two syllables, when they were put into classes for reading and spelling, these being the only subjects in which the pupils were taught collectively. For those in writing, the teacher usually set the headlines by hand, in addition to which he had in many instances to rule the paper, and make and keep in order the quill pens, which were the only kind in use. Steel pens were introduced sometime in the 'forties,' but did not come into general use until about 1850. To pupils in arithmetic, no two of whom were probably working in the same part of the book, the teacher had to give his attention individually.

"The First Books, or Primers, used were such as the fancy or caprice of the parents might dictate, and as they were not taught in classes, uniformity was not a necessity. After the Primers, Mavor's combined reading and spelling-book was in almost universal use. For the more advanced pupils, Cobb's, Webster's and Carpenter's spelling-books were employed by some masters, but their introduction never became general. In reading, the Bible, Testament and the English Reader were the principal, indeed the only, text-books, the last-mentioned being composed of selections from the most eminent authors in prose and verse, compiled by Lindley Murray, author of the well-known grammar. Verses of Scripture were committed to memory by the pupils. Before 1850 geography received comparatively little attention, which, in some respects, was perhaps not much to be regretted, as, previous to that, almost the only available books on the subject were by American authors, strongly anti-British, conveying the impression, as American publications usually do, that the United States was the greatest, and, in fact, almost the only country or nation worth mentioning on the face of the earth. Grammar was also much neglected, but, when taught, Lennie's and Lindley Murray's were the principal text-books, chiefly the former. In arithmetic, that of Francis Walkingame was mostly, if not exclusively, used, until superseded by the Irish National book about 1850, which, in turn, became obsolete about 1858; the introduction of the decimal currency about that time necessitating a change. In schools where a large proportion of the children were of Presbyterian parentage, the Shorter Catechism was taught by some teachers when requested by the parents, but the practice has long since been discontinued. On the whole, the schools of the period to which I at present have more special reference, in the first half of the century, were fairly efficient. The teachers, who were mostly Old Countrymen, often Scotsmen, ruled, perhaps, with somewhat despotic sway, enforcing their authority with a sometimes pretty free use of the birch, or rather the blue beech, a vigorous application of which now and then for purposes of discipline was thought to have a salutary effect. But whatever their faults in this respect (if they were faults), and however slender their attainments, the old-time teachers succeeded, to a fair extent, in imparting to their pupils the rudiments, at least, of a good education, and comparatively few of the children of those early settlers were to be found who could not, at any rate, read and write."

In the 18 x 24 log school-rooms, it will be readily understood, accommodation was not ample during the winter months when even the grown-up young people availed themselves of the opportunity afforded by slackness of work to attend school, more especially when, as sometimes happened, the reputation of the teacher stood high. Hats, caps and wraps of all sorts were stuffed into desks, for the want of nails and hooks on which to hang them. Windows were frequently destitute of several panes; chinking fell out; knot-holes in floors were covered with prominent patches; desks and benches became loose and creaky; doors ceased to fit their frames, or, perhaps, rather the frames ceased to fit the doors, for it was not uncommon for the whole structure to assume an appearance of utter recklessness, by sinking more or less to one side, and thus generally disarranging the simple architecture.* But even this condition of things was not without its compensations, chief of which was, perhaps, the advantages secured by way of ventilation.

Sometimes a second edifice of logs succeeded the original one in a section, but in most cases the first building was superseded by a frame structure, and more recently by one of brick or stone. With the advancement of time came also improvement in the grounds; neat fences and gates were supplied, trees were planted, respectable outhouses erected, and the water supply was attended to. In every instance these improvements have been found to "pay," both directly and indirectly, for not only does the task of discipline become thus a comparatively easy one for the teacher, but the effects are visible on the pupils in after-life.

* It was not unusual in the old buildings to protect the home-made ink of the pupils from freezing during winter, by burying the bottles nightly in a hole made under the floor.

Modes of punishment in the old days were barbarous. It is recorded of one teacher that he sometimes tied the thumb of one hand of a pupil to a string hanging from the roof or ceiling, while the other hand held a book, the pupil meanwhile having to stand on one foot until his task was finished, or his punishment thought sufficient.

The first school taught in the township was in the house of James Elliot, on lot 22, concession D, in the extreme north-west corner of the present section 9. This school was taught by a man named Pocock, an Englishman, in the year 1805. The first school-house built in the township was on the Springfield farm, near the line between lots 23 and 24, concession 1, within a few rods of where St. Andrew's Church now stands.

S. S. No. 1.—The first school-house was of logs, built on lot 31, concession 3, in 1817, and the first teacher was a Mr. Edward, who was followed by Messrs. John McFiggin, Jos. Maughan, or (according to one statement, Mr. Clark), Andrew McFarran, and Messrs. Hugel, Cooper, Muir, Leitch, Nealy, W. D. Fitzpatrick, John McConnell (afterwards Dr.), McKinnon, Tomlinson, Field, Ramsay, Quantz and Yeo.

The present trustees are J. Kennedy, J. C. Clark and Thomas Armstrong.

S. S. No. 2.—In 1830, the increase of population and the need of better facilities than were afforded by schools in distant parts of the township, led to the erection of a log school-house on lot 25, concession 3. The first teacher appointed was James Little.

This building continued to be used for nineteen years. A new one, also of logs, was put up in 1849, on the site of the present school-house, lot 22, concession 4; but it was burnt down in 1851. Temporary quarters were found until 1853, when the school-house now standing was erected. Estimated cost, $1,500.

The teachers following Mr. Little were Messrs. Upham, Cooper, McDonald, Mills, Eckroyd, McKinnon, McCaffrey, Wm. Irving (now Dr.), Steele, Lancaster, Martin, Macklin, McLean, Doherty, Whaley, Bruce, Ward, Yeo, Dean, and Misses Jeannie Elliot, Carrie Clifford and Agnes Moir.

Present trustees, Matthew Elliot, Alex. Macklin, James I. Stewart.

S. S. No. 3.—The first school was opened in this section in 1836, in a small log building on lot 17, concession 4, Markham Road, and the teachers in this old structure were James Park, Alex. Muir and — Hand.

A new frame school-house was erected in 1851, on lot 15, concession 3, on the corner of the Stirling farm. There was just enough ground for the building to stand, and the scholars had the Queen's highway as a play-ground.

In 1872 a brick building took the place of the frame one, on lot 15, concession 4, where an acre of land, at $250, was not thought too much for the wants of the young people. This building cost $2,500.

Since the erection of the frame school-house in 1851, the following teachers have been engaged: James Russell, Wm. Davison (4 years), George McKennell (5 years), E. R. Jacques (9 years), G. M. Jacques (8 years), J. B. Dunham, G. W. Ormerod, W. J. Clark (2 years), E. T. Young, John F. Stewart, Samuel Jewett, and the present teacher A. R. Jacques, now in his third year of engagement.

Present trustees, John J. Weir, Wm. Pearson and Charles Monk.

S. S. No. 4.—The first school section was a union one with Pickering, the school-house standing on the town-line, and the first teacher was a big Scotsman named Ferguson, of whom all that two of his old pupils now living can remember, is the force and frequency with which he applied the "taws."

Other teachers were Messrs. Reesor, Break, Clark, Spence, Johnson, and Misses Lawrie, Hewitt, Poole, Montgomery and Irwin. Present teacher, Mr. Wells.

Present trustees, Thomas Maxwell, Thomas Reesor and James Murison.

S. S. No. 5.—About 1823 or 1824, the first school was established in this section, the humble building having stood on the north-west corner of lot 26, concession 1.* A Mr. Carruthers taught here in 1824, a Mr. Dobson was teacher in 1830, a Mr. Hope in 1836, and these followed: Messrs. Clark, McFiggin, Muir, O'Reilly, Closson and James Russell.† When the township was divided into sections in 1847, a new frame school-house was built on the south-east corner of lot 30, concession 2. The present commodious building was erected in 1871, the builders being Thos. and David Forfar.

Present trustees, A. A. Forfar, Beebe Carnaghan and Thomas Pilkey.

S. S. No. 6.—The first school-house in the township was built within the bounds of the present Section

* Some say it was on concession 2, and one statement is to the effect that it was known as the Squaw Village school.

† Mr. Russell lived near the Rouge, 7½ miles from the school (which he taught in the early "fifties"), and as there were in those days no Saturday holidays, he had to walk ninety miles a week to and from school, to which, if we add another fifteen miles to and from St. Andrew's Church on Sunday, we have a total of 105 miles a week, or nearly 5,500 miles a year! For other particulars referring to Mr. Russell, see "Churches and Ministers."

No. 6. It stood on the Springfield farm, lot 23, concession 1, and was built of round logs with saddle corners, and one door in the end. It cannot now be ascertained with certainty who the first teachers in this school were. For some years it was used as a church. The next building in Section 6 was erected on lot 24, concession 1, on the corner of the grave-yard lot. The old men to-day speak of playing hide-and-go-seek among the tombs when they went to school here. It was made of hewed logs, with a door and two windows in the side, and a fire-place in the end. Here John Taber taught.

The third house was built on lot 19, concession 2. It was a frame building. John Muir taught here for many years. The present brick building was erected in 1863, on lot 18, concession 2. It has a senior and junior department.

Teachers in No. 6, as far as can be known, were — Anderson, John Taber, J. Muir, — Gibson, A. M. Sheriff, Alex. Muir, W. D. Fitzpatrick, H. M. Campbell, T. Macdonald, W. Purvis, — Smith, W. J. Clark, Miss Taylor, W. J. Coltman, Alfred Kennedy. In the junior department, Misses L. Dunsmore, — Hewitt, — Squire, L. Willis, F. B. Duncan and M. F. Pearson.

Present trustees, Robert Purdie, Robert Green and John Baird.

S. S. No. 7.—The first school-house was on the Fishery Road, and was an ordinary square building of plank, erected in 1832. The first teacher was John Wilson, a Yorkshireman.

The second building stood on lot 14, concession D, on the side-road. The Rev. Saltern Givens fre-

1
2
4
5
6
13
7
8
9
10
11
12

quently held Episcopal service here. Methodist ministers also held service here.

The third school-house was built on the West Hill, and is now the dwelling of the Camps family.

The present structure (frame) is on lot 9, concession 1, a little north of the Kingston Road. The school property is valued at about $2,000. There are nearly 150 children of school age in the section, and the number in attendance in 1895 was 122.

Present trustees, Jas. Neilson, Henry Westney.

S. S. No. 8.—Not fewer than six school-houses have existed in this section. One stood near the residence of George Taylor, close to the intersection of the Danforth Road and the side-road, between lots 26 and 27, concession C. Another was on lot 27, concession C, near the farm-house of Robert Martin, at present occupied by James Miller. No dates can be given in connection with these buildings. The site of a third school was on the side-road between lots 34 and 35, concession C, almost in front of Wm. Thomson's residence. This school was built about 1824, and was taught in 1826 by a Roman Catholic named Fitzgerald. After him came Mr. (afterwards Dr.) Carroll, an eminent Methodist minister, who died not many years ago. Still later, but prior to 1833, the teacher was Miss Hannah Fitzpatrick, and afterwards Wm. Thomson.

This building was removed to Moffat's Corners, and re-erected on the York side of the town-line.

Miss Fitzpatrick also taught in an old church which was removed to York, and thence to Wexford.

The fifth building used as a school stood on the north end of lot 32, concession C, near the residence of Alex. McCowan. The teacher was a Perthshire Scotsman named David Ogilvie. This was about 1835.

Another old school-house stood on the north end of lot 32, concession 1. It was erected, as nearly as can be ascertained, about 1838, of flattened pine logs, and measured about 18 x 26 feet. It was first taught by Miss Mary Branham, and afterwards by David Ogilvie, from 1842 to 1845; by an Englishman named Thomas Adams from 1845 to September, 1847; and for the rest of the year by A. Veysey. When the schools were re-arranged, in consequence of dividing the township into regular sections, the school was removed to the centre of the section, and Mr. Veysey continued teacher until the end of 1849.

The following is a list of teachers who have been in Section No. 8 since 1st January, 1850:

Thomas Cooper - - - -	1850, and part of '51.
Duncan McNair - - - -	Remainder of '51 and part of '52.
Mr. Leonard - - - - - -	" " '52.
*Timothy T. Coleman - -	1853, '54, and '55.
Duncan Fitzpatrick - - -	Part of '56.
Mr. McKay - - - - - -	Remainder of '56.
William R. Bain - - - -	1857.
†Alexander Muir - - -	1858 and part of '59.
James Poole - - - - - -	Remainder of '59, and 1860.
John McConnell - - - -	1861.
Henry M. Campbell - - -	1862, '63, '64, and '65.
‡John A. Wismer - - -	1866.
Martin Sutherland - - -	1867–'68.
§Thomas Hogarth - - -	1869, '70, '71, '72, '73, and '74.
Cranswick Craven - - -	1875–'76.

* Afterwards entered the medical profession, and was some time mayor of Seaforth.

† Now Principal of Gladstone School, Toronto.

‡ Now Commercial teacher of Jamieson Avenue Collegiate Institute, Toronto.

§ Now Principal of Leslieville School, Toronto.

William H. Bewell - - - -	1877, '78, '79, '80, '81, '82, '83.
Miss Mary E. Caldbeck - -	1884, '85, and part of '86.
Miss Elizabeth Armstrong -	Remainder of '86; '87, '88, '89.
Miss McCarten, Miss Yeomans, Joseph Paxton, - - - -	1890.
Miss M. E. Pomeroy - - -	1891.
Miss Catherine McMurchy -	1892, '93, '94.
Miss Fanny B. Duncan - -	1895–'96.

The present school-house is of brick, 54 x 36 feet, and cost $1,900. Its predecessor, which had stood from 1846 to 1863, cost $280. The present teacher is Miss F. B. Duncan.

Present trustees, Leslie Armstrong, Jas. Crichton, George McCowan.

S. S. No. 9.—The first school-house is said to have stood on lot 18, concession D. The second one was on lot 19, concession C, on the old Kingston Road. The third was on lot 14, concession D. Another building used as a school-house stood on lot 26, concession C, and here Mr. John Taber taught in 1835. The present school-house in Scarboro village was erected in 1861 at a cost of $1,400, exclusive of the site which was purchased for $400. In 1895, $642 was levied for school purposes; the average attendance having been 65, the whole number of school age in this section being 140.

Present trustees, Smith Wilson, William Patton, Andrew Young.

S. S. No. 10.—The first school-house in this section was built on Danforth Road, lot 26, concession C, on the farm owned by George Taylor, sen., about 1823. Wm. Bell, sen., Isaac Chester, sen., and Geo. Taylor, sen., attended school there. John Taber taught for some time. In 1833 the school-house was built on the Kingston Road near the Half-way House. Some years after this another school-house was built on the south-east corner of lot 29, concession C. This afterward gave place to the school-house on the site of the present one on the Danforth Road. The present building was put up in 1870. In 1894, S. S. No. 10 was enlarged by 500 acres from the south-east corner of S. S. No. 8. The section thus enlarged was divided into two, the one to the west next to York town-line being designated S. S. No. 12. Names of some of the teachers are the following: John Taber, Mr. Simmons, Mr. Cowan, Mr. Skelton; and teachers of later years were Isabella Findlay, Libbie Latham, A. P. Latter, Oscar Pickering, David Whiteside, Miss I. C. Gibson, G. R. Hodgson, and the present teacher, N. K. Walter.

Present trustees, Geo. Smith, John Heal, Jonathan Ashbridge.

S. S. No. 11.—Before 1836, the first log building used as a school-house was on lot 4, concession 1. The teacher, Mr. Sammons (or Salmons) boarded from house to house, but slept in the school-room, rolling his bed up every morning and placing it in a corner. In 1836, a building of planks was put up for a school-room, on lot 3, concession 1, Kingston Road. For its day this was rather a superior structure, with a cottage roof. It is now used as a dwelling. The builder was "Uncle Tommy Adams." From 1837 to 1843 the teacher was Hugh Graham, who was succeeded by William Steele, who remained until 1850. From 1850 till 1858 the teachers were William

Clark, Thomas Nealy, Miss Falls and Miss Jacobs. In 1850 Miss Dorothy Campbell became teacher, and through her efforts a more commodious and more sanitarily satisfactory building of stone was erected on lot 1, concession 1, in 1860. The trustees were Messrs. C. C. Sanders, Ed. Huxtable and Wm. Cowan. Since 1861, Miss Campbell's successors were Wm. Peart, Miss Lowry, Arch. Little, Thos. Hogarth, A. E. Annis, Wm. Fleming, W. B. Walker, Susan J. Huggard, R. B. Butler, C. Palmer, C. Craven, Miss M. Hewitt, John Stonehouse, A. Law, C. Craven (again for four and a half years), Geo. Tait, D. H. Campbell (3 years), J. E. Kelly, W. H. Closson, C. F. Ewers, E. W. Tonkin, C. F. Ewers, M. E. Smith from 1891 to 1895, and for the present year, Sara Norris.

The school-house is finished in modern style, and is equipped with maps, charts and globes. The school property is valued at $1,200.

S. S. No. 12.—Opened September, 1895. Building cost $2,200. Teacher, Maud Robertson.

Present trustees, Daniel Baldwin, George Bell, Francis Duffort.

In the old frame school that stood near Gates's tavern between 1840 and 1845, the teachers were Wm. Salmonds, Jas. McIntosh, Wm. Skelton, John Boyle, John Jackson and Thos. Moodie.

A. M. Sheriff once taught at "McHenry's," on the Danforth Road, one and a half miles east of Woburn.

Before the appointment of county superintendents, the gentlemen who acted as township superintendents in Scarboro were the Rev. Messrs. George, Belt, Laing and Fletcher.

In Smith's "Canada," published in 1851, reference is made in the Business Directory of Vol. I. to "W. H. Norris, Principal of Collegiate School, Scarboro," and to "A. F. Purcell, Classical Master of Collegiate School, Scarboro." As it has been impossible to find any record of this "Collegiate School," the inference is that Messrs. Norris and Purcell announced themselves as above, rather because they were willing to manage such a school, than that it existed.

The Alexandra School is conducted under the Industrial School Association of Toronto. It is situated on the eastern limits of Toronto, and is maintained for girls. It was established in 1890, and consists of two cottages. The school is reformative in character. There were twenty-four ward pupils at the Alexandra in 1895. The grounds are fourteen and a half acres in extent. Miss Walker is Superintendent; assistants, Miss Brainard and Miss Hill.

The Blantyre Industrial School is a Roman Catholic reformatory institution for boys. It consists of the old Blantyre mansion and grounds, the former having been remodelled and enlarged. The institution is beautifully situated and the extensive grounds afford ample employment to the pupils.

Among all the dominies who have exercised sway in this township, Thomas Appleton deserves special notice. He was a Yorkshireman and a Methodist, who came to Upper Canada in 1819, and began to teach school the same year in Scarboro, remaining here for twelve months. He next taught in King for four months, when he was appointed to take charge of the Common School in the town of York, where, after managing the school most satisfactorily for a year, the trustees, Dr. T. D. Morrison, Jesse Ketchum and Jordan Post, came into collision with the "Honorable and Venerable Dr. Strachan," whom Robert Gourlay characterized as a "monstrous little fool of a parson." Dr. Strachan, in the name and on behalf of Lieutenant-Governor Maitland, but quite illegally nevertheless, applied to the trustees for the school-house, in which he purposed placing a Mr. Spragg, whom he had brought from England to conduct a "national," *i.e.*, a Church of England school, on the Bell, or monitorial system. This application having been refused by the trustees, payment of Mr. Appleton's services ceased, on the plea that the legislative grant had been too much decreased to warrant the expenditure, although Mr. Appleton, with the consent of the trustees, continued to officiate for several years. Remonstrances, petitions and memorials were unavailing; but, with "John Bull" persistency, the ousted dominie maintained his claim for remuneration. Applications made to the Home District Board of Education were not even replied to, and no satisfaction could be obtained until the case was referred to a committee of the Legislature, which reported on the 18th of March, 1835, "That eighty-five pounds four shillings be paid to Thomas Appleton, teacher of the Common School of this place, in the years 1822, 1823, 1824, 1825, 1826 and 1827, for public moneys due to him, and withheld by the Board of Education, and for the interest accruing thereon." This report was signed by Wm. Lyon Mackenzie, David Gibson, Thomas D. Morrison and Charles Waters.

We have the case of Mr. Appleton to thank for the abolition of the old Provincial Board of Education, and for bringing to an end the efforts that had been so long and so determinedly made, to fasten on this Province, sectarian Protestant schools.*

The great difficulty of procuring exact information with regard to school affairs is a cause of regret. Too frequently the secretary of the board performs his duties carelessly, the minutes being either unrecorded or recorded only on loose sheets of paper. Even when books are kept, they are liable to be lost or mislaid, as changes take place in the board of trustees; and it is quite certain that this condition of things is not nearly so bad in Scarboro as in many other townships, where those in office have been, and are, less qualified to perform the necessary clerical labor.

The suggestion is here made that inspectors should be instructed by the Minister of Education to examine the minute-book of each school board at least once a year, preferably, perhaps, as soon as possible after the annual public meeting, and to make such suggestions as may be deemed necessary for the purpose of maintaining correct records. This course would ensure transference of all documents from old to new officials, and minute-books out of date, or filled up, should be deposited in the county registry office, or in some other place of security.

* Numerous references to the Appleton case will be found in the first two volumes of the "Documentary History of Education in Upper Canada," by J. George Hodgins, M.A., LL.D., Barrister-at-law, Librarian and Historiographer to the Education Department of Ontario, Toronto, 1894.

CHAPTER XII.

PUBLIC LIBRARIES.

"Books are not absolutely dead things, but do contain a progeny of life in them to be as active as that soul whose progeny they are ; nay, they do preserve, as in a vial, the purest efficacy and extraction of that living intellect that bred them."—*John Milton.*

SCARBORO PUBLIC LIBRARY.

JUST thirty-eight years after the cutting of the first tree, many of the pioneers having passed from the scene with the disappearance of the forest, a somewhat unusual and highly creditable movement in a purely rural community was successfully carried out. Perhaps without exception, every one of the "Fathers of the Settlement" had received, at least, a good elementary education either in the Old Land, whence most of them came, or in the United States, from which arrived a few representatives of the United Empire Loyalists. It has already been shown how heartily, and how self-sacrificingly, the original occupiers set themselves to the task of providing such schools as were possible in those days.

Most of the original settlers would have regarded with wonder the proposal to enact any law or regulation in favor of compulsory attendance at school, other than the parental form of it, to which they themselves had been subjected, and which, no doubt, they sometimes exercised over their Canadian offspring.

Now that sons and daughters of the "first families" became the parents of a new generation, they craved for mental food of a quality superior to that supplied by the text-books and by the weekly newspaper. Dr. George Birkbeck, in Great Britain, had shown the practicability of establishing libraries for the use of mechanics, and the movement was in its prime during the first half of this century. It is not unlikely that the yeomen of Scarboro were thus influenced, to some extent; but whatever the moving cause may have been, it is to their infinite credit that, on the 7th of April, 1834, a meeting was held in St. Andrew's Church to organize a public library, which continued to be known as the Scarboro Subscription Library for a period of forty-four years, until, in 1878, it was incorporated as a Mechanics' Institute under the Ontario Act.

The first meeting, which would appear to have been as harmonious as it was well attended, resulted in the election of R. D. Hamilton, M.D., as President; Robert Hamilton, Vice-President; Wm. Elliot, Treasurer; Arch. Glendinning, Secretary, and James A. Thomson, Librarian. Besides these, there were enrolled as members, the Rev. James George, Thomas Paterson, Andrew Johnston, William Glendinning, Simeon Thomson, Francis Johnston, Wm. D. Thomson, Jon. Thom, John Gibson, S. Cornell, Christopher Thomson, J. Brownlie, Wm. Forfar, jun., Wm. Paterson, George Scott, David Brown, Thomas Brown, Wm. Hood, John Muir, Adam Bell, John Stobo, Dr. D. Graham, J. Davidson, J. Findlay, John Elliot, John Tingle, Alex. Jackson, Andrew Paterson, Thos. Whiteside, John Martin, George Thomson, John

Glendinning, John Thornbeck, Daniel Ferguson, Marshal Macklin, Robert Tackett, Wm. Crone, T. Walton, sen., Wm. Findlay, Wm. Scott and J. Carmichael—a goodly number for a beginning, even where the population is comparatively dense at the present day; but here we find forty-six persons, chiefly farmers, living in some instances, as a matter of course, miles apart, uniting, more than half a century ago, to place themselves and their families in touch with the best thoughts of the best literary and scientific writers of that time and of past time.

In addition to the officers already named, a committee of twelve was appointed to manage the affairs of the library, and among the regulations they laid down we find that members were required to pay an entrance fee of five shillings (currency, presumably), and the same amount annually, in two payments, each half-yearly, in advance; and that a general meeting should be held half-yearly to choose "managers," examine books, and arrange for the purchase of new volumes. Each member was privileged to recommend the purchase of a book, but the decision was to be the result of a majority vote, and "no book of a seditious, deistical, or licentious character was to be allowed on the shelves, on any pretence whatever." Sedition and deism were terms which, sixty or seventy years ago, possessed a much wider range of application than they do to-day; and we can readily understand the solicitude and the horror that actuated the people of 1834 in their desire to preserve themselves from the very taint of disloyalty to Creator or to king, when we bear in mind that Voltairism, on the one hand, and republicanism, on the other, were openly advocated in many quarters. In Canada, Robert Gourlay had done much to unsettle public political opinion. William Lyon Mackenzie and Dr. Papineau were not throwing oil on the troubled waters; and as the men of Scarboro were all true Britons to the core, nothing could be more reasonable than that literature of the tendencies in question should be excluded from the library!

For fifty years the membership averaged forty-seven, and now stands at seventy—than which it would be difficult to adduce better proof regarding the uniformly judicious management of the library, and the steady, highly intelligent character of the people.

Although incorporated, as already mentioned, in 1878, it received no public aid until 1880, when a government grant of $400 and a municipal grant of $25 enabled the committee to make considerable additions to their catalogue, which now contains the titles of about four thousand volumes. The circulation amounts to 2,775 per annum, or an average of nearly thirty-three volumes to each member, and it is worthy of observation that the percentage of fiction is extremely low.

Some of the old minute books having been lost or mislaid, it is impossible to follow the record consecutively; but it is known that Jas. A. Thomson was president in 1860, perhaps also previous to that date, and continued in office until 1878, when Jos. Latter was elected, and held the position till 1888. David Martin was appointed president from 1888 to 1891, when he was succeeded by A. W. Forfar in 1892, and by Wm. Carmichael in 1893. Mr. Carmichael is still in office. Among those who have acted as secretaries may be mentioned G. M. Jacques, from 1875 to 1881; Henry Thomson, from that date until 1891; David Martin, till 1893; and D. W. Thomson, the present efficient secretary.

At the time of incorporation, upon careful examination, the library was found to contain 1,108 volumes in good condition, classified as follows: Biography, 124; History, 144; Fiction, 177; Works of Reference, 28; Literature, 131; Religious, 210; Travels, 121; Science and Philosophy, 77; Poetry and the Drama, 35; Miscellaneous, 61.

Since incorporation the number of volumes has increased to 3,651, classified under the following heads: Biography, 324; History, 382; Fiction, 874; Literature, 319; Science and Philosophy, 335; Travels, 363; Religious, 528; Miscellaneous, 382; Poetry and the Drama, 79; Reference, 65.

Number of volumes issued during the year ending April 30th, 1896: Biography, 120; History, 192; Fiction, 1,112; Literature, 639; Science and Philosophy, 78; Travels, 77; Religious, 338; Miscellaneous, 173; Poetry and the Drama, 40; Reference, 6.

Total issue, 2,775; number of members, 85.

Board of Management for current year: President, William Carmichael; Vice-President, George Elliot; Treasurer, David Martin; Secretary, David W. Thomson; Librarian, John Buchanan.

Directors: Robert Martin, John Parsell, Joseph Tingle, Isaac Chester, Archibald W. Forfar.

In 1846 a small frame library building was erected near St. Andrew's Church, and within a short distance of the spot on which David Thomson cut down the first tree. Although this unpretentious-looking little structure has answered an admirable purpose for half a century, it has long since ceased to be worthy of the treasures it contains, or to afford the accommodation required, and it is now certain that a new and commodious brick structure will be provided on a neighboring site nearer to the church and on the opposite side of the road. An edifice of this kind for such a use is one of which any community should be proud; the best situation in the locality is not too good for it, and there is little doubt that all will unite to make the new building worthy of its purpose, and to maintain the high state of efficiency so long held by the Scarboro Library.

As this goes to press, the building, a commodious structure 26 x 36 feet, is in course of erection, and will probably be completed in time to be inaugurated during the centennial, June 17th and 18th. The walls are of brick, on a stone foundation, and the edifice, though plain in exterior, will be commodious and attractive within, and must prove a source of much pleasure and a little pride to the patrons of the library. Mr. Carnaghan, Chairman of the Building Committee, has made himself most commendably active in his efforts to complete the erection.

HIGHLAND CREEK PUBLIC LIBRARY.

At the present day, owing to the vast number of newspapers, magazines and periodicals of various kinds, the want of books is not so likely to be felt as when there was a dearth of literature, and it is an evidence of a desire for something more substantial than mere news gossip, and monthly doles of from second or third to tenth-rate stories, when people feel the want of high-class books, including works of reference, history, biography, science and travel. Actuated by this spirit, and no doubt fully aware of the advantages so long possessed by their up-stream neighbors, the residents of the eastern side of the township resolved to establish a Mechanics' Institute Library, entitled to a "legislative grant per annum." A meeting of prominent persons was accordingly held at Highland Creek in December, 1889, when it was decided to ask for incorporation, and an active committee was appointed to canvass the neighborhood for subscribers at $1 per annum. Fifty-five names were procured, and on January 28th, 1890, the Institute was incorporated. The first annual meeting was held in Elliot's Hall, on Tuesday, the 13th of February following, when there were elected: Wm. Tredway, President; Robert Cowan, Vice-President; Henry Westney, Secretary-Treasurer; A. J. Law and T. C. Kirkham, Librarians; Chas. Humphrey, T. G. Parker, A. T. Elliot, J. H. Richardson, James Duncan, B. F. Closson, J. W. Stanion and L. Lewis, Directors; Arthur Reeve, sen., and James Pratt, Auditors.

The available funds were not large, consisting of $110, of which $25 was a grant from the Township Council, and $30 a donation from the Highland Creek Literary Society. On March 1, 1890, the Highland Creek Library was opened, and before the close of the year its membership numbered fifty-nine.

Beginning with 167 well-selected volumes, additions have been made annually, until at this date there are upwards of one thousand books in the library, with a circulation of nearly two thousand. The following table shows its condition, as per official statement for the year ending April 1st, 1896:

	No. of Vols. Purchased.	No. of Vols. in Stock.	No. of Vols. Issued.
Fiction	40	236	586
Voyages and Travels	18	201	555
History	34	175	499
Miscellaneous	40	190	421
Biography	10	82	102
Science	11	102	133
Poetry	5	24	35
Religious	6	20	42
Literature	..	8	20
Works of Reference	2	13	15
Total	166	1,051	2,408

Amount of money expended in books, $115.79; value of books in library, $758.30.

BEN. F. CLOSSON, *President.*
A. T. ELLIOT, *Sec.-Treas.*
MARK TAYLOR, *Librarian.*

CHAPTER XIII.

DOCTORS AND LAWYERS.

"No one is more estimable than a physician who, having studied nature from his youth, knows the properties of the human body, the diseases which assail it, the remedies which will benefit it, exercises his art with caution, and pays equal attention to the rich and poor."—*Voltaire.*

"Just laws are no restraint upon the freedom of the good, for the good man desires nothing which just law will interfere with."—*J. A. Froude.*

UNDER this heading we are limited mainly to the medical men of the township, the few lawyers connected with it, either by birth or other reason, finding more profitable centres elsewhere.

A very respectable list of medical practitioners, who have found Scarboro a desirable locality from an early period of its settlement, will engage our attention. Several are native to Scarboro, and of these a fitting opportunity serves at this juncture for giving their names, as well as the names of certain divines and lawyers who are, or were, sons of its soil.

Among the medical men we find: Opie Sisley, M.D., C.M.; Samuel R. Richardson, M.D.; Jos. Richardson, M.D.; Samuel Richardson, M.D.; Russell Taber, M.D.; Stephen Taber, M.D.; Wm. Lapsley, M.D.; Marshal Macklin, M.D., C.M.; David A. Clark, M.D., C.M.; William Irving, M.D., C.M.

Among the ministers: Revs. James Richardson, Ezekiel Richardson, J. J. Elliot, B.A., A. G. Bell, B.A., James Thom, and Albert D. Wheler.

Among the lawyers: John Bain, Q.C., Jas. Baird, B.A., G. W. Badgerow, T. A. Gibson, B.A., and John Thom.

DOCTORS.

In dealing with the medical men of Scarboro we find much that is not only characteristic of the men, but of the times to which they belonged, and certain of them demand a more enlarged notice than do those who, living in our own day, are governed by its conventionalities.

The township, as far as our records go, went on very well until 1829 without a resident doctor. At that date, R. D. Hamilton, M.D., a canny Scotsman from Lanarkshire, came over by way of New York to Canada, settling in Scarboro on the Danforth Road, near Bunker's Hill, but afterwards residing with his brother-in-law, John Torrance, on lot 24, concession D.

He was "a happy old bachelor who had loved and lost." Rather eccentric, and quite self-dependent, he could do his own cooking and mending, and sew on his own buttons. But notwithstanding his eccentricities, Scarboro loved him as she would a generous, noble-minded friend. He was at home everywhere, and used to say that no matter where the dinner-horn blew he knew there was a glad welcome for him.

Dr. Hamilton was a highly educated man and a great reader. He was also a writer, and produced a work in two volumes, on the principles and practice of medicine on the plan of the Baconian philosophy, quoting from, and criticising freely the works of, Hippocrates, Galen, Newton, Cullen, Lavoisier, Aristotle and Lord Bacon. Of some of the old writers he quaintly said: "They have written on the loss of health in the same romantic style as Milton on the loss of Paradise."

The stock of medicine carried by Dr. Hamilton, as compared with the present-day deluge of drugs, was very limited, consisting merely of a few powders stowed in his pockets, but a minimum assortment was balanced by a maximum dose. A pet nostrum of his, especially after bleeding, consisted of: calomel, 8 to 10 grains, and antimonial powder, 5 to 6 grains, given in one bolus. An ardent advocate of purgatives, no argument convinced him that their use could by any possibility prove harmful.

He had been an army surgeon, and had seen actual service at Corunna and in other engagements, and his army training, no doubt, accounted for his freedom with the lancet, and his advocacy of the then usual practice of bleeding, as a specific for "all the ills that flesh is heir to," especially diseases that were of an inflammatory nature.

It is told in this connection that on one occasion when old David Thomson had pneumonia, Dr. Hamilton bled him each day for nine consecutive days, taking at least a pint of the crimson fluid on each occasion. The hardy old pioneer not seeming to improve under this heroic treatment, Dr. Paterson, of Markham, was called in, in consultation, when they decided to bleed him again, making the tenth bleeding he had undergone. The patient appearing no better, hope was abandoned, and the relatives were summoned to the bedside. But the story concludes with Thomson's recovery, and a four years' longer lease of life for the patient.

An odd tale is told of another of Scarboro's hardy sons who, having had his ear bitten off by a horse, took the severed member in his pocket, and walked a very long distance to consult Dr. Hamilton, who successfully re-united the parts.

As the worthy old doctor never kept a horse, he had to be sent for, and taken home—generally on horseback—the messenger mounting with the doctor, or walking behind. It is said the horse was never put beyond a walk, however urgent the case.

He was conservative both in medicine and politics, and under the name of "Guy Pollock"* wrote some pungent articles in the city papers.

He died in 1857, at the age of fifty-seven years, and was buried in St. Andrew's graveyard, being put, according to his own request, twelve feet under ground. In his panegyric at the grave the Rev. J. Bain said of him, that he "was the beloved physician, the beloved of the country-side."

The next medical man to settle in Scarboro was Dr. Graham, who came to the township in 1834, and took up his abode at Gates's Hotel. He also was a Scotsman, from Lanarkshire, and, like Dr. Hamilton, lived a life of celibacy. He was of fair complexion, of a fine physique, tall, erect and athletic, with a prepossessing countenance and a courtly manner. He was very fond of sport, and kept a blood-horse, being in his element in a race, or in hot chase after a fox.

Dr. Graham's loyalty and conservative principles took him out as a volunteer in 1837. After the rout at Montgomery's Tavern, he, as did others, helped

*Guy Pollock, whose name Dr. Hamilton assumed, was a contentious blacksmith, but not at all of a literary turn. Reference is made to him in Chapter IX., Trades and Tradesmen.

himself to one of the horses left behind by the "rebels." He was then boarding with a Mr. Lawrie, of the opposite political stripe, who, on learning the facts of the case, would not allow the horse in his stable, nor the doctor to remain under his roof.

In his profession Dr. Graham was skilful and much liked; he was not so ardent an advocate of the lancet as his brother-physician, though he by no means neglected its use.

He died at a comparatively early age in 1847, and was buried in St. Andrew's graveyard, where a modest little monument marks the spot.

In 1842, or about that year, Dr. Winstanley took up his residence in Scarboro. He was an Englishman, and the son of an English Church clergyman who held a living in this province (some say in Scarboro township). The Winstanleys were of an aristocratic family, and the doctor was the first of his profession in Scarboro to keep a handsome turn-out, which consisted of an English dogcart and a fine horse in English harness. Like Dr. Graham, he was fond of hunting and sports in general, for which there were plenty of opportunities in the township at that period.

Dr. Winstanley remained in Scarboro but a short time, removing to Yonge Street, not far from Toronto. But he was fond of the beautiful scenery of the Heights, and built a delightful summer cottage on the acclivity a little west of Victoria Park, where he spent his summers for many years before failing health confined him to his town residence, where he died.

Dr. Hipkins, who came to Scarboro about 1849, was of English extraction. He established an excellent practice during the four years of his stay, and was very popular. He removed to Toronto.

Dr. Bain was born in Kirkaldy, Scotland, his father being Rev. Jas. Bain, of St. Andrew's Church, Scarboro. He began practice under his father's roof about 1856, but left the township about a year afterwards, and died at an early age.

Dr. Baker, who came to Scarboro about 1853, was a Canadian, and graduated from the Medical Board of Upper Canada, his degree being signed and sealed at Quebec by the Earl of Elgin and Kincardine, on the 25th April, 1853. The same year, in the pleasant month of June, he married Emily, the widow of Francis Earls, of Toronto, and commenced practice. Dr. Baker is said to have been the first medical man in Scarboro to carry a medicine case.

Six weeks subsequent to the birth of her first child (a son, who survived both father and mother, dying in England in 1889), Mrs. Baker died, and shortly afterwards Dr. Baker went to New York Hospital and took a two years' post-graduate course. Returning, he practised in Toronto and Scarboro until shortly before his death, September 25th, 1861.

Dr. Harvie, who settled in Scarboro about 1857, was an American who had formerly taken up his abode in Durham County, Ont., practising at Enniskillen, Darlington township. He stayed but a short time in Scarboro.

Dr. William Lapsley, a Scarboro boy who now resides in Toronto, carrying on a consulting and office practice, is a graduate of Toronto School of Medicine. In 1861 he settled at Woburn, in his native township, where he practised for twenty-seven years and established a fine connection, besides making a number of warm friends. In 1888 he went to Toronto, where he is frequently referred to as consulting physician. One of his sons is also a member of the medical profession.

Dr. Lorenzo Dow Closson, who was born near Chautauqua, N.Y., in 1829, was the successor of Dr. Hamilton, by whose influence it was that he received the appointment of surgeon to the 3rd Battalion of York militia. He has filled the responsible offices of coroner for the united counties of York and Peel, and medical health officer for the township of Scarboro. For upwards of forty years he practised in Scarboro and its vicinity, until his naturally strong constitution gave way under the continued strain of a large and laborious practice, and he was obliged to retire. Since then Dr. Closson has resided in Toronto, his elder son, Dr. John H. Closson, being in practice in that city. Dr. Closson's name is still a household word in Scarboro; no other physician ever spent so long a period in the practice of his profession in the township, and probably none whose time and talents were more cordially devoted to her welfare.

Dr. John Closson, an elder brother of the former, also practised here for several years, during the same period.

Dr. Duncan James Pollock came to the township in the first year of the American civil war, 1862. He was a son of Charles Pollock, of Hamilton, Ont., and settled at Ellesmere, occupying a brick cottage on the 1st concession. He was a bachelor, and his sister kept house for him. He commenced the practice of his profession very young, notwithstanding which he soon became popular, and his practice rapidly extended throughout Scarboro, and into the townships of York and Markham. He was also coroner of York township.

Dr. Pollock was an enthusiastic curler, and a member of the Ellesmere Club, and was at one time its president.

After about twenty years of residence in what half a century had made a populous township, the heavy labor of a rural practice began to tell on him seriously, and he retired to a less arduous field in Toronto; but, owing to a long period of overwork, an organic disease was developed which ended his bright career at a comparatively early age. He died in the south on the 26th November, 1879.

Dr. Samuel R. Richardson was born in Scarboro. He practised for a short time on the Markham Road, near Woburn, about 1882. He spent two years as assistant superintendent of the Toronto Asylum for the Insane, under Dr. Joseph Workman, the most distinguished of Canadian alienists, and was for two years professor of materia medica and therapeutics, and lecturer on diseases of the mind and nervous system in Victoria Medical School. Dr. Richardson has been in Eglinton for upwards of sixteen years.

Peter McDiarmid, M.D., born in the Ottawa Valley, began his medical profession in 1866, having selected Scarboro as his field of practice, choosing Malvern as his place of residence. Dr. McDiarmid succeeded Dr. Pollock, and continued his practice with marked success for four years (1871 to 1875). As a man he gained the respect and confidence of the community. His removal to the States was deeply regretted by his numerous friends.

One of the few medical men who have spent a quarter of a century in the practice of their profession in

Scarboro, is Dr. Duncan McDiarmid, elder brother of the last named. A man of a modest, unassuming manner, and of a kind and sympathetic nature, he wins the love and respect of his patients, and his opinion is commonly looked upon as final, so completely do they trust his professional judgment. Dr. McDiarmid was born near Ottawa, and came to Scarboro in 1870, where he is still active, hale and hearty.

Dr. William Irving, now of St. Mary's, was born in Scarboro in 1847. He taught school in section No. 2, and graduated at Trinity Medical College in 1874. He practised for a time in East Toronto, and subsequently in his native township, when he removed to Exeter, and afterwards to Kirkton. He has been in St. Mary's for eight years, and now enjoys a lucrative practice. He is an active politician, and is President of the Perth County Reform Association. Dr. Irving is credited with the belief that Ontario is the finest country in the world, and that Scarboro is by all odds the best township in Ontario.

Drs. Joseph and Samuel Richardson, the younger brothers of John Richardson, M.P.P. for East York, both enjoy lucrative practices, the former in Chicago, and the latter in Strathroy, Ont.

Dr. Hunter came here in 1888, settling at Woburn. His practice extended mainly toward the eastern part of the township and about Highland Creek, where he enjoyed a large patronage. He was a man of considerable ability. He left Scarboro in 1890.

Dr. George Robert Cruikshank was born at Weston, York County. He entered upon practice at Ellesmere in 1886, but after four years left to take a post-graduate course at Edinburgh. Returning to Canada, Dr. Cruikshank settled in Windsor, where he now resides.

Opie Sisley, M.D., C.M., was born in Scarboro in 1863. Matriculating in Arts in Toronto University, he entered at the same time the Toronto School of Medicine, graduating in 1888 and becoming a Licentiate of the College of Physicians and Surgeons of Ontario the following year. He first settled at Ellesmere, but moved to Agincourt in 1894, where he still resides. For four years Dr. Sisley has been coroner for the County of York and medical health officer for the township of Scarboro.

Dr. Clapp is the latest addition to the long line of illustrious physicians who have taken up residence in Scarboro township during the century that has elapsed since the first opening was made in the mighty forest. He came to the township in 1893, and settled at Scarboro village, where his health has materially improved, and he is able to attend to a good practice. More fortunate than the majority of his brethren in the profession, Dr. Clapp enjoys a private income, and in the season is able to indulge his fondness for hunting in the wilds of Muskoka, or the solitudes of Nipissing.

LAWYERS.

Thomas Alexander Gibson, B.A., youngest son of John Gibson, born June 22nd, 1866, studied at Markham High School and Toronto Collegiate Institute, matriculating at Toronto University in 1884 with first scholarship for general proficiency. Graduated with highest honors in classics in 1888, and at once entered upon the study of law with the firm of Fullerton, Cook & Co. Called to the bar in 1891, and formed a partnership with W. R. Cavell, under the firm name of Cavell & Gibson, with offices at 43 Adelaide Street

East, Toronto, where he continues the practice of his profession.

Matthew A. Hall is a Scarboro boy, who has won considerable success as a lawyer in Omaha, Neb., where he is partner in one of the principal legal firms in the city. Few men in the state are considered capable of rendering a sounder or more profound opinion on matters of law than he is, and his reputation as an honest lawyer is equal to his fame as a counsellor. Mr. Hall is one of the many young men that we are proud to connect with our township.

John Bain was the son of Rev. James Bain, of Old St. Andrew's Church. He was called to the bar in the Province of Ontario, in the year 1866, and appointed Queen's Counsel in the year 1887. Mr. Bain was solicitor for the Imperial Bank and other large corporations, and had a large and influential practice. He died at the age of forty-six, in the year 1893.

George Washington Badgerow was born May 28th, 1841, in the township of Markham, but spent much of his early life here, assisting his father in the management of a woollen mill, on lot 16, concession 2. At the Markham High School, where he ranked as the best student, he qualified for a public school teacher, and having secured a situation he walked eighteen miles twice a week after school-hours to take lessons in the higher departments from a tutor. He studied law in Toronto, and was called to the bar in 1871. He represented East Riding of York in the Local Legislature as a Liberal from the year 1879 to 1887, and was appointed County Crown Attorney for the county in 1887. Mr. Badgerow was an enthusiastic member of the United Workmen order, of which he was Grand Master for two years; Supreme Overseer in 1884, Supreme Foreman in 1885, and Supreme Master Workman of the A.O.U.W. of America, in 1886. He died 31st of July, 1892.

James Baird, a member of the firm of Lobb and Baird, was born in Scarboro village. He is a son of Jonathan Baird, who formerly kept hotel near the Grand Trunk Railway, in the village. He received his early education in S. S. No. 9, and went to Toronto Collegiate Institute in 1876, Toronto University in 1878, and graduated with the degree of B.A. in 1882, was called to the bar in 1885, and is now practising law in Toronto in the above firm.

John Thom, a Toronto lawyer, is also said to have been born in this township.

CHAPTER XIV.

SOCIETIES.

"To understand man, however, we must look beyond the individual man, and his action or interests, and view him in combination with his fellows."—*Carlyle.*

THE records of the various societies that have existed in Scarboro township from time to time, are not so full as could be desired, but such as we are able to give are most creditable to the moral sentiment of the township.

The first temperance society of which we have record, was instituted in 1834 in what is now School Section No. 5, by the Rev. James George, minister of St. Andrew's Presbyterian Church. The following is a partial list of the members: David Elliot, Walter Elliot, James A. Thomson, Adam Bell, Agnes McLevin, Margaret Reeve, Margaret Elliot, Thomas White, William Forfar, jun., Wm. Paterson, Mary Johnston, Margaret Glendinning, Catharine Bowes, Ellen Elliot, Agnes Bell, Teasdale Hall, Hugh Elliot, Thos. Paterson, Sophia Durham, Jane Reeve, Matilda Elliot, and Thos. Bell.

In S. S. No. 2, the first "regular" temperance organization was that of Mount Meldrum Division Sons of Temperance, instituted in 1855, on lot 24, concession 1.

It is still in a most flourishing condition, and has been a great power for good in building up a sound temperance sentiment in the community. Its numerous members, past and present, have carried its principles to almost every part of our Dominion.

The present place of meeting is Temperance Hall, Agincourt, lot 24, concession 3.

Its charter members were: John D. Thomson, David G. Thomson, James Elliot, Archibald A. Thomson, Andrew A. Thomson, Richard Ryan, Thomas A. Little, Samuel Harvey, James Scott, Archibald Elliot, Thomas Scott.

In 1862 Scarboro village had a Temperance Society Building, but no further record has been furnished.

School Section No. 2 can boast of a camp of the Sons of Scotland at Agincourt. Its charter members are William Johnston, John Johnston, James F. Elliot, David Wyper, Alexander Weir, James T. Stewart, William Docherty, Alex. Docherty, William Anderson, Wm. Green, J. Irwin, Wm. Crawford, John Chisholm, John Elliot, Joseph Irwin, George Baxter, Francis Weir, Wm. B. Davidson, John Martin, J. C. Angus, R. Craig, James Ogg, D. McDiarmid, M.D., Rev. J. A. Brown and Wm. Thomson.

Court Highland Creek, No. 1089, I.O.F., was instituted in June, 1892, with the following staff of officers: A. T. Elliot, C.D.H.C.R.; James Duncan, C.R.; W. J. Morrish, V.C.R.; J. R. Dale, M.D., Phy.; W. H. Closson, Fin.-Sec.; W. Stitts, S.W.; R. Parker, S.B.; W. H. Tredway, P.C.R.; John Plaxton, Chaplain; Robt. Cowan, Treas.; Henry Reeve, Rec.-Sec.; David Mosher, J.W.; James Atkinson, J.B. The court commenced with a charter membership of twenty-one and has had a steady growth ever since, having for its members the best citizens of the locality. Among the recently initiated brethren are Rev. John Chisholm and Chas. A. Drummond, M.D., the latter being elected as associate physician. There has not been a death in the Court since its commencement, and the applications for sick benefits have been very few. All the work is carried on in the name of Liberty, Benevolence and Concord, meeting fourth Tuesday of each month in Elliot's Hall.

There are three brass bands in the township :

Highland Creek Band, the members of which are J. Thorne, A. Collins, J. Gormley, A. Law, E. Collins, Geo. Sprunt, W. Bennet, A. Neilson, and C. Humphrey.

Scarboro Village Brass Band, the members being W. Collier, F. Secor, Geo. Sprunt, E. Cornell, J. Cornell, J. McIlmurray, J. Fawcett, J. Hammond, J. Chester, A. Taylor, and W. Miller.

Ellesmere Band, named the "Maple Leaf," includes W. Glendinning, Sidney Thomson, T. Whiteside, F. Bell, Richard Thomson, J. M. Thomson, Andrew Paterson, John Walton, Albert Mason, — Loveless, and Harry Thomson.

There is a Mouth Organ Band at Malvern, consisting of A. Callender, C. Callender, W. Bennet, Andrew Thomson, J. Clayton, E. Willis.

Another organization of a similar kind has recently been formed at Agincourt with a numerous membership, of which the leader is J. Dixon; Sec.-Treas., W. Young; President, N. White; and the players, J. Dixon, and W. Bennett (on the guitar), W. Gorman, W. Paterson, E. Heron, R. Johnston, J. Kennedy, W. Bennett, J. A. Johnston, S. Shedlock, L. Thomson, and L. Glendinning (on the mouth organ).

CHAPTER XV.

PUBLIC-HOUSES AND STORES.

"Whoe'er has travel'd life's dull round,
Where'er his stages may have been,
May sigh to think he still has found
The warmest welcome at an inn."
—*Shenstone.*

"What is true of a shopkeeper is true of a shopkeeping nation."
—*Tucker, Dean of Gloucester.*

PUBLIC-HOUSES during the pioneer days were places of very considerable importance. Many farmers on well-travelled roads turned an honest penny by providing "entertainment for man and beast." In most cases liquor was supplied, but not always. Among the first hosts in the township were David Thomson, Levi Annis and Jonathan Gates. The inn of the last-named was a noted stopping-place on the Kingston Road for many years, and on two occasions was thought to be of sufficient importance for circus exhibitions.* But besides the respectable hostleries, such as those mentioned, there were found at short intervals along the leading roads numerous places where whiskey might be procured; whiskey, too, on which had been paid neither duty to make, nor license to sell. About 1831, and no doubt for many years both before

* A wild beast show and circus was exhibited at Gates's in 1843; another in 1845.

and after that date, there is said to have been no fewer than twenty-four houses between Highland Creek and Pickering where whiskey could be had.

In 1835 Mr. John Bell, who came to Scarboro about 1820, from Durham, Eng., and settled on lot 29, concession C, erected the "Blue Bell Inn," which soon acquired a high reputation. After the building of the Nipissing Railway this famous old hostlery ceased to pay, and was pulled down about 1876.

Hockridge's Hotel, nearly two miles farther north, was built about the same time, but was opened slightly before the "Blue Bell." The building was destroyed by fire about 1878, but had ceased to be a hotel eight or ten years before.

In the fall of 1847, Richard Sylvester commenced hotel-keeping on the south-west corner of lot 34, concession 1. Ten years later Mr. Sylvester moved the building to the north-east corner of lot 35, concession D. The hotel business was discontinued in 1870, and in 1872 the house became the property of John Tingle, who forthwith moved his stock-in-trade into it, and in April of that year opened the old bar as a general store.

Elliot's Inn was on the Kingston Road, not far from where St. Margaret's Church now stands.

Mr. Moffat kept a hotel on the south-west corner of lot 35, concession C. This place was known as "The Royal Oak."

Another noted hostlery was the "Painted Post," on the Danforth Road, near the Scarboro and York town-line.

Sixty years ago the "William Wallace Inn" was kept by John Muir, on lot 16, on the old Kingston

Road, and about the same time a beer-shop and store stood on the road opposite the old log school-house between lots 18 and 19 on the south side. The owner of this place was Wm. Burton.

Mape's Inn on the Markham Road is mentioned in the municipal records of the Home District for 1849. But the first hotel between Toronto and Markham is said to have been kept by Richard Taylor on the Danforth Road, lot 26 (no concession is named).

John Malcolm's tavern, "Speed the Plough," was on the Markham Road, lot 19, concession 2.

Robert Malcolm succeeded him, and also kept a harness shop on his fifty-acre farm, early in the "fifties," but gave up the business about 1856.

Sisley's hotel was on lot 23, concession D, on the place known as Bunker Hill.

Dowswell's (now Woburn) was on lot 18, concession 1.

STORES.

A Mrs. Betsy Stafford is said to have been the first storekeeper in the township on the Pioneer Thomson farm, within a stone-throw of St. Andrew's Church and the Public Library; and it is thought that a store, opened in S. S. No. 8 about 1843, by Paul Sheppard, on lot 35, concession D, was the next. Sheppard was succeeded by Samuel Blackburn. This store was discontinued about 1846.

J. J. McBeth opened a store at Wexford in 1865, and gave up business in 1879. In 1865 John Tingle also opened a store at Wexford.

Wm. Burton kept a small store on the south side of the Kingston Road, opposite the school-house between lots 18 and 19.

CHAPTER XVI.

VILLAGES AND POST-OFFICES.

"I visit such tranquil spots always with infinite delight."

—*Oliver Wendell Holmes.*

"The post is the grand connecting link of all transactions, of all negotiations. Those who are absent, by its means become present; it is the consolation of life."—*Voltaire.*

THE selection of place-names by Euro-Americans is nearly always a matter of caprice, without the remotest reference to topography, hence the curious jumble presented by the names of post-offices in Scarboro, although it is in this respect not so bad as are many other townships.

In Agincourt, Armadale, Ellesmere, and Wexford, there is no *court*, no *dale*, no *mere*, or no *ford* (*fiord*). In the hybrid Bendale, the *ben* is missing. Other post-offices are Brown's Corners, Malvern, Woburn, Danforth, Highland Creek, West Hill, Wexford, Scarboro Junction, and Scarboro. Among all these names are represented England, Scotland, Ireland, and France, without any degree of propriety except in the two instances of West Hill and Highland Creek, although Danforth is allowable.

It is not too much to expect that the General Post-office authorities may yet see the necessity of exercising some measure of discretion in matters of this kind, and that they will give the preference to Indian names, or to English ones, which, if not characteristic of the localities, are at least less absurd than many already bestowed.

Highland Creek village is one of the oldest commercial centres of the few extremely modest ones that ever existed in the township, owing to the proximity of Toronto. At the eastern intersection of the Danforth and Kingston roads, it was once of more comparative importance than it now is, although yet a point where considerable local traffic is maintained. A Catholic, a Methodist, and a Presbyterian church are situated at short distances of the point at which the roads cross each other.

Woburn possesses the town hall.

Scarboro village comprises about forty acres, as shown on a plan registered in the registry office of the County of York, being the south-east part of lot 19, concession D. The property was owned by Isaac Stoner, and sold by him in the fall of 1855, by auction, in lots containing one-fifth of an acre up to one acre. Some choice quarter-acre lots sold as high as $428.

The Grand Trunk Railway erected a station at this point, at which a large business was transacted in the shipment of flour and grain during the years 1856 to 1859, when, in consequence of the heavy grade, the station was moved one mile farther west. Most of the lots have merged into farms and gardens.

The chief buildings here are a brick school-house, the Methodist parsonage, a building for the sale of every description of farming implements, a general store, a blacksmith shop, and a few dwellings.

The first post-office in the township was on lot 19, concession D, the first postmaster having been

Peter Secor, who held the position from the date of establishment in 1830, to 1838.* On the removal of the office to lot 17, concession D, Col. McLean became postmaster, and so continued until 1853. Other postmasters have been W. Tredway, Donald McLean, M. Rosebush, and the present official, J. Knights.

It may be mentioned as an evidence of how facts may become merely matters of tradition in a comparatively short time, that in the books of the Post-office Department at Ottawa, there is not a scrap of information pointing to the establishment of this office in 1830. Here, therefore, we are indebted to the memories of "oldest inhabitants" and to local documents.

Agincourt rejoices in having two railway stations—one on the Canadian Pacific, and the other on the Midland branch of the Grand Trunk. It is, next to Scarboro Junction, the most populous village in the township, and does a good local trade.

Agincourt post-office was opened June 1st, 1858, the first postmaster having been John Hill, who was succeeded by John Miller, who was followed by J. W. Kennedy. The present postmaster is W. A. Kennedy.

It is said that Mr. Hill, having made many vain endeavors to get a post-office established here in connection with his general store, happened one day when in Ottawa (perhaps on this business) to meet a member of parliament representing a constituency in Quebec, where Mr. Hill originally came from. Asking Hill if he could do anything for him, the desirability of a post-office was mentioned. The

* Mr. Secor's sympathy with Mackenzie was what led to this change.

M.P. said at once, "I'll put that through for you, but you must let me give the office its name." Within a short time Mr. Hill was appointed postmaster of *Agincourt*, pronounced locally *Aigincourt*, even the "*t*" being sounded.

Danforth post-office was opened on April 1st, 1859. Henry Hogarth held the office of postmaster until his death, on April 16th, 1883, when his daughter Agnes was appointed. Miss Hogarth is still in charge.

Scarboro Junction post-office was opened on July 1st, 1873, George Taylor being in charge. He was succeeded by Robert Davidson, on March 7th, 1876. He continued in office until February 20th, 1888, when the present postmaster, R. Bell, was appointed.

A considerable area of farm land has been laid out at the Junction as village or town lots, most of which as yet forms only an extensive common.

At this point the Midland branch of the Grand Trunk Railway unites with the main line.

Malvern has the largest public hall in the township, and here are held the principal political meetings in the district. With seating accommodation for 1,000 persons, it is in frequent demand for lectures and concerts. During the curling season, the basement of the hall affords capital rink-space for the Scarboro Club. In this village also there are blacksmith, waggon, and harness shops.

The other places are so small as to require no particular notice here, containing as they do little more than the post-office, a small store, a blacksmith shop, and sometimes a church and a hotel. Numerous incidental references to these little centres occur in the foregoing chapters.

POST-OFFICES IN THE TOWNSHIP OF SCARBORO, DATE OF ESTABLISHMENT, AND NAMES OF FIRST POSTMASTERS.

NAME OF POST-OFFICE.	DATE OF ESTABLISHMENT.	NAME OF POSTMASTER.
Agincourt	June 1, 1858	John Hill.
Armadale	April 1, 1869	Robert Harrington.
Bendale*	April 1, 1878....	William Forfar.
Brown's Corners	September 1, 1888	David Brown.
Danforth	April 1, 1859	Henry Hogarth.
Ellesmere	June 1, 1853	A. Glendinning.
Highland Creek	July 6, 1852.....	— Chamberlain.
Malvern	November 1, 1856	David Brown.
Scarboro	(No record in P.O.	Department, Ottawa)
Scarboro Junction ...	July 1, 1873	George Taylor, sen.
West Hill	June 1, 1879	John H. Richardson.
Wexford	March 1, 1865 ...	J. T. McBeath.
Woburn †	July 6, 1852	Thos. Dowswell.

The foregoing statement is from the department of the Postmaster-General, and may be considered, therefore, authoritative.

Beginning with the oldest, the order of seniority is as follows: Scarboro, Highland Creek and Woburn, Ellesmere, Malvern, Agincourt, Danforth, Wexford, Armadale, Scarboro Junction, Bendale, West Hill, and Brown's Corners.

* Formerly Benlomond. † Formerly Elderslie.

CHAPTER XVII.

MILITIA.

"Deeds Speak."
—*3rd Reg. York Militia Banner, 1812.*

"O heard ye not of Queenston Heights—
Of Brock who fighting fell—
And of the Forty-ninth and York,
Who 'venged their hero well?"
—*Mrs. S. A. Curzon.*

UPON the declaration of war by the United States against Great Britain and her colonies on June 18th, 1812, the men of Scarboro responded loyally to the call to arms.

From a letter written by Colonel Chewett, 3rd Regiment of York militia, to "Captain Thompson,"* in which reference is made to his company, in conjunction with the Pickering and Whitby companies, we gather that the Scarboro men were attached to that regiment, and from the family records of the township we know that they were with General Brock at Detroit, when Hull surrendered on August 16th, 1812.

From Burlington Bay to the shores of Lake Erie the road lay through the forest; but Brock's men were all volunteers and hardy woodsmen, accustomed to life in the New World and loyally devoted to the defence of their country. They often had to bake bread before they could have supper, when they halted for the

* This is evidently meant for David Thomson, the pioneer.

SCARBORO'S DEFENDERS.

night. Many rolled the dough hastily together and covered it with hot ashes; others, more patient and ingenious, impaled theirs on forked sticks, and setting them on end in the ground close to the fire, turned the dough about until it was baked, their patience being rewarded by having lighter and cleaner bread than that baked in the ashes.

Part of the way along the shores of Lake Erie before they reached Long Point, was narrow, and the waters of the lake so rough that it was often difficult for the men to avoid a wetting from the incoming waves. At one spot they were obliged to wait until they receded, and then run for a slightly wider margin before the succeeding swell could overtake them. General Brock, who was ever one with his men, enduring the same trials and discomforts, tried when his turn came, to follow the example of the men, but, being less nimble, the wave caught and drenched him thoroughly. He, however, endured the soaking quite good-naturedly, and hurried on as though nothing had happened.

The General embarked his men at Long Point in a number of small boats used by the settlers for the transport of their corn and flour, and after four days and nights of incessant toil reached Amherstburg, a distance of two hundred miles.

The passage was a stormy one, and the conduct of the men in the face of such difficulties won Brock's admiration.

After the surrender of Detroit, the volunteers returned to York, where some of the Scarboro men were retained as reserves during the campaign on the Niagara frontier, but the majority were with Brock at Queenston Heights. Several men from our township were badly wounded. John and Andrew Kennedy were of this number, the latter having had his leg shot away by a cannon-ball. The Secors, Wilsons and others received injuries. Upon the return of the regiment to York, the Scarboro company was with it when a banner,* worked by the women of Toronto, was presented to it by Miss Powell.

After York was taken by the Americans, on April 27th, 1813, many of the Scarboro men who were among those included in the articles of capitulation and therefore under parole until exchanged, returned to their homes; some of them, no doubt, taking advantage of enforced inaction to attend to the ploughing or seeding on their land. †

Tradition says that a number of Scarboro men were among "FitzGibbon's Tigers."

The graves of many of these early defenders of Canada are to be found in St. Andrew's cemetery.

Among the records of those who defended the country against the invaders in 1813, the name of Jas. Elliot occurs. Elliot was at home (about fifteen miles distant) when he heard the three cannon-shots, which were the pre-arranged signal intimating the approach of the American fleet. He ran all the way to

* A full account of this banner and its presentation is given by Miss M. A. FitzGibbon, in "Transaction No. 1 of the Woman's Historical Society of Toronto," 1896.

† This is not improbable, as, in his accounts of the campaign of 1813 on the Niagara frontier, FitzGibbon speaks of the militiamen and settlers who joined him when they heard firing in the woods. Others may have fought in the ranks with the 49th, known as the "Green Tigers." The militiamen were at that time frequently mingled with the regular regiments, fighting in the same ranks. The nature of the ground and the character of the warfare rendered this commingling of the men of the militia with the regulars a mutual support.

York, and arrived at the moment of the blowing up of the magazine. The concussion was so great that it loosened the plaster from Mr. Playter's house at Scarboro. Another account speaks of Wm. Pherrill who was detached as signal-man at the outlook post on Scarboro Heights, with orders to mount his horse and ride into York with the tidings the moment he spied the American vessels in the distance.

Although the story of Elliot's hastening to York upon the report of the signal guns comes from various sources, and is probably correct, he must certainly have reached the town before the blowing up of the magazine, as the guns were fired before eight o'clock on the evening of the 26th.

That our old defenders were jealous of the honor and integrity of the regiment to which they belonged, the following curious petition to Sir Peregrine Maitland, then Lieutenant-Governor of Upper Canada, testifies. It is copied from the original draft on the water-lined paper of the date:

"*To His Excellency Sir Peregrine Maitland, K.C.B., Lieutenant-Governor of Upper Canada and Major-General commanding His Majesty's forces therein, etc., etc., etc.*

We, the Undersigned Non-Commissioned Officers and Privates of the —— Company of the 2nd Regiment of York Militia, beg leave to approach Your Excellency with the purest sentiments of Loyalty and Attachment to His Majesty's Person and Government, who has given us an additional proof of his paternal care for this distant part of his extended Dominions in placing over us as his Representative an Officer of Your Excellency's distinguished Rank and Character.

Feeling as we do, that nothing can be nearer Your Excellency's Heart than the preservation of that

Honor and integrity in all ranks of the Officers of the Militia of this Province, which as a Military Character You must always have revered, we come before your Excellency with the more confidence to state what we humbly conceive to be derogatory to the Honor of the Corps to which we belong.

Captain Daniel Brooke,* who has been appointed to the command of the —— Company, has been publicly accused by his Brother-in-law with Felony and other heinous offences, which accusations have never to our knowledge been satisfactorily answered, in Consequence of which, without any evil Intention of opposing the Laws of the Country, we unthinkingly determined not to serve under a person of his Character.

We are now, however, fully convinced of the tendency our conduct had to Insubordination, and are sorry we should have been guilty of such Misconduct, and will in future faithfully discharge our duty under the orders of any person Your Excellency may appoint over us. Nevertheless, we shall feel much gratified should Your Excellency be pleased to grant us the Indulgence of placing another Officer in the room of Captain Brooke,* whom we can never respect as a Man, however we may be inclined to obey his orders [as] a Captain in the Militia of Upper Canada.

We are, with the highest sentiments of Esteem, Your Excellency's most obdt. and very humble servants:

Richard Thomson, Adna Bates, jun., Gideon Cornell, Earl Bates, George Cornell, Andrew Thomson, Thos. Sweeting, Wm. Jones, David Thomson, Archibald Thomson, Peter Little, Christopher Thomson, James Thomson, John Martin, James Taylor, Andrew Johnston, Joseph Secord, William Thomson, Levi Annis, John Miller, Thomas Adams, Wm. Robinson, John

* He owned the bush in York township which, in after years, formed a rendezvous for the notorious "Brooke's Bush Gang." This Brooke had no connection with a family of the same name in the township, one of whom was a well-known old stage-driver.

Crosby, James Daniels, William Thomson, John Thomson, James Thomson, Peter Secor, Amariah Rockwell, Isaac Secor, Peter Stoner, Jonathan Gates, John Laing, Stephen Pherrill, John Stoner, Abraham Stoner, Adna Bates.

Scarboro." *

The Scarboro militia met annually for drill on the King's birthday, June 4th, at Sisley's Hotel on the Danforth Road. In 1828, about 120 men assembled.

One of the features of the muster, after salute and roll-call, was treating the men to a drink of beer, which was carried round in a pail.

The men at this time were not very proficient in drill, and it is said that an Irish officer in command of one of the companies often remarked, "It is hard work to get them in order, even to give them a drink of beer."

In 1860 they were drilled at Woburn by the late Colonel R. Denison.

In 1836 the officers in command of the 3rd Regiment of East York or Scarboro militia were: Colonel, A. H. McLean (January 19th, 1836); Lieut.-Colonel, R. D. Hamilton; Major, Wm. Proudfoot; Captains, J. McDonnell, A. Glendinning, Wm. Thomson, J. Torrance, James Gibson, John Taber, G. H. Fitz-Gerald, Joseph Secor (January 9th), John Howell; Lieutenants, D. Graham, J. Willaghan, D. Knowles, David Stobo (or Stoner), Wm. Pherrill, J. B. Street,

* The document is not dated, and there is no record among the papers as to whether this unique petition was granted. It probably was, and a better man than the objectionable captain appointed. The petition of which this is a copy is in the possession of Mrs. W. Carmichael, who kindly permitted us to use it here. Mrs. Carmichael is a granddaughter of the pioneers David and Agnes Thomson.

John Wilson, Alex. Grant (January 20th), A. McDonnell; Ensigns, W. J. FitzGerald, Thos. Chester, James Wentand, John Elliot, John Kennedy, John Pilkey; Adjutant, G. H. FitzGerald. There is no Quartermaster or Surgeon. Limits: Township of Scarboro.

The men of Scarboro did not aid the "rebels" in any way during the outbreak in 1837. An old resident remembers seeing Matthews (who was a native of Pickering) and his followers going up the old Kingston Road at about nine o'clock one night. They carried a white flag, and endeavored to persuade all whom they met to join them, making prisoners of those who refused. Among the latter was a shoemaker named Small who, in his usual condition of *high spirits*, marched with them, singing "Rule Britannia," and when they stopped at Gates's, tried to burn their flag.

When the "rebels" threatened Toronto, the loyalty of the Scarboro men was practically expressed. They marched out four hundred strong. A number of these men are still living, including Hugh Elliot, Isaac Chester, James Weir (the two latter are over eighty years of age), and several others. They were enrolled and commanded by Colonel Allan McLean, formerly a captain in the 91st British Regiment. He had seen service in India, and was a very popular man in Scarboro.

Our Volunteer Rifle Company was organized in the autumn of 1861, largely through the efforts of J. R. Taber. The first meeting was held in a house built by G. Chester for J. Rose, directly opposite the Scarboro post-office.

The officers were: Captain, W. H. Norris; Lieut., J. R. Taber; Ensign, Wm. Tredway, who subsequently resigned, giving place to R. H. Stobo; Color-Sergt., H. Chester; Sergeants, Isaac Stobo, R. C. Bowen, David Atchison; Corporals, Jas. Allison, Jas. Law, Robt. Martin, Wm. McCowan; Bugler, Jas. Hartley. Rank and file: R. Cornell, J. Dowswell, T. Scholes, H. Chester, I. Stobo, R. Stobo, W. Taber, G. Rush, C. Bowen, H. Bowen, T. Bowen, W. Churchill, J. Cann, Wm. Hall, J. Atwell, J. Leslie, J. McHenry, J. Duncan, J. Lennox, A. Hatrick, J. Ellis, J. Brumwell, H. Callender, J. Huxtable, J. McCann, J. Bell, J. Dawson, J. Smith, W. Kizer, W. Collins, Wm. Purdie, J. Booth, R. Taber, R. Stoner. Total, 44.

At the first review held in Toronto after the Company was organized, and when it had been brought to its full strength of 64 officers and men, it received great praise from the inspecting field-officer for the excellence of the men's marching, and steadiness under arms.

Scarboro's patriotism was again severely tested at the time of the St. Alban's Raid. She sent a well-drilled company to the front, which remained at Niagara from January 1st till May 1st, when it returned to Toronto. It was sent to Dunnville in 1866 to guard the Grand River dam above the Welland Canal, and prevent threatened damage by rumored sympathizers with the Fenians. It remained there three months, being billeted on the townspeople.

They had returned home only nine days, when they were again ordered to the front to repel the Fenians.

They went from Toronto to Port Dalhousie by steamer, thence to Thorold by the road, and were detained there through lack of a sufficient number of railway cars. When they reached Frenchman's Creek they found the bridge had been burned by the enemy. On Sunday morning they marched into Fort Erie, in open order, double file, one hundred feet apart, forming the connecting link between the advance guard and Colonel Lowry's battery.

The Scarboro company was considered by both British and American officers the finest at the front, where it remained about six weeks. The average height of the men was 5 feet 10 inches. Wm. Purdie and Russell Cornell were sergeants of the company.

The following composed the Scarboro Rifle Company in 1865-6: Captain, W. H. Norris; Lieuts., J. R. Taber, R. H. Stobo; Color-Sergt., H. Chester; Sergeants, Isaac Stobo, R. C. Bowen, David Atchison; Corporals, Jas. Allison, Jas. Law, Robt. Martin, Wm. McCowan; Bugler, Jas. Hartley. Rank and file: W. Purdie, W. Allison, J. Allison, J. Smith, G. Burton, H. Callender, C. Rose Robinson, J. G. Kizer, A. Bertram, C. Gentleman, D. Hosken, G. Pherrill, W. Taber, J. Bowen, L. Higgins, J. O'Brien, R. Whittington, E. Moody, J. Secor, J. Lennox, R. Cornell, J. Post, W. Post, D. Galbraith, L. Armstrong, W. Roach, J. Bell, J. Ellis, sen., J. Ellis, jun., J. Acheson, J. Hartley, J. Leslie, J. Munro, H. Carrick, J. Chester, W. Wilson, J. Ormerod, L. Bowen, R. Bowen, H. Bowen, J. Brumwell, W. Hall, W. Churchill, J. Dowswell, W. Dowswell, G. Rush, J. Duncan, R. Williams, J. Scholes, M. Murdoch, T. Booth, L. Butler, W. Hewitt. Total rank and file, 55.

S. S. No. 9 has been the centre of organization and headquarters of the militia and volunteer company of Scarboro.

A number of commission papers, some medals and several swords are still held with loyal pride as heirlooms by families in the section as memorials of the military life of the township.

There is no militia company in existence now; but should there arise a need for men to defend the country, Scarboro would be as ready to prove her loyalty to the British flag as her sons were in the past.

NOTE.—Since the above chapter was written, a contemporary M.S. account, corroborative of some of the foregoing statements, has come to light. We quote:

"On Monday, the 26th April, about six o'clock p.m., we received intelligence that the enemy's squadron were in sight from the Highlands, standing in shore about ten miles east of York. The signal guns were fired. . . .

"Colonel Chewett was in command of the unembodied militia of the town and neighborhood. . . . Adjutant-General Shaw, who lived in the neighborhood and knew every foot of the ground, was commanded to lead the militia, in Major Allan's absence,* and prevent the enemy from turning our flank and to support the Indians.

"The fall of Captain McNeal, at the moment of making a charge against the enemy's riflemen, and the heavy loss sustained by the 8th, threw them into confusion. The militia driven back, retreated to the ravine in front of Elmsley's house.

"Then General Sheaffe decided to retire to Kingston with his staff and regular force, and deputed Colonels Chewett and Allan to make the best terms they could with the enemy."—*Jarvis Papers.*

* Major Allan having been sent in another direction by Major-General Sheaffe.

CHAPTER XVIII.

BIRDS AND BEASTS.

> **"He prayeth well, who loveth well**
> **Both man, and bird and beast."**
> —*Coleridge.*

MR. A. W. FORFAR supplies the following list of mammals and reptiles that have been met with in the township, but most of them are now seldom, or never seen:

"Black bear, wolf, lynx, carcajou, fox, raccoon, porcupine, skunk, woodchuck, otter, beaver, marten, mink, weasel, hare, black, red, grey and flying squirrels, chipmunk, four kinds of mice, two kinds of moles, and at least one kind of deer.

Reptiles were never very numerous; two kinds of turtle; black snake, milk snake, copperhead, garter snake, two kinds of small brownish snakes (one with the under side a bright crimson, and the other a light brown merging into a light yellow); three lizards (one very small, red; one about four inches long, brown; and one about nine or ten inches, bluish slate color, with large yellow spots).

There were, and are, also four kinds of frogs, and two of toads."

The last black bear was shot on lot 21, concession B, in the winter of 1885, after a very exciting hunt, by Isaac Stobo and Robert Callender. Bruin had located himself in a cave on the face of the high clay cliffs which border on the lake, and seemed determined to "hold the fort," from which he was dislodged only with great difficulty. Mr. Stobo retains the skin of this animal as a valuable, almost as an historical, keepsake.

Deer were plentiful. Even as recently as sixty years ago, small herds of them were often seen drinking together at the dams of the old saw-mills, and it is recorded that one man has shot as many as fourteen in a day. Two were observed on the lake shore in the winter of 1895.

Birds of all kinds were much the same as those in other similarly situated parts of the Province, except perhaps that eagles were more numerous about the Heights. An eagle shot there four years ago measured about seven feet from tip to tip of its wings. A few yet appear, but they are seen more seldom every year. Proximity to Lake Ontario brought immense numbers of water fowl up the numerous streams. Pigeons flew in such incalculable numbers that they were killed when flying over hills—men, women and boys knocking them down with poles,—especially when the weather was a little foggy.

Wm. Humphrey asserts that his father, in 1834-35, made more money shooting quail than he did when threshing grain with the flail, at the rate of every tenth bushel for his pay. The birds came to feed off the grain, and Humphrey disposed of his game at a remunerative figure in York.

Hundreds of sand-martins still nest along the precipitous portions of the cliffs, but not now in numbers comparable with those of former years, when less disturbed by man, and not at all by sparrows.

FISH.

The streams might almost be said to have been alive with fish, including sturgeon, suckers, mullet, shiners, alewives, whitefish, herring, salmon-trout, brook-trout, pike, maskinonge, perch, and black, white, and rock bass. It was not uncommon for farmers to lay in a stock from the Scarboro streams, and for this purpose anglers came from Markham and other places, to return only when they had secured one or more barrels of fish. A man named Tommy Young is said to have speared three barrelfuls during one night in Highland Creek.

The re-stocking of the township waters is a subject that ought to occupy attention. It would seem clear that sawdust was largely to blame in the first place for the depletion of the fish-supply, but latterly there is just as little doubt that the scarcity is owing to a disregard of times and seasons on the part of anglers, for the streams are now free from pollution. That the water becomes extremely low in the smaller creeks during summer is not a serious objection, for if fish-culture were undertaken in a business-like way, farmers, through whose lands the streams flow, might, at comparatively small cost, provide themselves with fish-ponds, the proprietorship of which should be as fully acknowledged as it now is in houses and cattle.

There is no reason why some scores of Scarboro farmers should not supply the Toronto market with brook-trout at remunerative prices. As in the case of other industries, fish-culture demands intelligence and skill. Of the former there is no lack here, and the latter would speedily be acquired.

CHAPTER XIX.

GAMES AND SPORTS.

"Who can enjoy alone,
Or, all enjoying, what contentment find?"
—*Milton.*

"If those who are the enemies of innocent amusements had the direction of the world, they would take away the spring, and youth; the former from the year, the latter from human life."—*Balzac.*

CURLING.

CURLING in Upper Canada, as a popular game, dates from about 1830. During the first half-century friendly contests on the ice were frequent, not only in Scarboro, but in Toronto, Bowmanville, Galt, Guelph, Fergus, Elora and other places where Scotsmen "most did congregate," emigration about that time having been largely influenced in consequence of the feeling of political unrest that prevailed in Great Britain, previous to the passing of the Reform Bill in 1832.

Numerous settlers brought with them their curling stones. Those who had failed to do so, and who were bound to curl, either fashioned field-stones for the purpose, or provided substitutes by sawing off sections from small logs of beech, or of birch.

Prominent among the early Scarboro curlers were the Clarks, Crawfords, Gibsons, Greens, Glendinnings, Youngs, Richardsons, Malcolms, Masons, Morgans,

Kennedys, Rennies, Patersons, Forfars, Sheppards, Stobos, Chesters, Thomsons, Hoods, Waltons, Elliots, Telfers, Raes, Badgerows, Broomfields, Bells, Smiths, Secors, Walkers, Martins, Purdies, Weirs, Lawries, Browns, Findlays, Nelsons, Crones, Scotts, Flemings,* Torrances, Hamiltons and Muirs, many of whom have long since crossed the "hog-score" in the great Rink of Time.†

Mrs. Wm. Purdie, of Malvern, has a distinct recollection of friendly matches having taken place about 1832 and 1833, and of seeing the players passing along the Kingston Road with their besoms.

It appears that an invitation having been sent by the Toronto curlers to those of the township on the "Front Road," John Torrance, of the "Back Road," agitated the formation of a rink embracing the players in his own neighborhood. Hence the rinks so-named.

The earliest club matches recorded came off in the winter of 1835-6, when the Torontos invited Scarboro to send one rink of eight players, and one stone each, as the game was then practised.‡

When this invitation reached Scarboro, there was considerable rivalry between the old and the young

*Andrew Fleming, one of the Auld Gang Siccars, possessed a marvellous ability in "running ports" and "chipping out" probable winners. His mastery of such tactics won for him the sobriquet of "The Duke," after the Duke of Wellington. It has been suggested that perhaps the word was originally connected with "jook" (Scot), *to dodge in and out*—among the other stones.

†"Pioneer David" himself was, no doubt, a keen curler, although circumstances prevented him from following the bent of his inclination. William Thomson (probably his father) was president of the Dumfries Curlers in 1772.

‡James Findlay's stone was known as "Loudon Hill," and John Torrance's as "Tinto."

CURLERS WHO PLAYED AGAINST TORONTO
IN 1835.

players as to representation on the challenged rink. The old hands referred contemptuously to the young fellows as "Wully Draigles," and the compliment was returned by the latter speaking of their seniors as the "Auld Gang Siccars." But this good-natured emulation was terminated by an agreement that the two parties should play against each other, the winners to enter the lists in opposition to the Toronto club.

The following is the result of this early match on Toronto Bay:

Auld Gang Siccars.	*Wully Draigles.*
James Findlay,	Walter Miller,
Robert Hamilton,	James McCowan,
Thomas Brown,	John Stobo,
Abraham Torrance,	James Green,
Archibald Glendinning,	John Gibson,
James Gibson, sen.,	Robert Scott,
Andrew Fleming,	James Weir,
John Torrance, skip...19	James Gibson, skip...27

Majority for the Wully Draigles, 8 shots.

In the match ultimately played with Toronto, Scarboro was confronted by Dr. Telfer, Alex. Ogilvie, Wm. Henderson, Alex. Badenach, John O. Heward, Hon. Justice Morrison, George Denholm, and Capt. Thomas Dick, skip, who, after four hours' hard play, were left lamenting to the tune of fifteen shots behind Scarboro, the score standing, Toronto, 16, Scarboro, 31, being within a shade of two to one.

Mrs. Thomas Patton distinctly remembers another curling match on the Highland Creek marsh, between Toronto and Scarboro. The men came in sleighs, and the horses were put into the barns, sheds and stables of her grandfather, Richard Beattie, who resided on lot 5, concession D. She thinks this match took place in the winter of 1841-2.

By the exertions of Robert Malcolm, of Toronto, an old Scarboro boy, a match was arranged for in the fine covered rink of the Maple Leaf Club at Ellesmere, on the 17th of March last, the anniversary of the saint whom Scotland bequeathed to the Emerald Isle. It was at first the intention that four of those who *skelpit* Toronto sixty years ago should take part in this game, Scarboro against Old Countrymen (chiefly Scots); but, unfortunately, James Gibson was unable to be present, and James Weir, though on the ice and intensely interested, did not play. The ages of the staunch old Britons averaged between seventy and eighty years, and of the Scarboro chiels, nearly sixty years. The game lasted three hours, and the ice was all that could be desired.

The score stood as follows:

Scarboro.	*Britain.*
R. M. McCowan.	Jas. McCowan, sen.
Wm. Patton.	S. Kennedy.
Geo. Elliot.	John Gibson, sen.
S. Rennie, skip........19	R. Crawford, skip....15
T. Gibson.	G. Empringham.
A. Bell.	A. Doherty.
R. Thomson.	Wm. Hood.
I. Stobo.	A. Fleming.
A. Malcolm, skip 15	R. Malcolm, skip 12
Total 34	Total 27

Much encouragement was given to the players by the presence of the genial, faithful and highly respected minister of St. Andrew's, the Rev. Donald Barclay Macdonald, and among the numerous spectators present, were: Mesdames D. R. Thomson, Christine Thomson, Anthony Ionson, Isaac Stobo, Adam Richardson, Robert McCowan, George Chester, Archibald Paterson, Robt. Forfar, Tilmuth Pherrill, Wm. Young, Thos. Weir and Wm. Doherty; Misses E. Hood, V. Forfar, A. Richardson and Nellie Carson; Messrs. Francis Armstrong, David Forfar, Thos. Whiteside, John A. Paterson, David W. Thomson, Isaac Chester, sen., Francis Glendinning, James G. Thomson, James G. Paterson, Robert Thomson, Lyman Kennedy, John C. Clark, Anthony Ionson, James Gibson, William Mason, Joseph Forfar, Francis Mason, Joseph Teeson, sen., William Allenby, Henry Kennedy, Andrew Young, jun., Archibald A. Forfar, Robert Galbraith, James Ley, Alex. McCowan, Archibald W. Forfar, Alex. Baird, William Green, John Marshall, Robert Chapman, Robert Forfar, Wm. W. Walton, Wm. Young, Robt. Rennie, Tilmuth Pherrill, George Chester, Arch. Paterson, Wm. W. Thompson, James Cherry, Thomas Weir, Wm. Doherty, Abner Abraham, Albert Mason, Lawrence Jackson, William Milner, Joseph Teeson, jun., Ernest Forfar, John Glendinning, Robert Mason, David Forfar, jun., John Malcolm, Charles Milner.

After the curlers had taken lunch, they were arranged outside and photographed by J. C. Clark.

A return match was played in the magnificent Victoria Rink, Toronto, on the 20th of March, only three days after the last game, when Scarboro repeated its victory of sixty years ago with considerable improvement on the score, which on this occasion stood exactly 2 to 1 in favor of the township men, thus:

Scarboro.	*Toronto.*
T. Gibson,	D. Gibson,
A. Malcolm,	W. Summerfeldt,
R. Crawford,	B. Chapman,
A. Hood, skip 23	W. Forbes, skip 12
Simpson Rennie,	D. S. Keith,
Richard Thomson,	Geo. Taylor,
Adam Bell,	W. B. McMurrich,
Jas. G. Malcolm, skip...10	Kay Roberts, skip ... 5
John Gibson,	G. Waud,
Jas. Gibson,	Hugh Miller,
And. Fleming,	John Bain,
R. Malcolm, skip 11	Dr. Richardson, skip.. 5
Total 44	Total 22

Majority for Scarboro, 22 shots.

A very hearty wish was expressed among the players on both sides, that similar veteran matches, but on a larger scale, should be played annually, and it is likely this desire will be realized.

The Markham *Economist*, January 3rd, 1861, has the following:

CURLING MATCH, MALVERN.—The annual curling match between the five Canadian players from the east and the five Canadian players from the west side of the Markham Road, took place on Badgerow's pond on Friday, the 28th ult.

. . . . . .

Below is a list of the names of the players and numbers scored by each party:

East.	*West.*
James Fleming,	William Purdie, jun.,
Robert Fleming,	Peter C. Secor,
Wm. Fleming,	A. Glendinning, jun.,
Andrew Fleming, jun.,	R. Thomson, jun., skip.26
A. Malcolm, jun., skip..29	

The paper does not explain how the *four* players from the west matched *five* from the east, but on such occasions it was customary for one or more of the minority to play extra stones, so as to make the number of throws on both sides correspond.

HEATHER CLUB.

The Heather Curling Club, an offshoot from the Scarboro Curling Club, was formed at Burton's tavern, Markham Road, on the 31st day of December, 1862, when the following officers were elected, viz., John Gibson, Pres.; Arch. Glendinning, Sec.-Treas.

On October 22nd, 1863, a meeting was held to take into consideration the propriety of erecting a covered rink. J. Gibson presided, and Adam F. Macdonald, now the indefatigable Principal of Wellesley School, Toronto, was secretary. At this meeting, a committee, consisting of the President, Robert Crawford and James Robertson, was appointed to solicit subscriptions for that purpose. On November 5th this committee reported, when it was decided to proceed with the erection of the said covered rink, the same to be built on the farm of William Clark, lot 30, concession 4, and a Building Committee, consisting of the President, Hugh Clark, J. L. Paterson, Robert Crawford and Adam Armstrong, was appointed to have the matter in charge. The building was completed, and curling commenced December 16th, 1863. This is supposed to have been among the first, if not the first, of covered curling rinks in the Province. The first members of the club were William Clark (honorary member), John Gibson, Andrew Young, Arch. Glendinning, Hugh Clark, Thomas Gibson, James

Robertson, Simon Kennedy, John L. Paterson, Wm. Crawford, Robert Crawford, Wm. Clark, John Crawford, Adam Armstrong, Jas. Paterson, Jas. Young, Robt. Cunningham, George Gibson, Lockhart Rogers, James Clark (of Kentucky), Henry Kennedy, George Morgan, Adam Bell, Dr. Pollock, Simpson Rennie, Andrew Hood, William Rennie, Robert Gibson and John Clark.

In 1866 Thomas Todd, of Markham, gave a coat of arms to be competed for between the Scarboro and Heather clubs, which was won by the Heather Club.

On the 25th day of March, 1869, it was resolved to join the Royal Caledonian Club, and the name of the Heather Curling Club first appears in the annual for that season. On January 6th, 1870, the Heather and Waverley (of Cobourg) clubs, competed for a R.C.C.C. medal, which was won by the Heather Club. In January, 1872, the Heather unsuccessfully competed with the Toronto Club for a R.C.C.C. medal. The following year they won a R.C.C.C. medal from West Flamboro. In January, 1875, another medal was won from the Thistle Club, of Hamilton. In 1876 the Heather Club won a pair of curling-stone handles, presented for competition among the three Scarboro clubs, by Robert Malcolm, of Toronto, between the years 1862 and 1869. The Heathers played 63 matches with outside clubs, winning 36, losing 24, and 3 were ties.

MAPLE LEAF CLUB.

The Scarboro Maple Leaf Curling Club was organized in 1874, by a number of players belonging to the old Scarboro and Heather clubs, on account of the great distance many of the players had to travel to

CURLERS AND QUOITERS.

meet with other members of the latter organizations. Ellesmere was selected as headquarters, and the first president chosen was W. Glendinning, A. Young, jun., having been appointed secretary.

In 1878 the Maple Leaf Club joined the Royal Caledonian Curling Club Association, and about the same time erected a covered rink. This building collapsed in 1881, but in 1883 another and more substantial one was put up, and much new interest was manifested in the game.

The club has met and divided honors with representatives from the Hamilton Mechanics, Hamilton Thistles, St. Mary's, Guelph, Brampton, Whitby, Newcastle, Cobourg, Port Hope, Markham; the Granite, Caledonian, Prospect Park and Moss Park clubs, of Toronto, and the home clubs.

It holds several valuable trophies, including three silver cups, five pairs of curling-stones, and half-a-score of medals.

For several years they have been among the finals for "the tankard," to win which is still regarded as "a consummation devoutly to be wished."

The officers of the club at present are: Wm. Green, President; R. McCowan, Vice-President; Rev. D. B. Macdonald, Chaplain; Committee of Management, H. Thomson, A. Paterson, W. Young, A. Mason, W. O. Walton, A. T. Paterson; Secretary and Treasurer, R. Forfar. Members: R. Thomson, A. Richardson, Robt. Green, F. Bell, J. Chester, George Chester, George McCowan, J. Stobo, W. Chester, N. Malcolm, Wm. W. Walton, and R. Buchanan.

The Maple Leaf stands ready to accept challenges from the world, to play on Ellesmere ice.

QUOITING.

This game has been played in the township with enthusiasm for upwards of sixty years. The first club was organized in 1858, and was the outcome of a championship contest held in Toronto, under the auspices of the Caledonian Society, when Messrs. David Johnston and A. Muir, both Scarboro men, carried off the medal. Instead of deciding as between themselves, they very public-spiritedly undertook to form a club, placing it in possession of the medal, to be held against all comers. Besides the two gentlemen named, there were Messrs. John Holmes, jun., Edmund Jacques, Richard Thomson, Simon Kennedy, Walter Glendinning, John Stark, and nearly fifty others. The first member of the new club to win the medal was John Holmes, jun., who also won a cup in a quoiting match. Messrs. A. Muir, E. Jacques and R. Thomson have since held the medal.

The length of pitch was arranged at 21 yards between hobs, with natural sod ends. After this club became defunct, a new one under the old name, "Scarboro Quoiting Club," was formed in 1870. President, Geo. Morgan; Secretary-Treasurer, David Brown; Umpire, Andrew Hood. In this club the length of pitch was regulated at 18 yards, clay ends.

Several contests between the home club and those of Galt and Ayr resulted invariably in favor of Scarboro.

In an international match against a picked team from various noted quoiting centres in the United States, Scarboro won by 365 points. Besides the officers of the club above named, other members were Geo. Sheppard, Simpson Rennie, Walter Glendinning,

Wm. Purdie, David Purdie, Richard Sylvester, Alex. Muir, James Patton, D. Lawson, D. Smith, W. Brotherson, R. McCowan, W. McCowan, J. W. Kennedy, J. Rippon, J. Ley, John Walton, T. Pilkey, J. Allen, Geo. Robinson and Isaac Thomson.

The membership having dwindled considerably, a new club was organized in 1891.

The largest prize which has come to Scarboro for quoiting supremacy was won by Wm. Purdie, jun., in a Toronto contest, when he carried off a $50 prize—$42 cash and a pair of steel quoits.

It is proposed that a match shall take place on the occasion of the present centennial celebration, between those who are over and those who are under forty years of age. Players are to be residents of Scarboro on one side, against all comers.

Among the earliest quoiters in the township was John Torrance, who won a championship silver medal at the Athletic Games in Toronto, in 1840, and which is still in possession of his descendants.

CRICKET.

Scarboro Cricket Club was organized over forty years ago with Alex. Muir as the first Sec.-Treas., John Muir as Captain at one time, and Chris. Moody at another.

Among the players were Chris. Moody, Guy Stoner, Ed. McGann, Ed. Stevens, David Secor, Ira Bates, Alex. Purvis, Isaac Fawcett, Dan. Scrivner, Joseph Armstrong, John Muir.

After some years, the club became greatly diminished on account of removals and deaths, but received a new lease of life, when the following names were added to its list of players: Peter, William, James and Sidney Purvis, D. Brown, W. Brown, James Patton, P. Ellis, T. Ellis, G. Ellis, John Clark, D. Stoner, D. Purdie, James Law, John Law; Captain, James Purvis. They played matches with Weston, Markham, Unionville, and Ellesmere.

There is now a good club, called by the same name and embracing some of the players of former clubs. Indeed, the present one is the continuation of the former organizations. The present captain is D. Beldam; players, Charles Beldam, Geo. Taylor, J. E. Spark, John Gormley, J. Ormerod, Harry Ormerod, R. Callender, C. Callender, D. Brown, Arthur Law and Ab. Law. Matches were played with Markham, Pickering, Toronto, Old Fort, East Toronto and West Toronto Junction. Out of ten matches played in last season, *i.e.*, 1894-95, eight were won.

There is another cricket club at Ellesmere.

FOOT-BALL.

There are five foot-ball teams: "The Aborigines," of Highland Creek; "Scarboro Village," "Rangers," "Maple Leaf" and "Union," all composed of alert, muscular young Scarboronians, who thoroughly enjoy a good "kick," and who maintain an excellent spirit of friendly rivalry among themselves.

CHECKERS.

There is no field of amusement in which her sons have taken a higher place than in the realm of checkers. We believe that no part of our broad Dominion has produced so many enthusiastic and ardent lovers of the game as has the township of Scarboro.

The first public match in Scarboro of which we can find any authentic account was played at Malvern, between East and West Scarboro in 1853. The players representing the west were Adam Core, John Muir, Wm. Mills, J. L. Paterson and Jas. Paterson. Those of the east were Andrew Fleming, sen., Robert Fleming, William Fleming, E. R. Jacques, Thomas Jacques, jun., and John Jacques. The West won the match.

Checkers was now quite extensively played, and local matches were of common occurrence for several years.

In 1859 Markham players challenged Scarboro to play a match in Markham village, with twelve a side; the Scarboro men went on the day appointed, but found no opponents. A bloodless victory!

The *Economist* (Markham), March 27th, 1862, says: "Early in the forepart of last year a movement was set on foot in the township of Scarboro for the purpose of making arrangements for a 'draught tournament.' . . . Thirteen competitors entered the lists. Four prizes were given: John Muir, sen., first and championship; James Fleming, second; Andrew Fleming, sen., third, and Alexander Muir, fourth.

E. R. Jacques, who competed for first, was debarred from contesting for second."

For some years after this time lively engagements for supremacy took place between the clubs of Scarboro and Toronto.

The *Economist*, April 2nd, 1863, says: "A highly interesting contest at 'draughts' between the players belonging to Scarboro and Toronto clubs, came off on the 28th of March, 1863, in the city of Toronto, resulting in favor of Scarboro by three games.

Scarboro.	Won.	*Toronto.*	Won.	Drawn.
Jas. Fleming	3	J. Arnold	3	0
R. Fleming	4	J. Cruthers	0	2
Jos. Purvis	3	J. K. Gordon	2	1
E. R. Jacques	4	D. McDonald	1	1
Andrew Fleming, sen.	1	J. Drynan	4	1
John Muir, sen	2	W. McDougall	4	0
Total	17	Total	14	5

A return match was played at Malvern on May 25, 1863, and resulted in another victory for Scarboro by three games. The Scarboro players were John Muir, sen., Andrew Fleming, sen., E. R. Jacques, James Fleming, Jos. Purvis and R. Fleming.

The Toronto players, unwilling to accept defeat at the hands of a country club, challenged Scarboro to a third contest, with twelve players a side. The match was arranged for October 16th, 1863, at Woburn. Only three of the Toronto club put in an appearance —their best three. The following is the score:

Scarboro.	Won.	*Toronto.*	Won.	Drawn.
J. Muir, sen	1	M. Rooney	1	4
E. R. Jacques	4	J. Jeffrey	0	2
R. Fleming	1	J. K Gordon	1	4
Total	6	Total	2	10

Majority for Scarboro, 4 games.

This, as the score indicates, was a closely-contested match, but was another decided victory for Scarboro.

In the winter of 1864 the Grand Draughts Tournament was arranged in Toronto, where the best players of Canada met to measure their strength. Scarboro was represented by John Muir, E. R. Jacques, and Robt. Fleming. Five prizes were offered. R. Fleming secured the second.

The year 1867 witnessed another match between Scarboro and the metropolis of Ontario—two players a side. E. R. Jacques and Wm. Fleming represented Scarboro, and Dean and Varcoe, Toronto. The match took place in Toronto, and six games were played with each opponent, making twenty-four games in all. Scarboro won 17 games, Toronto 3, and 4 were drawn.

After Mr. Fleming left the township in 1869, and Mr. Jacques's death in 1872, checkers from occupying a prominent place, seemed to have died out for a time, although the township was never without its "remnant" of good players and playing. Lately the game has again come to the front, and Scarboro to-day may be said to be a township of checker-players. There is a board in almost every house, and there are organized clubs at Ellesmere, Woburn, Malvern, and Hill Side, each with a large membership. Out of these numbers there will no doubt yet arise some David to slay the present Goliaths, and win for this Scarboro of ours the proud title of "champion of the world."

Among the chief players who have made the name of Scarboro famous in connection with the "Dambrod"* mention should be made of Adam Bell, who still lives on lot 22, concession 2; John L. Paterson, lot 27, concession 3; Adam Core (a native of Biggar, Scotland), who may be called the father of checker-playing in this township; James Jackson, now of

* From *dame*, or *dam*, any woman, or a lady, each piece of old being so designated; and *brod*, a board. Until quite recently the game was known by no other name in Scotland.

Orillia; John Jackson, millwright; John Elliot, from Newcastle-on-Tyne; James Lawrie, of lot 12, concession 3; Walter Hood; William, his son, now champion of Manitoba and the North-West Territories; the late George Morgan; George Chester; John Muir, the champion of 1862; Joseph Purvis; E. R. Jacques, who composed and published numerous games and positions, and was for many years recognized as Canada's greatest player; Dr. Thomas Jacques; Andrew Fleming, who settled on lot 9, concession 3, in 1834; Robert Fleming, son of Andrew, now of Dunedin, New Zealand, where his influence in furthering the game has been very marked; and William Fleming, his brother, born in Scarboro in 1841. Further reference to the last-named gentleman may not be out of place. When only twelve years of age he played in a match between East and West Scarboro, drawing two games out of six played against Adam Core. A few years later he played in several team matches against Toronto, and invariably won. In 1867 he made a tour of Canada, during which he lost but one game out of about two hundred, winning all the rest with the exception of ten or twelve draws.

In 1868 he held the championship of Canada, since which time he has defeated almost every noted checker-player in the Dominion. He has published a large number of original games, and is the author of many critical positions, which have been highly spoken of by the best authorities.

In 1887 Kelly, of Winnipeg, challenged him for the championship and $100 a side. Kelly resigned without having won a game. In the same year Kelly repeated the challenge with a stake of $50 a side, and this time Fleming defeated him with a score of 6 to 1.

WILLIAM FLEMING,

CHECKER CHAMPION.

Having held the championship of Canada until opposition to his claim had ceased, he resigned the proud title in 1890, with the record of not having lost a match in twenty-two years.

The names of some of Scarboro's present players are Wm. Young, J. Reynolds, Wm. Miller, Adam Bell, Alex. McCowan, Joseph Teeson, jun., Wm. H. Paterson, Wm. Paterson, A. W. Forfar, Robert Galbraith, Robert Thomson, Albert Mason, Thos. Walton, Frank Bell, James Ley, David Marshall, Lawrence Jackson, Robt. Forfar, John Malcolm, Frank Hancock, John Martin, Robert Martin, Joseph Teeson, sen., Walter Green, William Milner, Horace Thomson, Charles Milner, Hugh Doherty, Ernest Forfar, Alexander Doherty, William Doherty, T. Ramsay, John Lowry, Robert Jackson, James Maxwell, David Brown, Wm. Irwin, James Clayton, George Hough, T. L. Willis, Emerson Maxwell, John Weir, James Weir, Thos. Weir, Robt. Sisley, Joseph Ormerod, John Lawrie, Robert Sellers, A. McPherson, Alex. Neilson, Wm. H. Jacques, James Murison, James McCreight, Andrew Murison, Arthur Wells, Donald Reesor, Fred. Collins, Miss M. Collins, Frank McCreight, Robt. Collins, John Murison, William Stotts, Robert Neilson, H. A. Burrows, Wm. Patton, Geo. Chester, Russell Cornell, Robert Green, William Carmichael, Vipond Sparks, W. H. Chamberlain, Wm. Green, F. Wheler, H. White, W. White, L. Morgan, James Paterson, J. L. Paterson, John Lawrie, Jas. Lawrie, sen., Wm. Closson, Wm. Morrish, David Leslie, Wm. Stephenson, James Shackleton, J. H. Richardson, W. J. Haycraft, W. Latham, Rt. Callender, Miss Fanny Callender, and E. L. Oliphant.

SHOOTING.

Shooting has always been a favorite sport in this township. Here, as elsewhere, it is to be feared that the right to use fire-arms has sometimes been exercised irrespective of the rights of the lower animals, which, indeed, were not supposed to have any.

Our birds are no longer subjected to indiscriminate slaughter, and public sentiment condemns the old-time practice of shooting at the protruding heads of living turkeys and geese through a hole in the top of a box. In those days competitors drew lots to decide the order of firing, and he who first shot off the exposed head received the fowl as his prize. A target now takes the place of the bird, the winning shot, as a matter of course, being that which hits nearest to the centre.

Mr. J. C. Clark supplies the following information relative to the township rifle club:

The Scarboro Rifle Club was organized in 1886. The preamble sets forth, "That we, the members of the Scarboro Rifle Association, desiring to encourage and foster the sport of rifle shooting, and to develop accuracy in the use of that weapon, and to engage in friendly competition with like associations, do hereby adopt the following as our Constitution, by the terms of which we each and all agree to be governed."

The officers were: S. Rennie, Pres.; T. M. Whiteside, Vice-Pres.; A. W. Granger, Sec'y; and J. W. Kennedy, Treas.; with about forty members.

A silver cup was given for competition by W. M. Cooper, of Toronto, and a silver medal by the President, S. Rennie. It was arranged to shoot for the medal at ranges of one hundred and two hundred yards, off-hand, and for the cup at ranges of four hundred, and five hundred yards, any position, head to the target, the medal or cup to be the property of the member winning it three times. The medal was won by A. H. Canning, and the cup by J. C. Clark. A diamond scarf pin was won by J. E. Angus in a club competition, at ranges of one hundred and two hundred yards.

In 1889 the Association joined the Ontario Off-hand Rifle Association, and shot in the various matches of the season, competing in the annual tournament at Orillia, where they secured third place, members also winning valuable prizes in individual competitions.

In 1892 a challenge appeared in the sporting columns of the Toronto papers, from the Howard Club, of Ridgetown, to shoot any club in the Province, distance one hundred yards, with a rest. This was promptly accepted by the Scarboro Club, and conditions were arranged accordingly, teams to consist of fifteen men a side, to shoot five shots each, result to be determined by string measure.

The Scarboro Club succeeded in beating their opponents by about forty-five inches. Their scores were: Jas. Rennie, 3¼ inches; A. Paterson, 4⅝ inches; B. Dixon, 5¼ inches; R. Rennie, 5¼ inches; Thos. Hood, 5⅜ inches; J. W. Kennedy, 5¾ inches; J. F. Davison, 6¼ inches; G. Chester, 6¼ inches; S. Rennie, 6⅜ inches; A. H. Canning, 6⅝ inches; Wm. Rennie, 7½ inches; J. E. Angus, 7⅞ inches; J. Chisholm, 10¾ inches; R. McCowan, 11⅞ inches; R. Canning, 12 inches.

The present officers of the club are: A. McPherson,

President; J. Chisholm, Vice-President; J. C. Clark, Sec.-Treas.

The rifles in most common use are Winchester, Martin, Bullard, Ballard, and Remington, of 32-40, 38-55, 40-60, 40-56, 45-75 calibre. The target of the Dominion Off-hand Rifle Association is used for ranges of one hundred and two hundred yards.

LAWN TENNIS.

Lawn tennis as a club game is of somewhat recent date in Scarboro as in most parts of the Province, although for many years previous to the formation of the Agincourt Lawn Tennis Club, a number of ardent adherents of other field sports met frequently on the private lawns of J. C. Clark, near Agincourt, and the first tennis of the township was played there.

Prominent amongst the lovers of field sports who assembled there were that veteran baseball enthusiast, Geo. H. Ramsay, B.A., Dr. D. A. Clark, W. D. Skelton, J. M. Field, B.A., R. S. Rennie, Geo. H. Deane, J. C. Clark and a few others, who formed the nucleus of the very prosperous club which organized in 1892 under the following officers: Honorary President, Dr. O. Sisley; President, J. C. Clark (J. P.); Vice-President, W. A. Kennedy; Secretary, Dr. D. A. Clark; Treasurer, G. H. Ramsay; Captain, G. H. Deane; and practice was continued on the lawns of J. C. Clark and Dr. Sisley, Agincourt.

Many matches were played during that season with uniform success against Weston, Deer Park, East Toronto, Stouffville, Thornhill, Lindsay and Uxbridge, the club suffering defeat at the latter place only.

In 1895, the courts of the club were constructed at

Agincourt, the membership materially increased, and much was done to popularize the game, which now bids fair to be one of the leading sports of the summer season.

A series of handicap matches was arranged and played amongst the individual members, G. H. Deane being the winner.

The present officers are: Honorary President, J. C. Clark, Esq.; President, O. Sisley, M.D.; 1st Vice-President, W. A. Kennedy; 2nd Vice-President, A. J. Smith; Secretary, G. H. Deane; Treasurer, R. S. Rennie.

From the contents of this chapter it will be seen that the people of the township participate largely in the recreative. Indeed it may be in some measure on this account that they enjoy their present general prosperity. Social friction rubs off the rough corners, and friendly intercourse, with consequent exchange of ideas, leads to improvement æsthetically as well as materially.

Games and amusements in Scarboro have never been allowed to degenerate to the merely mercenary level. They are indulged in, not as ends, but as means, and the results may be seen in all the best of the numerous happy homes that dot the township, from York to Pickering, and from Markham to Lake Ontario.

CHAPTER XX.

ODDS AND ENDS.

"Those scraps are good deeds past."—*Shakespeare.*

MR. JOHN GOLDIE, an eminent Scottish botanist, set out on a pedestrian tour from Quebec, on June 4th, 1819, for scientific purposes; and on the 25th of that month he made the following entry in his diary:

"As I did not intend to go into York, I travelled to-day but slowly, sometimes in woods and sometimes in cleared land. Before mid-day I passed a creek which lay very low, so that the road is very steep on each side. All the declivity on the east side was completely covered with the *Penestemon pubescens*,* such a quantity of which I never expected to see in one place. For a number of miles to-day I passed through barren, sandy, pine woods, which it is probable will never be cleared. In the morning I met a number of Indians and squaws. One of them was very drunk. He told me he was crazy with taking too much bitters this morning. One of them had no clothing upon him, except a piece of cloth about a foot in length and breadth, which hung before him.

"I stopped for the night six miles from York, there being no other inn upon this road nearer to it. As I

* The common beard-tongue. The flower has some resemblance to foxglove.

SCENES IN SCARBORO.

was only a short distance from the lake, I went to it, but found the shore at least two hundred feet high, and very abrupt, in some places almost perpendicular, so that it was with considerable difficulty that I could approach the water. Having bathed in the lake, I returned to my lodging. This day was very pleasant, there being a considerable breeze, which both kept a person cool, and kept off those tormentors, the mosquitoes. Thermometer, 76."

The foregoing extract is made from the manuscript, by the courtesy of Dr. J. Caven, son of Principal Caven, and grandson of Mr. Goldie.

The old house now standing near Scarboro post-office, and formerly the residence of Col. McLean, was erected by Capt. Richardson, who, while living here, built the steamer *Canada*, at the mouth of the Rouge.

The first brick house was built on lot 24, concession B, in 1831, by Stephen Pherrill.* It is still in good repair. About the same time the late James Jones built one on lot 28, concession C, having made his own bricks.

The first house in school section No. 7 was built of planks by Wm. Cornell. It was afterwards used as a hotel. Mr. Cornell also made the first clearing in this section.

A schooner, laden with marble slabs and tea, was wrecked on the beach, off the cliffs, about forty years ago.

* One writes that the name was Adna Pherrill, and the number of the lot 25, not 24, concession B.

Wheat, flour, potatoes, and produce of various kinds were formerly shipped from the mouth of Highland Creek to ports in New York State. At a still earlier date the settlers took their wheat by boat from this point to the Bay of Quinte, and brought back flour. The round trip required from one to two weeks.

The south eighty acres of lot 34, concession B, bore an important part in the examination that took place in 1846, relating to the mismanagement of King's College affairs. Jas. Dark bought the lot in 1835 for £140, of which he paid only a small sum. On his death the lot was left to his wife Charlotte, who sold it to her son Edwin. Other sons were James and Matthew.

It was largely on account of an investigation regarding the attempt made by a King's College clerk named Hawkins to secure possession of this land from the Darks, that other shady transactions of a similar character were brought to light.

During the early part of the century the mail for Mariposa left Scarboro twice a week (on horseback), the time required being from 6 a.m. to 8 p.m. Jacob Brooks carried this mail for thirty years, first on horseback, and subsequently in a vehicle. Brooks served in the war of 1812, and received a Fort Detroit medal. He was succeeded by his son-in-law, Inglis, who drove the Markham stage from Toronto for upwards of fifteen years.

John Waller was probably the first mail-carrier to employ a conveyance for the use of passengers between York and Kingston.

The annals of Scarboro present examples of some changes that have taken place in surnames.

Cornwell has simply been abbreviated to Cornell by the elision of the *w*. But *Pilkey*, from Pelletier, is a clear case of corrupting a French word to make it easy for English pronunciation (see "Pioneers," page 51). A similar change seems to have been effected in this word elsewhere, for in the Buffalo *Express* of March 28, 1896, there is a reference to "Thomas Pelkey, a jolly and corpulent French-Canadian," and an "Alfred Pelkey," as members of a party bound for the gold-fields of Alaska. Farther east in Ontario the form Pelkey also appears. On the Pilkey medal it is "Pelkie." (See page 270.)

Macklin, the present form of a name distinguished in the township, has appeared as Macklim and Macklem. The name of Macklin, the well-known actor, was originally Maclachlin, or Maclaclan.

G. W. Badgerow's grandfather was a Parisian Frenchman, who, when he settled in Pennsylvania, had the name of Bergeron!

Malcolm, for some years, degenerated into Malcom, but the second *l* has been restored, showing the connection with MacCallum and Gillichallum, "the servant of St. Columba."

Secor, which in Scarboro families has retained its original form, takes now the spelling of Secord elsewhere, *e.g.*, Laura Secord (see "Pioneers," page 51).

"Coonet," or "Koonet," as applied to a kind of house, or fire-place, was originally VanKoughnet, an old settler (see "Domestic Life," page 103).

The "Coonet" log-house was so constructed that a yoke of oxen could enter at one side and pass out at the other when drawing logs to supply the huge fireplace at one end of the building.

The district comprised in S. S. No. 1 (the northwesterly part of the township) is known as the L'Amaroux Settlement, a family of that name having early settled in this locality, on lots 33 and 34, on the 4th concession, and lot 33, in the 3rd concession. The venerable Rev. Dr. Scadding conducted religious services in this settlement in its early days.

The first cooking stove, a "Birr," or "Burr," is said to have been brought into the township from New York, by William Cornell, who reached Scarboro by schooner.

Old Tommy Adams ("Uncle Tommy") was the pioneer flax-grower in 1825. It was scutched, heckled and spun here by primitive methods, being chiefly made into bags, mattresses and ropes. The ropes were used on his schooner, plying between Port Union and Oswego.

Straw-plaiting was a favorite occupation among the women in early days. Thirty yards made a good hat. The Misses Nancy and Jenny Perry (yet living, at a very advanced age, in a cottage on the Kingston Road) were regarded as most proficient and expert plaiters and hat-makers.

A correspondent who has supplied numerous interesting scraps of folk-lore, writes: "The modern craze for church parties was totally unknown in early days. Churches then were used solely for devotional purposes. The only entertainments of the early settlers were the hoe-down and dance, which generally took place in the evenings after logging-bees, raisings, etc. The celebration of the monarch's birthday was not so enthusiastically observed until the *regime* of our beloved Queen. Long may she reign!"

The Methodist Church at Highland Creek was enlarged in 1868 by building an addition to the front end, thus making it look long and narrow. A jocular minister used to refer to it as "the shooting gallery."

Bunker, or Bunker's Hill, seems to have been whimsically applied to what was formerly known as Sisley's Hill. It has been suggested that the name was bestowed on account of the number of "engagements" that used to take place here in connection with town-meetings, fairs, trainings, etc., John Barleycorn being always an active participant, and often the instigator.

In 1802 the population was 89; in 1820 it had reached 477, and ten years later it was 1,135.

In 1803 the township owned 5 horses, 8 oxen, 27 cows, 7 young cattle, and 15 swine; but as it is credited with only three houses, it is puzzling to know where all the people lived, for they must have numbered nearly a hundred.

In 1842 Scarboro contained 2,750 inhabitants, 1 grist-mill, and 18 saw-mills. In 1850 there were 3,821 inhabitants, 3 grist-mills, and 23 saw-mills.

Robert Hamilton, a Scottish weaver, who came here in 1825, was the pioneer total abstinence advocate in the township. On the occasion of his first "raising" he absolutely refused to provide whiskey, and those who came to assist refused just as positively to touch a stick on this account. The dead-lock was overcome by his giving the boss carpenter authority to manage the business as he pleased, and the exercise of this pleasure brought the work to a successful termination.

A correspondent supplies the three following extremely interesting paragraphs:

"In evidence of the primitive state of the country in the later 'twenties' or early 'thirties,' Mrs. Jos. Workman once told me of an advertisement which she remembered of Mr. (afterwards Sir Francis) Hincks, informing the public at large that he had imported a half-dozen of gentlemen's white shirts, which would be found of good quality and at reasonable prices. The mother of the writer remembered seeing even empty waggons stuck in the mud on King Street East, within a hundred yards of the market, between 1825 and 1830.

"About 1830 a saw-mill was owned and run by a Mr. Taylor at Highland Creek, who at that time was a local preacher amongst the Methodists. He was converted to Mormonism by the Mormon missionaries in the early 'forties,' and rapidly rose in Utah until he became Brigham Young's right-hand man, and finally succeeded to the presidency of the Mormon body. At last accounts he had six other wives besides the one he took from Scarboro.

"The early settlers were all extremely hospitable,

and in nearly every house was a supply of whiskey or ale, and the social glass was a matter of course, being rarely absent. At the same time drunkenness was very rare. Amongst those few who indulged too freely was a farmer in the east of the township, who, however, lived to the good old age of ninety-eight. A few years before he died, a temperance lecturer, to emphasize his contention that temperance was conducive to longevity, cited the case of this old gentleman, of whose age he had been told a few minutes before, as that of one where temperate habits firmly followed produced such a green and vigorous old age. His eloquence was brought to a sudden stop by roars of laughter, and then he learned, to his disgust, that his pattern old man had been anything but a temperate liver for more than seventy years. Now no more abstemious or law-abiding township exists in the Dominion than old Scarboro is."

Victoria Park, a well-known summer resort for picnic and pleasure parties, is situated at the south-west angle of the township. It consists of fourteen acres, partly cleared and partly woodland, on the lake shore. In 1877 this property was leased for a park by J. H. Boyle, of Toronto, from Peter Paterson, of Blantyre. It is now the property of Thos. Davies, of Toronto.

"Squaw Village" was so called from the fact that on one side of the road there lived a family consisting in part of nine extremely candid young women, somewhat swarthy in complexion, while on the opposite side was another bevy somewhat less numerous but equally frank.

Scarboro's magisterial bench is composed of the following Justices of the Peace: Jeremiah Annis, Jos. Armstrong, Geo. Chester, J. C. Clark, Wm. Helliwell, Richard Knowles, Jas. Lawrie, John Milne, Simpson Rennie, A. M. Secor, John Richardson.

The silver medal mentioned in the chapter on militia matters as being in the possession of the Pilkey family, is for service in the British army between 1793 and 1814. Medals of this kind were issued in 1848, and bear on one side a bust of Her Most Gracious Majesty Queen Victoria. The Pilkey medal has on the clasp, the words "Fort Detroit." This, however, means, not that the soldier performed service nowhere else, but that the capture of Detroit was the most memorable event of the campaign. The family tradition that the medal was presented to Pierre le Pelletier for "blowing up a fort" may be correct, and may refer to the explosion of the York magazine.

Medals bearing "Fort Detroit" on the clasp are among the most valuable in the whole series of British war issues.

On the rim of the medal is engraved, "P. Pelkie, Canadian Militia."

Mrs. Wm. Forfar had on one occasion an extremely exciting wolf experience. She and her brother, when children, were attending to the boiling down of sap one night, when a pack of some eight or ten wolves made their appearance, and, notwithstanding the fire, showed a desire to become quite too intimate. Young Forfar, who was the elder of the two, managed to lodge his sister in a small tree beyond the reach of immediate danger, and in this position she remained for many hours, while her brother treated the venturesome brutes to repeated applications of hot syrup from the sugar kettles. This mode of defence was a novel one, and one also which no doubt proved as embarrassing as it must have been painful to the wolves, which, towards daylight, retired from the place.

The "Fishery Road," mentioned elsewhere, is only a by-way leading from Kingston Road to the lake shore, chiefly used by "Old Portwine," a Dutch fisherman.

The "Kennedy Road," one of the chief highways extending from the front to Markham town-line, received its name from the Kennedys, several families of whom reside in the neighborhood.

The last lynx seen in the township was captured by the two sons of David Martin, on lot 31, concession D, in 1891 or 1892. This animal was a large one of its kind, and may be seen as a mounted specimen at "Aberfoyle" farm-house—Mr. Martin's residence.

In the Thomson family there is a "Fort Detroit" medal granted to Richard Thomson for his services during 1812. In the same family are also retained several old military weapons of this date.

CHAPTER XXI.

THE CENTENNIAL CELEBRATION.

"Time will discover everything to posterity: it is a babbler, and speaks even when no question is put."—*Euripides.*

WITHIN the last twenty years several notable centennials have been held in Ontario. In 1884, Toronto and other cities celebrated the settlement of the United Empire Loyalists in the Province. In 1892, Niagara, Kingston and Toronto commemorated the setting off as a separate Province of Upper Canada, and the summoning of its first Parliament by Lieutenant-Governor John Graves Simcoe. At the same time Niagara celebrated the organization of its first Church of England parish by the name of St. Mark's, and two years later (1894) saw the centennial of St. Andrew's, the first Presbyterian congregation in the old town. In 1894, too, the settlement of Glengarry a century before by the faithful Highlanders from the Mohawk Valley was celebrated, and it is certain that the coming quarter century will see more of these commemorative events as time brings our most wealthy and prosperous towns and townships to the centennial anniversary of their birth, or recalls the circumstances of great issues.

In 1881 the idea of a township celebration was suggested by Edmund Jacques, and supported by A. W. Forfar and D. W. Thomson, but not much beyond desultory talks on the subject took place until

1891. In that year, at a social held in St. Andrew's Church, Robert Malcolm, of Toronto, an old Scarboro man, delivered an address on the subject. The result of this was the appointment of a committee to consider what should be done. The Committee was composed of a number of old settlers, the Rev. D. B. Macdonald being chairman. The subject was kept alive, and suggestions in reference to it considered, but nothing definite proposed until 1894, when A. W. Forfar and D. W. Thomson were again to the front in its behalf. At a meeting of the Board of Directors of the Mechanics' Institute, held in November, 1894, the proposal to hold a celebration under the auspices of the Mechanics' Institute was broached by Mr. Forfar, and a committee was named to consider the matter and report before Christmas of that year, Wm. Carmichael being chairman. This committee never met to report.

During the fall of 1895, A. W. Forfar and D. W. Thomson again agitated the question. Together with John Buchanan, they laid the proposition before the Township Council. The result was the circulation of a petition amongst the ratepayers, and a public meeting was called, by proclamation, at Woburn, on October 23rd, 1895. A fair representation of the people responded. Among those present were David Martin, D. W. Thomson, A. W. Forfar, James Chester, Isaac Chester, Alex. Baird, Andrew Young, J. C. Clark, James Ley, Geo. Elliot, Thomas Thomson, John Gorman, W. F. Maclean, M.P. (East York), J. M. Thomson, Arthur Thomson, A. M. Secor, W. D. Annis, W. W. Thompson, Francis Armstrong and Rev. D. B. Macdonald.

The meeting being called to order, the Reeve read the proclamation and explained why he issued it.

PROCLAMATION.

TO THE INHABITANTS OF SCARBORO IN THE COUNTY OF YORK,

And all others, Her Majesty's subjects, whom it doth or may in any wise concern:

WHEREAS, I, James Chester, Reeve of the Township of Scarboro, having received a requisition signed by Rev. D. B. Macdonald, Thomas Hood, James Ley, Levi E. Annis, Archibald W. Forfar, Beebe Carnaghan, Isaac Chester, David Martin, D. W. Thomson, Alex. McCowan, Adam Richardson, W. A. Heron, Lyman Kennedy, Wm. Carmichael, Robert Martin and eighty others, who are freeholders of the said township, having a right to vote for members to serve in the Legislative Assembly in respect of the property held by them within the said township, requesting me to call a public meeting on or about the 23rd day of October next, to be held at Woburn, in the said township, for the purpose of taking into consideration the advisability of celebrating, in a suitable manner, the

ONE HUNDREDTH ANNIVERSARY

of the settlement of the township, which will occur in June, 1896;

AND WHEREAS, I have determined to comply with the said requisition, now, therefore, I do hereby appoint the said meeting to be held at

WOBURN,

in the Township of Scarboro, on

WEDNESDAY, OCTOBER 23RD, 1895,

at 7 o'clock p.m., of which all persons are hereby required to take notice.

AND WHEREAS, the said meeting has been so called by me in conformity with the provisions of Chapter 187 of the Revised Statutes of Ontario, entitled "An Act respecting Public Meetings," and all persons who attend the same will therefore be within the protection of the said Act, of all which premises all manner of persons are hereby, in Her Majesty's name, most strictly charged and commanded at their peril to take especial notice and govern themselves accordingly.

(Signed) JAMES CHESTER,
Reeve.

By order, THOS. CRAWFORD,
Township Clerk.

He then declared the meeting open for business.

On motion, Mr. Chester was called to the chair and A. W. Forfar appointed secretary.

The Rev. D. Barclay Macdonald being called upon, moved the first resolution, as follows: "That in the opinion of this meeting the residents of Scarboro should honor, in a fitting manner, the hundredth anniversary of the settlement of their township, in June next."

The reverend gentleman pointed out the value of this movement, and showed how much the people of the present day are indebted to their forefathers. The resolution was ably seconded by Geo. Elliot, supported by W. F. Maclean, M.P., and carried with much enthusiasm.

The second resolution, "Recognizing the great educational value of a public library, and the urgent need of a suitable place for our present valuable collection of books, amounting to upwards of 4,000 vols., therefore be it resolved, that we do forthwith proceed to the erection of a memorial building, to be called the 'Scarboro Centennial Memorial Library,'" was moved by James Ley and seconded by Dr. Opie Sisley. After a warm discussion it carried by a large majority.

Rev. Mr. Macdonald, being again called on, moved and strongly supported the third resolution:

"Recognizing the interest which would be awakened by, and the value to the cause of education and patriotism of, a series of Canadian local histories, therefore be it resolved—if the committee to be appointed report favorably upon the project—that we proceed to the issue of a history of this township, in such form as may hereafter be determined."

This resolution was seconded by Dr. Sisley, and

after being cordially supported by other gentlemen present, was enthusiastically carried.

On motion the following gentlemen were appointed an Executive Committee, viz.: Messrs. J. C. Clark, James Ley, Adam Richardson, L. E. Annis, George Chester, sen., Geo. Elliot, David Brown, John Lawrie, Wm. Tredway, and Rev. D. B. Macdonald.

On motion of D. W. Thomson, a Committee on Information was appointed.

Messrs. A. M. Secor, W. W. Thompson, and Alex. Baird were named a Committee on Finance.

The meeting adjourned.

Before separating the first meeting of the Executive was called for organization, to meet in St. Andrew's Manse on October 29th, 1895.

The Executive Committee met according to appointment. Organization was effected, and the following became permanent officers: Chairman, Rev. D. B. Macdonald; Secretary, J. C. Clark; Treasurer, A. M. Secor.

The Executive set to work with vigor to accomplish the work entrusted to it. A majority of the members were faithful in attendance at meetings, and gave valuable assistance in the work of the Committee. Two leading points engaged their attention: (1) The production of a history of the township; (2) The preparation necessary for a fitting celebration of the Centennial.

At a later date the Information Committee met for organization at Woburn. On motion, John Richardson, M.P.P., was called to the chair permanently, and Levi Annis appointed secretary. The Committee was divided into twelve sub-committees, one for each school section, and a chairman named for each, as follows:

No. 1.—Simpson Rennie, Chairman; J. C. Clark, Thos. Hood, Alfred Mason, F. G. Morgan, Rev. J. A. Brown, Thos. Crawford (township clerk), Dr. O. Sisley, John T. Paterson, R. Skelton, E. Wood, Thos. Armstrong.

No. 2.—Lyman Kennedy (reeve), Chairman; George Elliot Alex. Macklin, James Stewart, Hugh Elliot.

No. 3.—David Brown, Chairman; R. Harding, James Weir, Jas. Sterling, A. R. Jacques, R. Jackson, Thos. Ormerod, Adam Russell.

No. 4.—William Milne, Chairman; Andrew McCreight, P. Reesor, N. Reesor.

No. 5.—A. W. Forfar, Chairman; A. Young, F. Glendinning, W. Walton, Beebe Carnaghan.

No. 6.—A. M. Secor, Chairman; W. Carmichael, Adam Bell, John Johnston, Francis Scott, Wm. Green, Rev. D. B. Macdonald, Richard Thomson, Thos. Pilkey, D. W. Thomson, Amos Thomson, R. Purdie, Jonathan Baird.

No. 7.—Wm. Tredway, sen., Chairman; B. Closson, Wm. Helliwell, R. Neilson, W. Humphrey, H. Westney.

No. 8.—David Martin, Chairman; W. W. Thompson, Francis Armstrong, Alex. McCowan, Anthony Ionson, Jos. Armstrong, Robt. Martin (also in No. 10).

No. 9.—L. E. Annis, Chairman; F. Wheler, D. Pherrill, Rev. W. G. Stevenson, Rev. T. Walker, John Richardson, M.P.P., Geo. Chester, sen., Isaac Stobo, Jas. Humphrey.

No. 10.—A. J. Reynolds, Chairman; Robt. Martin (see also No. 8), Robt. Bell, Jonathan Ashbridge, Geo. Taylor.

No. 11.—Richard Knowles, Chairman; Andrew Annis, W. W. Stotts, R. Cowan.

No. 12.—D. Baldwin, Chairman; A. Moffat, G. Bell, J. Richardson (York), A. Heron.

A Toronto contingent was appointed, chiefly composed of former residents of Scarboro: Robt. Malcolm, Chairman; Dr. Closson, Alex. Muir, A. Hood, R. Swan, Hugh Miller, W. Christie, E. M. Morphy, T. E. Champion, and H. M. Campbell.

The chairman of the Executive was requested to prepare a circular giving an outline of the information necessary for the history. This circular was accordingly prepared, and issued to all sub-committees. Copies of it were also sent to interested persons in various parts of the Dominion.

It was at first intended that one or more of the Committee should undertake the preparation of the Centennial volume, but it was soon felt that for various reasons it would be more advantageous to have this done by someone not connected with the township, and after a little discussion the following resolution, moved by James Ley and seconded by George Elliot, was adopted: "That someone outside of the township be engaged to edit the volume, and that the Chairman, the Secretary, and L. E. Annis be a committee to select and engage an editor."

At next meeting this committee reported in favor of David Boyle, Curator of the Ontario Archæological Museum, of Toronto, and this selection was confirmed by resolution.

The following programme, prepared by the Executive Committee, will be carried out as nearly as possible on the days of celebration, June 17th and 18th, 1896:

WEDNESDAY, JUNE 17th.

1. SPECIAL MEMORIAL RE-UNION SERVICES in St. Andrew's Church, 10.30 a.m. to 12 noon. During these services the past will be reviewed; short addresses will be given by old residents of the township and of other parts of the Province. Appropriate services of praise will be sung by the choir.
2. DINNER-HORN CALL TO THE TABLES. Dinner from 12.15 to 1.30 p.m.

Band Music.

3. BUGLE-CALL TO ASSEMBLE AT THE PLATFORM.
   Hymn: "Before Jehovah's Awful Throne."
   Prayer: Rev. G. W. Stephenson.
   Choir: "Let the Hills Resound."

4. SHORT ADDRESSES: John Richardson, M.P.P., and Mr. Simpson Rennie, representing the farmers.
   Interlude: Mouth-organ Band.
   Choir (250 voices, Mr. Stouffer leader): "Raise the Flag." —*Nelson.*

5. SHORT ADDRESSES by Messrs. James Ley and Wm. Tredway, representing the trades.
   Interlude, concertina and organ, followed by Choir: "Wake the Song of Jubilee."

6. SHORT ADDRESSES by Rev. J. A. Brown, Dr. D. McDiarmid and Mr. Alfred Jacques, representing the professions.
   Instrumental Interludes. Last speaker to be followed by full chorus, "Rule, Britannia"—Band and Choir.

7. ANNOUNCEMENTS.—National Anthem.
   Closing Prayer: Rev. Father E. F. Gallagher.
   Bag-pipe Selections, ten minutes.

8. FIRST FOOT-BALL CONTEST. Play to last one hour. Band Music at half-time and close of game.

9. TEA served at five o'clock.
   Band Music.

10. SECOND FOOT-BALL CONTEST. Bag-pipes at half-time and at close of match.

CONCERT at 8 p.m., in the Large Tent.

Children's Games will be arranged at suitable times during the day.

THURSDAY, JUNE 18th.

1. COMMEMORATIVE SERVICES continued in St. Andrew's Church from 10.45 a.m. to 12 o'clock noon.

2. DINNER-HORN CALL. Dinner from 12.15 to 1.30 p.m.

3. BUGLE-CALL TO ASSEMBLE AT THE PLATFORM, 2 p.m.
   Anthem: "Praise ye the Lord."
   Hymn: "Holy, holy, holy, Lord God Almighty."

4. CHAIRMAN'S ADDRESS preparatory to hoisting the Union Jack and Dominion ensign.
   Choir: "Raise the Flag." Flags will be run up to the mast-head.
   Band: "Three Cheers for the Red, White and Blue," followed by the Choir and Children, the latter of whom will take up the song with appropriate flag exercise.
5. ADDRESS by His Honor Geo. A. Kirkpatrick, Lieut.-Governor of Ontario, in response to the Salutation of the Flag.
6. ADDRESSES by W. F. Maclean, M.P., and H. R. Frankland, Esq.
   Interlude: Violin and piano.
   Children and Choir: "The Maple Leaf."
7. The platform being honored with the presence of a number of old people belonging to the township, addresses in their name will be given by Mr. Elias Wood and D. B. Read, Q.C., a "York Pioneer."
   Choir: "O God of Bethel."
8. ADDRESS: O. A. Howland, M.P.P., Chairman Canadian Historical Celebration Committee."
   Choir: "This Canada of Ours."
9. ADDRESS: David Boyle, Secretary Canadian Historical Celebration Committee, and Editor of the Scarboro Centennial volume.
   The People (led by the Choir): "Auld Lang Syne."
10. ADDRESS: Hon. Dr. G. W. Ross, M.P.P., Minister of Education.
   Choir: "Hark the Song of Jubilee."
11. CHAIRMAN'S CLOSING REMARKS.
   Choir: "God be with you till we meet again."
   Closing prayer by the Chairman.
   The People (led by the Choir): "God Save the Queen."
12. HORN-CALL TO TEA, at 5 p.m.
13. FINAL FOOT-BALL CONTEST.

REV. D. B. MACDONALD, *Chairman.*

During the day arrangements will be made for bowling and quoiting contests between Scarboro players and others.

By the courtesy of William Fleming, of Markham, an old Scarboro boy, the two organs and piano to be used in the musical part of the programme have been supplied.

Subjoined are copies of some letters received in response to invitations extended by the Centennial Executive Committee to prominent persons, asking them to take part in the proceedings of the celebration.

The Lieutenant-Governor writes:

"GOVERNMENT HOUSE,

TORONTO, *May 24th*, 1896.

DEAR SIR,—It gives me great pleasure to accept the invitation of the Executive Committee of the residents of Scarboro township, to be present at the celebration of the Centennial on June 18th proximo.

I heartily commend the action of the Committee in preparing and publishing a volume containing the history of Scarboro from 1796 to 1896, and I shall have much pleasure in accepting a copy of the volume as a memento of the occasion.

The history of our province and country can best be preserved by histories of localities and early settlements such as you propose.

Very soon we shall miss from among us those venerable men and women, to be met with in every county, who delight us with stories told to them directly by the early settlers of the Province, one hundred years ago—thrilling stories of suffering, privation and toil, all met and overcome by heroic endurance, and a firm hope and belief, soon afterwards realized, in the fertility and resources of the country, in the salubrity of the climate, and in the happiness and prosperity of the people who were to be the possessors of this great province. These stories and traditions should be crystallized into history now, while those who heard them at first hand are able to relate them. The names of many of our townships contain a history which should be known to every child in the township, but, alas! very few can tell whence the name came, or why it was given.

I trust that every township, and certainly every county, in this province will follow the example of Scarboro and encourage the preparation of histories of the various townships and counties, which must prove not only interesting to the people whose history is given, but of incalculable value to the future historian of our country.

Wishing you every success, I am,

Yours very truly,

GEORGE A. KIRKPATRICK.

The REV. D. B. MACDONALD,
St. Andrew's Manse, Bendale, Ont."

The Minister of Education, Dr. G. W. Ross, replies:

"TORONTO, *April 30th*, 1896.

MY DEAR MR. MACDONALD,—I am very glad to notice that you propose to hold a centennial celebration of the settlement of the township of Scarboro. I believe such celebrations tend to increase the interest of our younger people in the growth of Canadian institutions, and, as a consequence, secure their attachment to the land in which we live. Besides, I think that we, who are the descendants of the pioneers of Canada, can in no better way show our appreciation of the great services they rendered to this country than by occasionally meeting to recall their early courage and endurance in order that we may be moved to imitate the qualities of citizenship which, under adverse circumstances, they manifested so patiently and so nobly.

I shall be glad to receive a copy of your memorial volume. I am sure it will be worthy of a wide circulation.

It may be impossible for me to be with you at the date of your celebration on account of the Dominion elections. Other engagements, however, permitting, I shall do myself the pleasure of attending.

Yours truly,

G. W. ROSS.

REV. D. B. MACDONALD, Bendale."

From Principal Grant, Queen's University, Kingston, Canada:

"*April 24th*, 1896.

MY DEAR MR. MACDONALD,—I would like to be with you at the celebration of the Centennial for many reasons, but absence from Canada at the time will make it impossible. I am so thankful that you are going to make your celebration contribute to what is greatly needed in Canada—the formation of material that is indispensable to Canadian history-writing. We are deplorably ignorant of the real past of our province, for its real past is to be found, not in the records of legislative bodies, nor in military annals, but in the actual experiences of our pioneers, and in the story of municipal development, and of social, religious, educational and industrial life. There are to be found the hidden springs of our national character, and the forces which are shaping our destiny.

Scarboro has a history, and I rejoice that it is to be given to us. May your example incite other townships and counties to issue similar local histories, perhaps to offer prizes for them. With all best wishes, believe me,

Sincerely yours,

G. M. GRANT."

From O. A. Howland, M.P.P., Chairman of the Canadian Historical Exhibition Committee:

"TORONTO, *April 27th*, 1896.

Rev. D. B. Macdonald.

DEAR SIR,—Many thanks for your kind letter inviting me to be with you at your admirably conceived centennial celebration on the 17th and 18th of June. I am very much pleased with the admirable circular of instruction and suggestion which your Committee issued preparatory to the work of compiling a township history. It cannot fail to have the effect of producing a great awakening of mind throughout the township regarding the interesting facts which lie dormant even in our most modern industrial communities. The study of development is the chief occupation of modern scholarship, and when applied, as you induce the people of your township to do, to the study of the stages by which their industrial and social civilization has arrived at its present state, it ought to have good effects on the minds of those who pursue and contribute to the study, as well as on the minds of those who come to witness the surprising collected results.

No small part of its good fruit may be found in its tendency to renew a vision of the sacrifices of the past, which have led to the prosperity of the present, and to the revival of a becoming veneration for the honesty, courage and single-mindedness of those worthy and industrious ancestors who initiated the task of making the wilderness blossom as the rose.

I shall certainly be with you if it should be at all possible.

With the most sincere wishes for your success, and that of your committee, believe me, dear sir,

Very truly yours,

O. A. HOWLAND."

From Rev. Dr. H. Scadding:

"TORONTO, *May 2nd*, 1896.

DEAR MR. MACDONALD,—It is very kind of you and the Committee to desire my presence at the approaching celebration in Scarboro, but I regret being obliged to decline the invitation. I am, however, in complete sympathy with you and the Committee in the undertaking. I sincerely wish that all our municipalities would follow the example of Scarboro; all of them might at least make out an accurate list of the first patentees in their respective districts. In the Crown Lands Department there is, I think, a register kept, entitled 'The Domesday Book,' which would be of assistance in doing this. To be a descendant of one of the 'First Patentees' is, in some points of view, as considerable a distinction as the being a descendant of the first United Empire Loyalists.

Believe me, dear Mr. Macdonald,

Very faithfully yours,

HENRY SCADDING."

BROWN'S CORNERS
MALVERN
WOBURN
HIGHLAND CREEK
SCARBORO
LAKE ONTARIO
MAP of the TOWNSHIP of SCARBORO
In the County of York and Province of ONTARIO.
BY ARTHUR THOMSON.

APPENDIX.

A.

THE "FIRST FAMILIES."

The following list, copied from the books in the Ontario Crown Lands Office, supplies information with regard to the original patentees of the land in Scarboro. The spellings are given just as they occur in the entries.

CONCESSION A.

Lot 27. Sarah Ashbridge (all)	May 16, 1799.
" 28. King's College (all 18a)	January 3, 1828.
" 29, 30. Capt. Wm. Mayne (all)	May 6, 1796.
" 31. Charles Watkins (N. pt. 47a)	April 14, 1852.
" 31. Septimus Auburn (S. pt. 40a)	April 9, 1874.
" 32, 33. John White (all)	August 24, 1796.
" 34. Rev. H. Addington Simcoe (front pt. 70a)	November 24, 1840.
" 34. Canada Company (N. ½ 100a)	July 18, 1831.
" 35. King's College (all)	May 16, 1835.

CONCESSION B.

Lot 19. Submission Gallaway (all)	May 17, 1802.
" 20. Parshall Terry, jun. (all 25a) ..	May 20, 1801.
" 21. King's College (all 100a)	January 3, 1828.
" 22, 23. David Fleming (all)	April 30, 1799.
" 24. Parker Mills (all 132a)	May 17, 1802.
" 25. Stephen Pherrill (all 140a)	April 11, 1832.
" 26. Jonathan Ashbridge (front part 100a) ..	August 8, 1799.
" 26. John Adair (N. part 100a)	August 8, 1799.
" 27. Sarah Ashbridge (all 200a)	May 16, 1799.
" 28. King's College (200a)	January 3, 1828.
" 29, 30. Capt. W. Mayne (all)	May 6, 1796.
" 31. Thomas Palmer (N. ½ 100a)	July 4, 1839.
" 31. Thomas Walton (S. ½ 100a)	May 29, 1847.
" 32. Andrew Templeton (rear ½)	June 17, 1799.
" 32. Richard Thornbeck (N. pt. of S. ½ 37a) ..	October 18, 1842.

Lot 32.	John White (S. pt.)	August 24, 1796.
" 33.	John White (S. pt.)	August 24, 1796.
" 33.	Robert Tait (rear ½ 100a)	May 17, 1802.
" 33.	Andrew Heron (N. pt. of S. ½)	November 11, 1842.
" 34.	King's College (N. ½ 120a)	January 3, 1828.
" 34.	King's College (S. pt.)	May 16, 1835.
" 35.	Henry Webster (all 200a)	August 18, 1810.

CONCESSION C.

Lot 10.	(Included in 10 D, *q. v.*)	
" 11.	King's College (all)	January 3, 1828.
" 12, 13.	Donald McLean (200a)	March 29, 1805.
" 14.	William Osterhout (all)	July 8, 1799.
" 15.	James Humphrey (all 98a)	October 17, 1844.
" 16.	Wm. Osterhout (all)	July 8, 1799.
" 17, 18.	Nicholas Smith (all 248a)	July 24, 1799.
" 19.	Submission Gallaway (all)	May 17, 1802.
" 20.	Parshall Terry, jun. (all 200a)	May 20, 1801.
" 21.	King's College (all 200a)	January 3, 1828.
" 22, 23.	David Fleming (all)	April 30, 1799.
" 24.	Thomas Hewett (all 200a)	June 17, 1799.
" 25.	Thomas Walton (all 180a)	May 6, 1841.
" 26.	Elisabeth Dennis (all 200a)	August 10, 1801.
" 27.	John Adair (all 200a)	August 8, 1799.
" 28.	King's College (all 200a)	January 3, 1828.
" 29.	Elizabeth Thompson (all 200a)	May 16, 1799.
" 29.	John Weaver (all 200a)	August 8, 1799.
" 30.	John Weaver (all 200a)	July 8, 1799.
" 31.	James Palmer (W. ½ 89a)	September 7, 1854.
" 31.	Wm. Phirrill (S. E. ¼ 50a)	June 16, 1846.
" 31.	Joseph Hough (N. E. ¼ 50a)	September 4, 1846.
" 32.	Andrew Templeton (front ½)	June 17, 1799.
" 32.	Thomas Cornwell (N. ½ 100a)	October 23, 1809.
" 33.	Robert Tait (front ½ 100a)	May 17, 1802.
" 33.	John Haacke (N. ½ 100a)	April 2, 1817.
" 34.	King's College (all 200a)	January 3, 1828.
" 35.	Wm. Devenish (all 200a)	May 18, 1803.

CONCESSION D.

Lot 1.	Joseph Ketchum (all)	March 23, 1798.
" 2.	Charles Coxwell Small (all)	June 9, 1835.
" 3, 4.	Joseph Ketchum	March 23, 1798.
" 5.	King's College (all 152a)	January 3, 1828.
" 6, 7.	John Richardson (all 400a)	June 6, 1806.

Lot	8. Alex. Neilson (E. ½ 80½a)		May 19, 1847.
"	8. Alex. Nelson (W. ½ 82½a)		October 3, 1854.
"	9. Charles Rice (all 200a)		May 17, 1802.
"	10. Samuel Heron (all 200a)		May 20, 1801.
"	11. King's College (all 100a) [?]		January 3, 1828.
"	12. James Hoghtelling (all 200a)		September 1, 1797.
"	13, 14. John McGill (400a)		May 27, 1797.
"	15. James Humphrey (200a)		October 17, 1844.
"	16. Elizabeth Osterhout (200a)		April 6, 1805.
"	17, 18. Robert Isaac Dey Grey (400a)		August 10, 1801.
"	19. Donald McLean (E. ½ 100a)		March 29, 1805.
"	19. Alex. McDonell (W. ½)	300a	June 12, 1806.
"	20. Alex. McDonell		
"	21. King's College (200a)		January 3, 1828.
"	22. James Elliot (200a)		July 8, 1799.
"	23. David Robertson (200a)		July 8, 1799.
"	24. Samuel Heron (200a)		July 8, 1799.
"	25. John Taber (N. ½ of N. ½ 50a)		March 16, 1848.
"	25. Isaac Chester (S. ½ 100a)		June 8, 1838.
"	25. Jane McBride (S. ½ of N. ½ 50a)		October 1, 1838.
"	26, 27. Robert Isaac De Grey (400a)		August 10, 1801.
"	28. King's College (200a)		January 3, 1828.
"	29. Hon. John Richardson, *et al.* (200a)		November 5, 1827.
"	30. Martin Buckner (200a)		May 16, 1799.
"	31. David Ferguson (S. ½ 100a)		May 1, 1838.
"	31. John Martin (N. ½ 100a)		October 26, 1844.
"	32. Thomas Cornwell (S. ½ 100a)		October 23, 1809.
"	32. Dorcas Hendrick (N. pt.)	200a	June 12, 1798.
"	33. Dorcas Hendrick (N. pt.)		
"	33. Ephraim Payson (S. ½ 100a)		July 8, 1799.
"	34. Elsa Cole (200a)		November 26, 1807.
"	35. James Molloy (200a)		December 31, 1798.

CONCESSION 1.

Lot	1. Joseph Ketchum (200a)	March 23, 1798.
"	2. Charles Coxwell Small (277a)	June 19, 1835.
"	3, 4. Joseph Ketchum (400a)	March 23, 1798.
"	5. King's College (200a)	January 3, 1828.
"	6. John Small (200a)	October 22, 1807.
"	7. John Coon (200a)	May 16, 1799.
"	8. Wm. Helliwell (200a)	July 18, 1856.
"	9. Joseph Forsyth (S. ½ 100a)	September 4, 1800.
"	9. John Haacke (N. ½ 100a)	April 2, 1817.
"	10. Mary McGill (200a)	April 6, 1797.

Lot	11. King's College (200a)	July 3, 1828.
"	12. George Irvin (N. ½ 100a)	April 5, 1797.
"	12. James Hoghtelling (all 200a)	September 1, 1797.
"	13, 14. John McGill (400a)	May 27, 1797.
"	15. Wm. Fawcett (S. ½ 100a)	September 30, 1850.
"	15. Frances Faucet (N. ½ 100a)	June 4, 1857.
"	16. Lt. Miles McDonell (200a)	July 8, 1799.
"	17. Wm. Jones (200a)	March 26, 1804.
"	18, 19, 20. Robert Isaac De Grey (600a) ..	August 10, 1801.
"	21. King's College (200a)	January 3, 1828.
"	22. Ebenezer Cavers (200a)	May 17, 1802.
"	23. Andrew Thomson (200a)	May 17, 1802.
"	24. David Thomson (200a)	May 17, 1802.
"	25. William D. Thompson (N. ½ 94a)	October 7, 1857.
"	25. Andrew Thompson (W. ½ of S. ½ 47a) ..	April 5, 1861.
"	26, 27. Robert Isaac De Grey (400a)	August 10, 1801.
"	28. King's College (200a)	January 3, 1828.
"	29, 30. Wm. Pickard (400a)	July 24, 1799.
"	31. Daniel Galbraith (S. ½ 100a)	September 23, 1836.
"	31. Robert Galbraith (N. ½ 100a) ..	September 23, 1836.
"	32, 33. Capt. Wm. Demont (400a) ..	May 1, 1798.
"	34. King's College (200a)	January 3, 1828.
"	35. Capt. Wm. Demont	May 1, 1798.

CONCESSION 2.

Lot	1. Zipporah Roebuck (200a)	May 17, 1802.
"	2. Wm. Eadus, *et al.* (200a)	April 6, 1797.
"	3. King's College (200a)	January 3, 1828.
"	4. Joseph Ketchum (200a)	March 23, 1798.
"	5. Owen McGrath (200a)	October 24, 1798.
"	6. Thomas Chester (S. ½ 100a)	June 18, 1856.
"	7. Owen McGrath (200a)	October 24, 1798.
"	8. Elizabeth Davis (200a)	December 31, 1798.
"	9. Canada Company (S. ½ 100a)	November 29, 1844.
"	9. Canada Company (N. ½ 100a)	February 14, 1834.
"	10. Susannah Harris (200a)	July 24, 1799.
"	11. John Segar (200a)	July 8, 1799.
"	12. Wm. Westney (S. ½ and N.E. ¼ 150a) ..	June 18, 1856.
"	12. Wm. Anthony (N.W. ¼ 50a)	January 30, 1857.
"	13. George Irvin (200a)	April 5, 1797.
"	14. Amos Merrit (200a)	April 15, 1797.
"	15. John Markley (200a)	July 8, 1799.
"	16. King's College (200a)	January 3, 1828.
"	17. Richard Hatt (200a)	July 24, 1799.

Lot 18, 19. Richard Hatt (400a)		November 1, 1808.
" 20. James Bowes (N. ½ 100a)		December 29, 1858.
" 20. Joseph Hall, *et al.* (S. E. ¼ 50a)		October 14, 1859.
" 20. Andrew Johnson (S. W. ¼ 50a)		June 21, 1859.
" 21. Andrew Johnston (200a)		July 8, 1799.
" 22. Jacob Fisher (200a)		May 17, 1802.
" 23. Valentine Fisher (200a)		March 8, 1803.
" 24. King's College (200a)		January 3, 1828.
" 25, 26. Archibald Thompson (S. ½ 100a) ..		May 16, 1799.
" 27. John Walton (N. ½ 100a)		December 19, 1835.
" 27. John Thompson (S. ½ 100a)		October 10, 1856.
" 28. Archibald Thomson (S. ½ 100a)		May 16, 1799.
" 28. John Henry Kahman (N. ½ 100a)	300a..	July 8, 1799.
" 29. John Henry Kahman		
" 30. Canada Company (200a)		July 9, 1829.
" 31. Eliphalet Hale (200a)		May 24, 1799.
" 32. Capt. Wm. Demont (200a)		May 1, 1798.
" 33. Ichabod Vradenburgh (N. ½ 100a) ..		November 27, 1850.
" 33. Andrew Fitzpatrick (S. ½ 100a)		September 30, 1836.
" 33. Louis Simon (N. ½ 100a)		February 18, 1850.*
" 34, 35. Capt. Wm. Demont (400a)		May 1, 1798.

CONCESSION 3.

Lot 1. Eliza Small (all)	February 10, 1797.
" 2. Clarissa Thompson, *et al.* (N. ¾ 150a) ..	March 3, 1857.
" 3. Eliza Small (all)	February 10, 1797.
" 4. John Robert Small (200a)	June 30, 1801.
" 5. Canada Company (N. ½ 100a)	August 21, 1835.
" 5. Canada Company (S. ½ 100a)	February 17, 1837.
" 6. Wm. Eadus, *et al.* (200a)	April 6, 1797.†
" 7. Eliza Small (all)	February 10, 1797.
" 8. John S. Palmer (200a)	July 29, 1862.
" 9, 10. James Whitton (400a)	October 24, 1798.
" 11. King's College (200a)	January 3, 1828.
" 12. Elizabeth Vanderlip (200a)..	October 24, 1798.
" 13. Sarah McDougall (200a)	July 8, 1799.
" 14. Nathan Osburn (200a)	July 8, 1836.
" 15. Alex. Sterling (N. ½ 100a)	October 9, 1857.‡
" 15. Thomas Walton (S. ½ 100a)..	March 8, 1859.

* Voided by the Heir and Devisee Commission, July 20, 1850.

† "This lot is omitted in the Record of the Patent bearing date March 8th, 1832, but is supposed to exist in the original." (MS. note in Crown Lands Register, page 117.)

‡ Patent to Andrew Sterling—Cancelled.

Lot 16-20. John McDougall (1,000a)	.. ..	August 20, 1804.
" 21. Canada Company (200a)	.. .. ..	July 9, 1829.
" 22. John McDougall (200a)	.. .. ..	August 20, 1804.
" 23, 24. John McDougall (400a)..	.. ..	May 17, 1802.
" 25. John Elliott (S. ½ 100a)	.. .. ..	January 7, 1846.
" 25. Robert Hamilton (N. ½ 100a)	.. ..	September 25, 1847.
" 26, 27. Nicholas McDougall (400a)	.. ..	May 17, 1802.
" 28. King's College (200a)	.. .. ..	January 3, 1828.
" 29. Margaret Ryckman (200a) ..	.. ..	July 24, 1799.
" 30. Richard Flack (200a)	.. .. ..	July 8, 1799.
" 31. Jacob Snider (rear pt. 100a)	.. ..	May 27, 1839.
" 31. Thomas Rogers (front pt. 100a)	.. ..	May 27, 1839.
" 32, 33. Capt. Wm. Demont (400a)	.. ..	May 1, 1798.
" 34. King's College (200a)	.. .. ..	January 3, 1828.
" 35. Capt. Wm. Demont (200a) ..	.. ..	May 1, 1798.

CONCESSION 4.

Lot 1, 2. Eliza Small (400a)	.. .. ..	February 10, 1797.
" 3. Canada Company (200a)	.. .. ..	August 31, 1831.
" 4. Eliza Small (200a) ..	.. .. ..	February 10, 1797.
" 5. John Robert Small (200a) ..	.. ..	June 30, 1801.
" 6. King Park (S. ½ of S. ½ 50a)	.. ..	July 5, 1856.
" 6. James Ross, the Elder (N. ½ of S. ½ 50a)..		May 3, 1848.
" 6. Abraham Reesor (N. ½ 100a)	.. ..	June 18, 1856.
" 7. James Thompson (200a)	.. .. ..	December 31, 1798.
" 8. John White (all) ..	.. .. ..	August 24, 1796.
" 9. Canada Company (S. ½ 100a)	.. ..	March 8, 1832.
" 9. Canada Company (N. ½ 100a)	.. ..	February 14, 1834.
" 10, 11. John White (all)	.. .. ..	August 24, 1796.
" 12. George Hamilton (200a)	.. .. ..	June 18, 1845.
" 13, 14 (E. ½). John Hewett (300a)	.. ..	July 16, 1797.
" 14. George Hamilton (W. part of E. ½)	..	September 4, 1837.
" 14 (W. ½), 15. Eva Bradt (300a)	.. ..	July 24, 1799.
" 16. King's College (200a)	.. .. ..	January 3, 1828.
" 17, 18. Elizabeth Thompson (400a)	.. ..	June 12, 1798.
" 19. Lieut. Miles McDonell (200a)	.. ..	July 8, 1799.
" 20. Joseph Harrington (S. ½ 100a)	.. ..	September 25, 1847.
" 20. Wm. Nash (N. ½ 100a)	.. .. ..	May 10, 1855.
" 21. John Smith (200a) ..	.. .. ..	July 10, 1801.
" 22. Barnabas Eddy (200a)	.. .. ..	July 8, 1799.
" 23. Ernest Martin (N. pt. 100a)	.. ..	[No date.—D.B.]
" 23. Nancy Wintemute (S. ½ 100a)	.. ..	July 29, 1833.
" 24. Canada Company (200a)	.. .. ..	July 9, 1829.
" 25. Azariah Lundy (200a)	.. .. ..	July 8, 1799.

Lot 26. David Thompson (200a)	.. .. ..	May 17, 1802.
" 27. Thomas Kennedy (N. ½ 100a)	.. ..	May 2, 1838.
" 27. Jairus Yeamans (S. ½ 100a)..	.. ..	June 22, 1838.
" 28. Andrew Thomson (200a)	.. .. ..	May 17, 1802.
" 29. Archibald Thompson (200a)	.. ..	May 16, 1799.
" 30. Andrew Kennedy (S. ½ 100a)	.. ..	November 1, 1817.
" 30. Andrew Kennedy (N. ½ 100a)	.. ..	May 17, 1828.
" 31, 32. Capt. Wm. Demont (400a)	.. ..	May 1, 1798.
" 33. Isaac Christy (S. ½ 100a)	.. .. ..	May 27, 1836.
" 33. John Rogers (N.W. ¼ 50a) ..	.. ..	September 1, 1845.
" 33. John McCready (N.E. ¼ 50a)	.. ..	September 1, 1845.
" 34, 35. Capt. Wm. Demont (400a)	.. ..	May 1, 1798.

CONCESSION 5.

Lot 1, 2. Peter Reesor (all 128a) ..	.. ..	February 4, 1812.
" 3. Benjamin Wm. Eaton (all)..	.. ..	June 26, 1812.
" 4, 5. Andrew Mercer (all)	.. .. ..	August 8, 1811.
" 6. George Kuck (all) ..	.. .. ..	April 13, 1812.
" 7. Andrew Mercer (all)..	.. .. ..	August 8, 1811.
" 8. John Oliver (rear part)	.. .. ..	March 5, 1840.
" 9. George Kuck (all) ..	.. .. ..	April 3, 1812.
" 10. John Oliver (rear part)	.. .. ..	March 5, 1840.
" 11. John Oliver (rear part)	.. .. ..	March 5, 1840.
" 12. George Kuck (all) ..	.. .. ..	April 3, 1812.
" 13. [No entry for this lot.—D.B.]		
" 14. Andrew Mercer (W. ½)	.. .. ..	August 8, 1811.
" 14. George Hamilton (W. pt. of E. ½)..	..	September 4, 1837.
" 15. Andrew Mercer (all)..	.. .. ..	August 8, 1811.
" 16. King's College (all 68a)	.. .. ..	January 3, 1828.
" 17-19. Andrew Mercer (all)	.. .. ..	August 8, 1811.
" 20. Benjamin Wm. Eaton (all) ..	.. ..	June 26, 1812.
" 21, 22. Andrew Mercer (all)	.. .. ..	August 8, 1811.
" 23. King's College (all) ..	.. .. ..	May 16, 1835.
" 24. Helen Fenwick (all)..	.. .. ..	February 13, 1812.
" 25-26. James Osburn, jun. (all)	.. ..	August 7, 1811.
" 27. Helen Fenwick (all)..	.. .. ..	February 13, 1812.
" 28. John Kennedy, sen. (all 64a)	.. ..	February 1, 1812.
" 29. James Osburn, jun. (all)	.. .. ..	August 7, 1811.
" 30. Helen Fenwick (all)..	.. .. ..	February 13, 1812.
" 31, 32. John Wintermute (all) ..	.. ..	June 30, 1801.
" 33. Benjamin Wm. Eaton (all)..	.. ..	June 26, 1812.
" 34, 35. John Wintermute	.. .. ..	June 30, 1801.

B.

The statistics of Scarboro for 1795 would be peculiarly interesting at this time, but unfortunately there was no statistician, because there were no taxes to collect, and even if there had been, there was nobody to pay them. Had Lieutenant-Governor Sir John Graves Simcoe appointed some one or more intelligent Mississaugas to furnish him with an estimated return of the township's natural wealth and resources, it might have stood somewhat thus: Mr. and Mrs. Sauga and family, 7; Wigwams, 1; Pines, 6,295,631; Oaks, 2,587,600; Maples, 4,759,989; other trees, 41,214,108; Bears (resident), 102; (non-resident), not known; Wolves (resident), 423; (non-resident), very large number; Deer (transient), 1,025; Game-birds, numerous; Fish, uncountable; Income and personal property of the Sauga family, inappreciable; Days of statute labor, none.

Exactly fifty years after this the figures prepared for the use of the Home District Municipal Council stood as follows: Resident lands, uncultivated, 22,313 acres; cultivated, 16,913 acres; value of land, £21,375; value of stock, etc., £22,054; tax on land and stock at 1d. in the pound, £180 19s. 1d.; School taxes, £135 13s. 3d.; total, £316 12s. 4d.; and there were about 650 heads of families (in 1848 there were 654).

The following table will show how matters stood at the close of the next half-century, according to the township assessment roll for 1895:

		Value.	Average Value.
Number of persons assessed	1,410	....	....
" acres (resident)	42,773	$2,174,567 00	$50 84
" acres (non-resident)	208	41,545 00	199 64
Total	42,981	$2,216,112 00	$51 56
Taxable income	$2,900 00		
Personal property	4,400 00		
		7,300 00	
Total		$2,223,412 00	

Number of Persons in families	3,816
" Children between 5 and 16 years	845
" " " 7 and 13 years	494
" " over 16 and under 21 years	267
" Cattle	3,615
" Sheep	1,838
" Hogs	1,958
" Horses	2,013
" Dogs	416
" Bitches	22
Acres of Woodland	1,800
" Swamp, marsh or wet land	3,642
" Orchard and garden	876
" Fall wheat	1,521½
Days of statute labor	2,249

C.

SCARBORO OIL COMPANY SHAREHOLDERS.

Wm. Allison, Highland Creek.
Jerry Annis, Scarboro.
David Annis, Scarboro.
Thos. Adams, sen., Highland Creek.
Andrew Annis, Port Union.
Jane A. Annis, Scarboro.
Wm. Armstrong, Rouge Hill.
Emily Annis, Port Union.
Jos. Bowden, Woburn.
Wm. Booth, Highland Creek.
Jane Bennett, Highland Creek.
Martin Badgerow, Malvern.
Jas. Brandon, Dunbarton.
Rev. W. B lt, Scarboro.
Jas. Bennett, Highland Creek.
Margt. Bell, Highland Creek.
Jacob Brumwell, Highland Creek.
Wm. Bell, Danforth.
Wm. Bellchamber, Dunbarton.
Edward Burton, Stouffville.
A. V. Bussick, Stouffville.
Fanny Burton, Stouffville.
Geo. Castle, Scarboro.
Jos. Covey, Toronto.
Russell Cornell, Scarboro.
J. H. Colegrove, Scarboro.
Chas. Cornell, Scarboro.
Geo. Chester, Scarboro.
Dr. L. D. Closson, Scarboro.
Wm. Collins, Scarboro.
Edward Clark, Scarboro.
Jabez Collins, Cherrywood.
Fred. Chinn, Stouffville.
Jno. Collins, Highland Creek.
Jessie Chapman, Scarboro.
Stephen Closson, Highland Creek.
Jno. Chellew, Scarboro.
Mary Courtice, Pickering.
A. J. Courtice, Pickering.
J. W. Chapman, Highland Creek.
Ann Clark, Highland Creek.
Jas. Carnaghan, Scarboro.
Jno. Duncan, Highland Creek.
Robt. Dixon, Port Union.
Thos. Ellis, Highland Creek.
Thos. Elliot, Highland Creek.
Jno. Elliot, Highland Creek.
Geo. Ellis, Highland Creek.
Wm. Fawcett, Highland Creek.
W. A. Fawcett, Highland Creek.
John Ford, Highland Creek.
J. Francisco, Highland Creek.
Andrew Fleming, Highland Creek.
Jno. Fisher, Dunbarton.
Ann Ferguson, Dunbarton.
W. S. Finch, Toronto.
J. R. Foster, Toronto.
Wm. Galloway, Highland Creek.
Ignatius Galloway, Highland Creek.
Nelson Gates, Scarboro.
Mary Guthrie, Scarboro.
B. W. Gossage, P.L.S., Toronto.
Wm. Helliwell, Highland Creek.
Geo. Hane, Highland Creek.
Mary Hodgins, Highland Creek.
Jos. Humphrey, Scarboro.
Jas. Humphrey, jun., Scarboro.
Edward Huxtable, Highland Creek.
Frank Helliwell, Highland Creek.
Arch. Heron, Danforth.
Chas. Hood (the contractor), Toronto.
Thos. Ireson, Belford.
Jos. Ireson, Belford.
Thompson Jackson, Scarboro.
Thos. Jacques, Scarboro.
Chas. Justis, Highland Creek.
Wm. Keeler, Highland Creek.
Stephen Keeler, Highland Creek.

Harry Key, Highland Creek.
Jas Keeler, Highland Creek.
Orson Keeler, Highland Creek.
Simon Kennedy, Agincourt.
Chas Ley, Highland Creek.
Alf. Lailey, Highland Creek.
Hy. Lanktree, Highland Creek.
Thos. Laskey, Highland Creek.
Sarah Dickson, Highland Creek.
Jas. Lawrie, Malvern.
Chas. Mabley, Scarboro.
Saul Mighton, Scarboro.
Alex. Moffat, Scarboro.
Jas. Mitchell, Port Union.
Jos. Moon, Port Union.
L. Mordan, Stouffville.
Jno. Morrish, Highland Creek.
Jno. May, Highland Creek.
Chas. McIntosh, Highland Creek.
Arch. McAllister, Highland Creek.
Donald McLean, Scarboro.
Thos. McMahon, Scarboro.
Robt. McHenry, Scarboro.
Peter Nesbit, Dunbarton.
Jno. S. Palmer, Dunbarton.
Thos. Parker, Highland Creek.
Jno. Pearce, Highland Creek.
Jordan Post, jun., Highland Creek.
Richard Pearce, Highland Creek.
Hy. Lee Pallen, Port Union.
W. H. Paterson, Port Union.
Geo. Pearce, Rouge Hill.
Mary E. Richardson, Scarboro.
J. M. Read, Scarboro.
Wm. Rolph, Woburn.
J. S. Reason, Woburn.
Samuel Richardson, Scarboro.
James Richardson, Scarboro.
Wm. Richardson, Scarboro.
Ezekiel Richardson, Scarboro.
Hy. G. Rutledge, Toronto.
Chas. Robertson, Toronto.
Thos. Skelding, Highland Creek.
Gilbert Smith, Norway.
D. Secor.
W. B. Sanders.
W. Somerville.
Wm. Size, Unionville.
Thos. Stephenson, Highland Creek.
John Stoner, Highland Creek.
Eleanor Seeker, Dunbarton.
D. G. Stephenson, Highland Creek.
James Smith, Toronto.
Hy. Moore, Toronto.
Joshua Tripp, Highland Creek.
Wm. Tredway, Highland Creek.
Jos. Telfer, Scarboro.
Smith Thompson, Malvern.
Geo. Topper, Malvern.
Jas. C. Taylor, Malvern.
John Wright, Highland Creek.
John H. Wilson, Markham.
Thos. Walton.
Martin Willis, Malvern.
Wm. Westney, Highland Creek.
David Wallace, Highland Creek.
Eliz. Wallace, Highland Creek.
John Wilson, Highland Creek.
Edward Wheler, Stouffville.
Matthew Walton, Toronto.
Thos. Young, Highland Creek.
James Young, Highland Creek.
Adam Yule, Port Union.

INDEX.

www.ingramcontent.com/pod-product-compliance
Lightning Source LLC
Chambersburg PA
CBHW021116270326
41929CB00009B/907